W##HAT OTHERS ARE SAYING ABOUT
E##CHOES FROM MEDIEVAL ##

In a time (
such as th
connectic   ake
with the p   a remarkable
job of hel]   ing people together, es   on of the soul.
                    —Diana L. Paxson, Author of *The White Raven*,
                    the *Wodan's Children* trilogy, etc., and the origi-
                    nator of the SCA

The costumed celebration of the Renaissance Pleasure Faire brings
our history to vibrant life. Barbara's book opens the door to even
more fascinating possibilities. Could it be that many who have taken
living history as a hobby are drawn to specific eras because of their
past lives?
                    —Phyllis Patterson, creator of Renaissance
                    Pleasure Faires

Some children are obsessed with particular periods of history, acting them out in their play, drawings, and stories. The fascinating case
studies of medieval reenactors in Barbara Lane's book will convince
you that some of these obsessions are actually memories of past
lives.
                    —Carol Bowman, author of *Children's Past
                    Lives*

Echoes from Medieval Halls helps to establish the link between past-
life events and our fascination with specific time periods. Gradually
we are becoming aware that we are on a journey of the soul and that
previous lives dictate many of our interests and, at times, determine
our companions along the way.
                    —Winafred B. Lucas, Ph.D., Diplomate ABPP,
                    author of *Regression Therapy: A Handbook for
                    Professionals*

Barbara Lane's work with "living history" reenactors represents an
exciting breakthrough in reincarnation studies. The case histories
presented in her two excellent books strongly suggest that, contrary
to popular ideas about karma, we do not come back as the "opposite" of what we were in a past life. I highly recommend her "Echoes"
books for everyone who wants to gain a deeper understanding about
reincarnation.
                    —Rabbi Yonassan Gershom, author of *Beyond
                    the Ashes* and *From Ashes to Healing*

Barbara Lane has done it again! Her second book, *Echoes from Medieval Halls*, is absolutely fascinating. You won't be able to put it down!

—Dr. Richard Levy, psychologist and author

This book is a must for anyone interested in past lives or who has an open, inquisitive mind. These accounts are "validations" of the concept of reincarnation and show how current interests are derived from lives we have lived before. A compelling, fascinating book . . . and an important book.

—Edith Fiore, Ph.D., author of *You Have Been Here Before*

Fascinating stories, skillfully woven into a fabric as rich as the ancient tapestries that adorned medieval halls. Barbara Lane combines scholarship and storytelling into a compelling tale.

—Chet Snow, author of *Mass Dreams of the Future*, past president of the Association for Past-Life Research and Therapies, Inc.

Echoes from Medieval Halls is an important contribution to literature on past-life recall. It provides useful anecdotal information which can be replicated and authenticated by researchers who want to hold regression evidence up to clinical standards.

—Bettye B. Binder, teacher, author, and president of the Association for Past-Life Research and Therapies (APRT)

This remarkable book peels back the layers of fantasy and fun experienced by historical reenactors to reveal a past-life reality which explains their passions and behaviour. A fascinating and compelling study.

—Roy Stemman, editor of *Reincarnation International Magazine*

Barbara Lane's *Echoes from Medieval Halls* is a karmic pu-pu platter of fascinating and well-researched past lives.

—Bruce Goldberg, D.D.S., M.S., author of *Soul Healing: Past Lives, Future Lives, and the Search for Grace*

Barbara Lane has produced another fascinating history of the past lives of living individuals. For all history buffs, her research into medieval life, customs, and culture is highly praiseworthy and adds powerful evidence for the validity of reincarnation. Read it for pleasure and a wealth of information regarding medieval history.

—Hazel M. Denning, Ph.D., author of *True Hauntings: Spirits with a Purpose*

Echoes
from
Medieval Halls

Also by Barbara Lane:

Echoes from the Battlefield:
First-Person Accounts of Civil War Past Lives

Echoes from Medieval Halls

Past-Life Memories from the Middle Ages

Barbara Lane

A·R·E PRESS

ASSOCIATION FOR
RESEARCH AND
ENLIGHTENMENT

A.R.E. Press • Virginia Beach • Virginia

A.R.E. Press
Sixty-Eighth & Atlantic Avenue
P.O. Box 656
Virginia Beach, VA 23451-0656

Library of Congress Cataloging-in-Publication Data
   Lane, Barbara, 1947-
   Echoes from medieval halls : past-life memories from the
Middle Ages / by Barbara Lane.
        p.   cm.
   Includes bibliographical references.
   ISBN 0-87604-390-2
   1. Hypnotism—Case studies. 2. Reincarnation—Case stud-
ies. 3. Society for Creative Anachronism. 4. Biography—
Middle Ages, 500-1500—Miscellanea. I. Title.
BF1156.R45L35   1997
133.9'01'35—dc21   97-6281

Cover design by Richard Boyle
Cover photographs by David H. Morse

Dedication

This book is dedicated to my loving parents,
John and Kathleen Lane; to all those touched
by medieval times; to those who are striving to
purify and transform individual and collective
psychic or karmic residue; and to the visionar-
ies of the past, present, and future.

Contents

Acknowledgments

With joy and gratitude, I want to thank those who supported my research and writing, particularly Ann Longmore-Etheridge for her professional editing assistance and historical expertise; historical expert Susan Reed, for helping me to organize the study, to recruit its participants and historical commentators, and to give me a crash course on the history of medieval reenacting. I am also grateful to my other historical experts: Bruce Blackistone, Stephen Hicks, Kathy Norvell, Paula and Larry Peterka, Lisa Steele, and especially Dr. Joann Moran, professor of medieval and Renaissance history at Georgetown University.

Thanks also to Jon Robertson of A.R.E. Press for his gentle guidance and support; Katherine Lauder, for offering her home as a writing haven; and Shirley Meyer, for helping make the Middle Ages come alive by sharing a mystical medieval European adventure with me. I appreciate my parents, John and Kathleen Lane, for unwittingly kindling my passion for metaphysics, and my mother for copyediting; Karen Beary, whose medieval garb transformed me into an elegant fourteenth-century lady; and the Markland Viking Camp, for letting me experience its ninth-century lifestyle. A heartfelt thank you to members of the Society for Creative Anachronism (SCA), living historians, and Renaissance Festival actors who were courageous enough to share in this book their stories and enthusiasm for the Dark Ages, Middle Ages, and Renaissance.

Preface

Mystical Medieval Threads

"Spring of vision. . ."
—Vernon Watkins, *Welsh poet*

January 1996. The entire eastern seaboard had been crippled—cut off, closed, and locked down by the worst blizzard in nearly a century. Weather was the lead story—the only news story. Hazardous conditions deterred the bravest from venturing out onto the roadways. Everywhere, people affected by the storm were gathered around television sets, eager for the latest update. And we were no exception.

Members of the Society for Creative Anachronism,

Inc. (SCA), were still dressed in their medieval garb, waiting to learn their fate. Would we be able to leave what had been planned as a weekend of kingdom-wide Twelfth Night festivities? We'd already been stranded at the Bavarian-style hotel an extra day. The television meteorologists did not seem hopeful that we would be heading home anytime soon.

The snow outside the Red Lion Inn in rural Blacksburg, Virginia, had long since buried our cars, making them into gravelike mounds in what had been the parking lot—now a white morass, unblemished save for the futile attempts of a few "Scadians" (members of the SCA) to dig out. Others gave in more gracefully to fate and offered to help the weary and equally stranded staff at the inn. One woman delivered fresh towels. Her Royal Majesty, Queen Brigit of the Kingdom of Atlantia, set a shining example for her subjects by mopping the kitchen floor.

A newcomer to medieval reenacting events, I was already convinced that I couldn't have been stranded with a nicer, more talented, self-sufficient, resourceful group of people.

I peered out the window and watched the white flakes fall in a heavy curtain. Despite the motion of the storm, an odd stillness prevailed.

I found myself imagining what the world had been like when the folk who inspired these medievalists, and the Pre-Raphaelites[1] before them, were flesh and blood—walking real steps upon earth. Perhaps a woman of the Middle Ages once peered outside into a similarly snowbound world, stranded after her own Twelfth Night had drawn to a close.

Twelfth Night was a medieval holiday celebrating the arrival of the three wise kings in Bethlehem. Twelfth Night was the twelfth day after Christmas, when gift-giving and celebration took place. Christmas Day still retained an air of religious solemnity.

I visualized the ancient snowbound medieval party-goer, occupying herself much as I had been. In one room, previously filled by reenactor merchants peddling their wares from cloth to armor, people now hunched over tables spread with games of military strategy. Others clustered around a fabric board to play the popular period game "Nine Men's Morris," in which a player strategizes moves in tic-tac-toe fashion to reduce his or her opponent's arsenal to only two men. At other tables, people pondered their next moves in a riotously popular modern card game called Magic™, which, to my novice eyes, appeared complicated, mystically based, and somewhat akin to Dungeons and Dragons™. Here and there, lone craftspeople dotted the room, silently painting or drawing.

Another room, used during Twelfth Night to display medieval crafts from calligraphed parchments to ornate needlework, and from armored helmets to homemade mead, had now been converted into a dance hall. Musical instruments being played included recorders, a lute, a shawm (a relative to the modern oboe), and a psaltery (a harplike instrument that sits on the lap and is played with a bow). The musicians accompanied dancers, who twirled, stepped, kicked, and glided while onlookers kept time. In slow, stately, formal line dances, such as the "pavan," couples promenaded in a processional designed to display their fancy clothing. These were interspersed with circle dances called "bransles."

Elsewhere, hypnotic drumbeats kept pace for belly dancers who shimmied and shook seductively, their costumes jangling and their zills (metal finger cymbals) beckoning to those within hearing range.

Bards, singers, and storytellers congregated near a fireplace in the lobby, hot flames crackling, the burning wood shooting sparks. I settled down on the stone hearth to listen. The pungent smoke stung my lungs and my eyes. A woman with a spinning wheel sat across from me. She worked quietly with flax and wool she had hand-dyed using period techniques. She told me that her resulting creation would be the softest merino wool that she would then knit into a hood. Occasionally, she would stop her work to lift her voice in song with the others.

The singers were accompanied by a Celtic harpist and guitarist as they sang lilting Irish ballads and folk songs. The rest of us would pipe in for the simple, often bawdy choruses. The melodies warmed the soul, while the heat from the fire warmed the body.

The previous evening had been full of pageantry and feasting. Dressed in heavy woolen floor-length cloaks, we had trudged through two feet of snow to the banquet hall.

Once relieved of our cloaks and baskets of tableware, we seated ourselves at long wooden tables. As everyone assembled, I was awed by the color and complexity of the revelers' garments. There were few, if any, peasants, since they consider themselves a part of the non-noble gentry, unless an individual consciously chooses a peasant persona.

Wide, sweeping gowns of velvet and brocade swished the floor. Some were high-necked; others showed substantial cleavage. Headpieces included turbans, hoods, veils, and the cone-shaped "hennins" of Walt Disney princesses. There were Elizabethan court gowns, highlander's kilts, and people dressed as huns, knights, nuns, and monks.

As servers brought the many courses of the feast to the table, goblets were raised and hearty shouts of "Vivat! Vivat!" rang through the banquet hall to honor the cooks. The fare included Welsh rarebit and succulent roast beef, chicken and sage pie, and agurkesalt (a cold cucumber salad), and had been prepared by a head cook and a squad of volunteers. King Cuan and Queen Brigit of Atlantia presided over the lengthy meal. Afterward, they held court to honor their exemplary subjects for their skills or service. These subjects came from the far corners of the kingdom, hailing from North Carolina, South Carolina, Virginia, Maryland, and Washington, D.C.

As a guest, I had chosen a temporary French persona, "Jeanne Vivienne," and was dressed in a white cotton cotehardie, over which was a sideless surcote of deep purple-black brocade. The sideless surcote, an overdress with the sides cut out to show the shape of the hips, was commonly referred to as the "Gates of Hell," because it was considered sinfully risque. To complete the outfit, I wore a linen veil and small velvet headpiece. At first, my outfit seemed peculiar, but after a weekend, I felt freer and more beautiful than in a sweater and slacks. This world and its charming affectations were seductive.

After another night at the hotel, I cast my lot with a small group who decided to made a break for home before the next predicted snowfall began. Although forecasters warned against such attempts, we caravaned toward the metropolitan Washington, D.C., area. We inched our way back home along a highway strewn with wrecks and abandoned cars. When I left, I had no idea how I'd get all the way home, as my ride was not going anywhere close to my location. Fortunately, another driver offered to take me to a Metro train stop. An hour later, when I got off at my Metro home stop, the surprised station manager told me that I had been the only person to detrain there all day.

The sidewalks of Alexandria, Virginia, were nearly impassable. Few moving cars or pedestrians were in evidence. As I struggled toward my home, a policeman pulled up in a patrol car and offered me a ride to my door. Gratefully, I accepted. It had been an oddly charmed trip, from start to finish.

Relaxing at home, I reflected on a study I had done two years before as part of my master's thesis. The study concerned Civil War reenactors, and why they would come home from work and so anxiously slip into the Confederate or Union past. Using my skills as a regression hypnotherapist, I wanted to see if I could discover any direct connections between their obsession with history and their past lives. Now, I realized that others, many of whom spend their days interacting with computers, spend their evenings retreating into the Middle Ages. Some of them actually research, design, and sew their own garb. Some weave their own cloth, while others learn to embroider, make their own chain mail or armor from wire and sheet metal. They take classes in combat archery, period fencing, sword and shield, dancing, playing period instruments, singing, storytelling, making mead and ale, feast preparation, and courtly etiquette.

Who are these people who surf the Internet by day and re-create the Middle Ages by night? Among other groups, they are members of the SCA, participants in Renaissance festivals, and denizens of living history camps, such as those of the East Coast-based Markland Medieval Mercenary Militia. This phenomenon had caught my attention, and I was intrigued to know why these people are drawn to re-create slices of a very distant age (from A.D. 500 through A.D. 1600), rather than a single event of such immense magnitude as the Civil War—almost within reach of living memory.

I wondered if I would have the same results as I'd had with regressing Civil War reenactors, if I regressed the medievalists. Would I detect any substantive differences between the two groups of reenactors and their recalled past lives?

Luckily, one of my Civil War reenactors led me to Susan Reed, the then Baroness of Ponte Alto (a swath of land corresponding to the inner suburbs of Northern Virginia) who invited me to attend a sewing circle at her home. But instead of being armed with needle and thread, I came with a tape recorder and note pad.

The night I drove to her "castle," I immediately identified the home by a banner bearing the herald of the "Barony of Ponte Alto." The house was cluttered with books, which the participants of the sewing circle referred to as they planned their attire for the upcoming 24th Annual Pennsic War. "Pennsic," I quickly learned, was "the" event of the year.

Pennsic is a two-week campout that draws nearly 10,000 Scadians to Pennsylvania each August to partake in warfare, shopping, ritual court gatherings, and competitions in science, arts, and crafts. Torches and bonfires light the night sky, while chance meetings at camp parties ignite romances known to lead to marriage.

In conversing with the women of the sewing circle, I found that they did not use their "mundane" present-day names, but rather used made-up medieval monikers, speaking as the characters of their "personas." Listening to Susan speak as "Teleri, the Cupbearer," the character she was playing at the time, I wondered about the past lives that would be revealed by subjects already used to acting and speaking as other personas. I also wondered about the difficulties I would face trying to verify past lives that spread over a millennium and across a vast geographical area. I couldn't travel to sites and archives all over the world, so I would need to recruit experts with specialties such as costuming and warfare, who could give me scholarly opinions on both the events and my subjects' descriptions of the everyday surroundings of their recalled identities.

That sultry evening in July 1995 I also learned that I was dealing with folk of a different mind-set from my Civil War subjects. As the women discussed their hobby,

I observed that they were somewhat less intense toward strict authenticity than the Civil War reenactors. While some participants took their research and portrayals very seriously, others enjoyed the events for the costumes, entertainment, and food. The range of interests was broad: while some enjoyed the privation of medieval life, others enjoyed it in its details.

I also learned about Renaissance festivals, a network of for-profit fairs run annually around the nation. I made a mental note to interview some of these festival participants, mostly paid actors, to see if their past lives—assuming they recalled them—could add important information to the study.

Along the way, I would eventually discover the other category of medievalist groups, including the Markland Medieval Mercenary Militia, the German Landsknechts, and others, which compete for authenticity awards at living history events. To analyze their recalled past lives along with the others seemed of major significance. Would those lives be any richer in detail, perhaps reflecting the greater depth of their conscious historical knowledge, than the other groups?

With Susan's help, I began to assemble the questions for my regression subjects, who I decided should include both veterans and relative newcomers to medievalist events. Susan also helped by spreading the word of my search for regression subjects.

In a matter of weeks, the study had taken on a life of its own. The phone rang off the hook with calls from volunteers. I selected a mix of men and women with varying involvement levels in the SCA, Renaissance festivals, and living history groups, and then began interviewing my new subjects.

As it would turn out, all thirteen could recall lifetimes in the Dark Ages, Middle Ages, or Renaissance, just as my Civil War subjects, who all remembered their past roles in the events of the early 1860s. Was it possible that the medieval past lives I tapped into revealed the hidden motivations that prompted these medievalists to re-create this time period? Could this, then, be a possible clue to what we experience in our lives today?

After the regressions were complete, I took the transcripts to Dr. Joann Moran, professor of medieval and Renaissance history at Georgetown University, Washington, D.C. Professor Moran found most of the regressions she reviewed to be fascinating, plausible, accurate in overall details, and generally consistent with historical fact. Moran specializes in the social and intellectual aspects of medieval history, has authored several books on the age, and has lectured on topics such as Arthurian legend, the lives of medieval women, and mysticism in the Middle Ages. In addition to Professor Moran's feedback, I decided to draw on the wealth of knowledge accumulated by various expert living history reenactors such as Dark Ages scholar Bruce Blackistone, of Oakley Farms, Maryland. I also asked for feedback from several subjects who each had his or her area of historic expertise.

My thirteen subjects included seven women and five men, whose ages ranged from twenty-four to forty-two. Their careers were diverse. Ten had spent between one and sixteen years as members of the SCA. Six had spent between two and fourteen years working at various Renaissance festivals. Three had spent between one and sixteen years as living historians.

With the help of Moran and Blackistone, and the comments of the subjects themselves, I would probe what drives these reenactors to participate in a hobby that consumes their time and money, and guides their personal relationships. In my search, I may have glimpsed a mystical thread connecting them to the past. Perhaps through reenacting, these medievalists had also unconsciously stumbled upon a portal to their past. Now together, we had passed through the gateway of their sub-conscious—allowing for the magnification of their own muffled echoes from medieval halls. I, too, was transported as I heard their echoes from a distant age.

Author's note: With the exceptions of Dori, Nick, and Helen, all the reenactor regression subjects have given permission to use their real names. The actual texts of the regression narratives have been, in places, condensed and edited to enhance readability. Only the dialogues of lifetimes pertaining to my medieval research have been included. While this book includes the past-life narratives of some of their members, neither the author nor A.R.E. Press represent that the philosophy of reincarnation is officially or unofficially sanctioned by the Society for Creative Anachronism, Inc., Renaissance Festivals, Inc., Markland Medieval Mercenary Militia, Ltd., The Markland Viking Camp, La Belle Compagnie, Das Teufels-Alpdrücken Fähnlein (Landsknecht Mercenary Reenacting) or other organizations or individuals named herein.

1

Dreamers and Dream Sellers

"Socket of all men's eyes . . . "
—Vernon Watkins, *Welsh poet*

The Society for Creative Anachronism, Inc. (SCA): Reinventing the Past

"If there is a single SCA motto," says longtime SCA member Susan Reed, "it would be 'In service to the dream.' Of course, each participant has his or her own interpretation of what the 'dream' is.

"For some," she says, "it's a commitment to Victorian medievalism—grand romance and chivalry in a pure, yet artificial form." Indeed, the ideals of the Society are perhaps more Pre-Raphaelite than truly medieval, centering on the Arthurian Round Table virtues of chivalry, courtesy, and honor.

Members of the SCA strive to recapture the ambiance of the Middle Ages and Renaissance, rather than the often stark and harsh realities, as do the diehard Civil War reenactment units with which I am familiar. According to Reed, many Scadians prefer the past the way "it should have been"—without the grinding poverty, illiteracy, and early deaths from childbirth, the plague, and other medieval diseases. Some even allow such anachronisms as charcoal grills, flush toilets, and deodorant.

The SCA is a nonprofit organization which currently boasts more than 20,000 paid members in the United States, Canada, Australia, Great Britain, and other European countries. Reed estimates that additional "players" more than double the figure. Although a few Scadians now portray life in the middle and lower class, members generally portray the upper class and enjoy court life prior to A.D. 1600.

SCA members think of modern times as the "Current Middle Ages," and the modern world as divided into thirteen geographical areas or kingdoms. Each kingdom is ruled by a king, who has won the title in combat, and his chosen queen. A kingdom may be subdivided into local branches, called provinces, baronies, and shires.

Barons and baronesses, like Susan Reed and her husband, are official representatives of the Crown within their territory. There are seneschals to oversee daily affairs; autocrats to organize events; marshals to supervise fighting and related safety rules; exchequers to assist with bookkeeping; chroniclers to keep the populace informed through newsletters; and chatelaines to welcome newcomers, provide loaner costumes (called "garb"), and interface with the public.

Even with anachronisms in this medieval reality, Reed says that through reenactments, Scadians do experience hands-on learning in areas such as spinning and dyeing, sewing, leather work, smithing, and cooking. Through research, members learn about medieval customs. At feasts, for example, Scadians come prepared to savor medieval delicacies. Some use their best medieval manners—eating with their fingers, using finger bowls between courses, and toasting the Crown and the cook. After dinner, they play medieval games and dance to period music.

During feasts and other events, Reed explains, Scadians refer to themselves and their colleagues by the historically plausible names of their characters or "personas." They use archaic language to refer to modern objects: cars are "dragons," telephones are "far speakers," and electronic stereos are "minstrels in boxes."

When not feasting and reveling, Scadian activities turn to tournaments of combat where every safety precaution is taken—including the padding of combatants and the use of hand-made rattan weapons.

"Since volunteerism is integral to the organization," Reed says, "an award structure is in place to acknowledge, reward, and thank members." Scadians who excel in areas of combat service, or the arts and sciences, are recognized for their excellence—for example, kingdom-level Awards of Arms and Peerage Awards. Peerages—rarely bestowed, according to Reed, recognize distinguished accomplishments, well-roundedness within the Society, as well as qualities such as service, self-discipline, courtesy, compassion, and generosity.

Seminars, classes, and craft guilds further Scadian knowledge. Medieval magazines, such as the *Renaissance Herald*,[1] *The Chivalry Sports: Renaissance Catalog Magazine*,[2] and *Smoke and Fire*,[3] provide both editorial content and advertising aimed at the SCA member.

Society members also stage events to share their color and knowledge with the public. Susan Reed says she believes that, as members of the SCA "walk, not backward into the future, but forward into the past," their personal and historical discoveries help themselves and others as well.

Renaissance Festivals: Dream Sellers

Between February and November 1994 3.2 million people—some bedecked in Renaissance attire, others crowning their twentieth-century jeans and shorts with flower garlands—strolled about some seventy Renaissance festivals spread throughout the United States.

At the Renaissance festival in Tuxedo, New York, during the 1994 season, Queen Winifred and her entourage, including "William Shakespeare," made a visit to the village of Sterling in the year 1589. Robin Hood wed Maid Marian, while a "living chess game" pitted Robin Hood's merry band against members of the court, with players who fought with swords to win their squares. For the classically inclined, there were performances of Shakespeare's *Merry Wives of Windsor* and Chaucer's *Merchant's Tale.* Visitors interacted with jocular royal madrigal singers, glass blowers, jugglers on stilts, and the wandering town rat catcher.[4]

Farther down the seaboard, in Annapolis, Maryland, a festival in the village of Revel Grove had been declared in honor of His Majesty King Henry VIII and his fourth bride-to-be, Anna of Cleves.

Revel Grove's own Globe Theatre presented the time-honored tale of two warring families, the Montagues and the Capulets, and the forbidden love of Romeo and Juliet. Audiences gasped as Johnny Fox, swordswallower extraordinaire, drove a sharp blade down his throat. Children squealed with delight at Horn's *Punch and Judy Show.* Hungry spectators gnawed on mammoth smoked turkey legs and dropped by the White Tavern Inn to lift a pint to the busty Bawdy Balladeers. Artisans and merchants displayed their wares from silver jewelry to pottery to entice shoppers to reach into their pouches for bills, while armored knights on horseback jousted with real swords as a prelude to the pageantry of the royal wedding at day's end.

Admittedly, the public scarcely notices the historical discrepancies—that Shakespeare's *Romeo and Juliet* would not yet have been written or that turkey legs were a yet undiscovered New World avian.

How did this Renaissance revelry begin? In 1963, Phyllis Patterson put on the first Renaissance Pleasure Faire, in Southern California. The former secondary schoolteacher and drama coach originally created it to educate and delight youngsters. Patterson answered an advertisement in the *Laurel Canyon Crier* to work in a summer theater workshop for eighty children under twelve. Determined to involve every child in the production, she decided to perform a history of theater from stories of a prehistory hunt to the 1960s musical *Oklahoma*. Each child was soon able to repeat the Victorian phrase that became the program's theme: "Ontogeny recapitulates phylogeny"—individuals' growth repeats the evolution of their ancestors through history.

While researching theater in the Middle Ages, Patterson stumbled on Pierre Ducharte's *Italian Comedy: The Improvisation, Scenarios, Lives, Attributes, Portraits, and Masks of the Illustrious Characters of the Commedie Dell'arte*.[5] What she found was the story of comedians who traveled from town to town in burro-drawn carts performing plays where servant-characters poked fun at their wealthy masters. As forerunners of the *Punch and Judy Shows*, the actors were experts at improvisation.

With a cart for their stage, Patterson's ten year olds stepped into the shoes of these medieval comedians. The theater program was such a hit that many of the children returned later to Patterson's terraced backyard for more improvisation experience. Some of her groups performed at the American National Theater in Los Angeles.

Armed with a new vision of theater for the people, Patterson proposed a faire as a fund-raiser for Pacifica Foundation, which sponsored America's first public radio station. Patterson, who had worked in television and radio, was given air time to ask for volunteer help and the first Renaissance Pleasure Faire, near Laurel Canyon, became a reality.

Having herself left a town of 300 as a youngster, Patterson told me she had wanted to re-create an atmosphere "where the whole town is your playground; you know everybody, and they take care of you." Sensing that people had a desire to return to their agricultural roots, she endeavored to keep that ambiance by including homemade crafts, personal interactions, and folkways at the Renaissance Faire, even though it eventually became a "town" of 4,000 inhabitants, including 1,000 actors.

Today, Patterson's son is the manager of the two Renaissance Pleasure Faires in California for the Renaissance Entertainment Corporation. It owns five festivals, including Northern and Southern California; Bristol Run, Wisconsin; New York State; and Fredericksburg (Virginia).

Patterson says she has seen families with three generations of faire actors. Most are volunteers who undergo a month of intensive training followed by an eight-weekend commitment in Southern California and, after completing another training program, a six-weekend commitment in Northern California.

Patterson notes that for many festival participants, history becomes a consuming passion and that many of her most enthusiastic participants are actually computer programmers or practice other seemingly incompatible trades, but who are driven to re-create the past. For them, she has seen the Renaissance Faires create a balance in their lives and offer a sense of community. Many were liberal arts majors in college.

Believing that learning should be a circus with all the senses excited, Patterson had a goal to help others realize that "history is about people's lives, not the Congressional Record." For this reason, local school children dress up and attend workshops on-site during the week.

Patterson says she believes that a lack of celebration causes an imbalance in the modern world. She has designed her faires to compensate. She has set the stage for visitors to come, dress up, and directly participate in the experience. "The heart of our success is that we attempt to blur the line between visitor and participant. All the faire's a stage," she told me.

Patterson concurs with the view of James Redfield, author of *The Celestine Prophecy*, of extending our consciousness of historical time. In his book, Redfield's characters discover that one must learn how the everyday view of the world developed over time and how it was created by the reality of the people who lived in previous ages. "To really understand where you are today, you must take yourself back to the year 1000 and then move forward through the entire millennium experientially, as though you actually lived through the whole period yourself in a single lifetime."[6] Having experienced this longer history, Redfield says that you now live in a "longer now."

Nearly a decade after Patterson had begun her faires, a vendor took the Renaissance festival concept to Minnesota. Today, Minnesota is the most well-attended faire in the country, drawing 315,000 visitors over fourteen days. Also rated among the largest for attendance are the faires at Scarborough, Texas, and Houston, Texas. Renaissance festivals in Toronto, Canada, and Richmond, Virginia, are two of the newest festivals to open the gates to the past.[7]

The Maryland Renaissance Festival celebrated its twentieth season in 1996. In 1995, over nine weekends, more than 250,000 people flocked to the site near Annapolis, Maryland.

According to the Maryland festival's administrator, C. J. Crowe, unlike most other faires, it allocates the largest budget for entertainment, pays their actors, provides actors' costumes, and keeps an entertainment director and staff year round. Actors audition before a panel and are judged on projection, delivery, articulation, and improvisation. Ninety-five percent of those selected are local actors with professional training. They are showcased in the royal court, stage shows, skits, or musical performances developed in-house, while most other festivals depend heavily on performers who "do the circuit."

"At first, it's just a gig for the actors. But those who love what they're doing get bitten by the history bug," said Crowe.

Living Historians: Facing the Past
Markland Medieval Mercenary Militia

Many living historians have cut their historical baby teeth on the Renaissance festivals, later graduating to organizations such as the SCA, then onto groups like the Markland Medieval Mercenary Militia, of College Park, Maryland. The nonprofit organization is specifically devoted to the studying and reenacting of all aspects of life from roughly A.D. 1 to 1500 with the goal of public education. While trying to stay close to historical roots, members learn history firsthand and share their knowledge.

New Marklanders can choose to participate in several different living history camps: Roman, Celtic, Viking, Anglo-Saxon, and fifteenth-century. The camps attempt to re-create the lives of commoners, including their crafts, games, rituals, and customs.

The organization's agenda has evolved since its 1969 inception, growing more and more focused on strict authenticity. Markland's first event took place when some fencing club members from the University of Maryland celebrated the 903rd anniversary of the Battle of Hastings with a reenactment. The event proved so successful that the battle has been reenacted each autumn ever since. The group has also branched out from the University of Maryland at College Park to the majority of the northeastern seaboard with members and events.

Markland business meetings are called "Althyngs," as were those of the Viking Icelanders who began what is today's oldest surviving democracy. Markland social gatherings are called "Fyrdmoots"—"Fyrd" is an old Norse term for "folk" or "the people."

In addition to public living history events and competitions, battle reenactments, and demonstrations at schools and museums, Marklanders' nonpublic events include feasts, wars, and an educational camp-out called "Camp Fence," where spinning, weaving, carving, and other disappearing arts are taught.

Marklanders can participate in several forms of combat: recreational ("rec") fighting and fratricidal ("frat") fighting. Rec fighting is a choreographed battle staged for the public with authentic, albeit unsharpened, steel weapons. Some fighters take on the role of major figures, such as Duke William of Normandy or King Harold at the Battle of Hastings, and have lines to speak as noncombatant Marklanders narrate the events of the battle to the crowd. Frat fighting is full-contact fighting with padded rattan weapons that must be constructed to meet acceptable safety standards and in which the rules of fighting conduct must be obeyed.

The Horse Guild, another Markland subgroup, participates in equestrian sports, and the Longship Company owns and sails its own clinker-planked Viking ship and a smaller ferrying vessel.

La Belle Compagnie

Another group of living historians, La Belle Compagnie, portrays English life during the time period of the Hundred Years' War, portraying an indentured company of archers, armed men, and men-at-arms in the service of a fictional English knight, Sir Geoffrey Peel. His lady and the rest of the civilian household and skilled craftsmen attached to a medieval knight are also portrayed.

The Landsknechts

These colorfully clad sixteenth-century German pike troops were instrumental in changing the face of warfare, forever ending the era of the mounted knight. This was the beginning of the end of war as a rich man's game, according to Paula Peterka, who with her husband, Larry, started a Landsknecht reenactment group on the East Coast in the early 1990s. Like its sister organizations in California and Pennsylvania, Das TeufelsAlpdrücken Fähnlein is a nonprofit corporation devoted to promoting historical education about the Landsknecht mercenary companies, circa A.D. 1495-1648, through living history performances.

These German soldiers were mercenaries and made an excellent wage. They were obligated, however, to be on reserve for the Holy Roman Empire and promised not to take any contracts against the Hapsburg dynasty. The troops brought their wives and children with them to their field encampments. When wandering through a Landsknecht camp, visitors will hear German spoken by the garishly costumed and bejeweled troops and their womenfolk. Many modern military organizations trace their origin to the German Landsknecht infantry.

The Middle Ages

The term "medieval" comes from the Latin "medius," meaning "middle," and "aevum" meaning "age." The Middle Ages, then, refers to a period of European history between ancient and modern times. Although historians differ, many identify the period as beginning with the decline of the Roman Empire in the fifth century and running into the 1500s. During the Middle Ages, Europe included the Holy Roman Empire, England, France, Scandinavia, Spain, Italy, Ireland, and a number of Eastern European states.

The early Middle Ages, from the 400s to the 900s, are usually referred to as the Dark Ages, when only a few church and palace schools kept the knowledge of the Romans alive. Many artistic and technical skills were lost, only to be rediscovered hundreds of years later. In the first half of the eleventh century, Western Europe began an economic, cultural, and political revival, leading to the glories of the High Middle Ages.

The Renaissance

The time period can be loosely defined as the late fifteenth and sixteenth centuries. As a great cultural movement, the Renaissance began in Italy in the early 1300s, with scholars, philosophers, and artists studying the classical antiquities of Greece and Rome. Gradually spreading throughout Western Europe, the period of "rebirth" ended about A.D. 1620, having included the discovery of, and expansion into, the New World; the marvels of Leonardo da Vinci; and the timeless works of William Shakespeare.

2

Past-Life Therapy—
Historical Perspectives on Healing

"Of love and of sound mind . . . "
—New Testament, *II Timothy 1:7*

In early May 1996 past-life regression professionals attended the sixteenth international spring conference of the Association for Past-Life Research and Therapies, Inc. (APRT), in Rockville, Maryland. Attendees directed their collective focus on past-life therapy as it relates to potent periods and events in history.

While attending as one of the speakers, I discussed medieval past lives with several presenters and also the benefits of investigating past lives. I was surprised to learn that, not only had they discovered medieval lives among their clients, but they had experienced such lives themselves.

One prominent speaker, therapist Dr. Joseph Costa, told me of his own past life as a crusader dressed in armor on a battlefield. Costa said he remembered feeling a spear being driven into his back and lodging between his ribs. The tip broke off inside his armor and squeaked as he continued to swing his sword. In this life, prior to this regression, he had experienced chronic pain in the area where his former self had been wounded.

As a past-life therapist, Costa has seen a substantial percentage of his clients return to the age of monks, castles, and devout religions. In some cases, he said, they recall lives as religious zealots. Costa believes that he has found a correlation between some of the more religiously oriented lives and issues concerning money in this lifetime. He explains that healers and people with a spiritual focus in this life and in similar lives long past, often ignore taking care of their own needs and have difficulty developing a steady income. He believes they must alter their past-life patterns and expand their current belief system to become successful.

In his past-life regression therapy practice, Costa says he focuses on solving what might be termed "soul lessons" and claims to have chased recycled, unresolved issues back to the prehistoric. He says that the experiences of his clients have led him to believe that souls don't think in terms of morality, or good and evil. Instead, the soul is making a desperate attempt to balance positive and negative energies. As for groups with the same soul essence who reincarnate to experience the same energy cycles and lessons, Costa believes that group learning occurs, as well as the resolution of soul lessons.

Rabbi Yonassan Gershom, who also spoke at the con-

ference, has himself participated in SCA events. Search-
ing for an historic Jewish persona, the Rabbi finally re-
sorted to dressing as a monk for his own (medieval
Jewish persona's) protection. "For the Jews, the Middle
Ages bore no resemblance to a Renaissance festival," the
Hasidic Rabbi said. "During the thirteenth century, Pope
Innocent III was responsible for first shutting up the
Jews in segregated ghettos. This was part of the 2,000-
year history of persecution of Jews in Europe leading up
to the Holocaust."

In his books, *Beyond the Ashes* and *From Ashes to Healing,* Gershom shares dozens of the many accounts he has
collected of past-life deaths at the hands of the Nazis
during the Holocaust[1] and believes that he and other
Jews have led previous past lives in the Middle Ages and
earlier historic periods—as Jews. As a collective, Gershom
says, Jewish connections survive beyond the grave,
forming a kind of Jewish tribal identity. If these souls
appear to incarnate again and again within the same
culture, even though they risk persecution—this begs
the question, why? The apparent freely made choice is a
constant conundrum and frequent fodder for those who
doubt the feasibility of reincarnation. "If I could have
chosen," such a person would say, "I would never have
chosen a life like that!"

To this question, Rabbi Gershom would reply that being Jewish involves far more than simply being persecuted. Those who return as Jews do so because they
resonate with beautiful rituals, ceremonies, and songs
of Jewish culture and religion. The positive aspects of
Jewishness far outweigh the suffering.

The Jews are one group which tends to maintain connections with each other from one incarnation to the
next. Another such group was the Native American Indi-
ans. Recently, past-life regression therapist Janet Cunningham conducted a series of regressions revealing that

some of her subjects had incarnated as members of the Native American Oglala tribe of what is now the Dakotas. She chronicled the experience in her book, *A Tribe Returned*.[2] In it, she told of the anger-filled and anguish-producing murders of the tribe members who carried resulting feelings of futility into their current incarnations. She also reported on the healing process that ensued as some of the reincarnated soul group members were reconnected and worked together through their rage and grief. "To me, personally and spiritually, it's a story of love transcending time and space," Cunningham said.

Another group of more than fifteen people, most from the Lake Elsinore, California, area, recalled under hypnosis having lived in the rural Virginia town of Millboro during the Civil War. The story was told by Dr. Marge Rieder in her book *Mission to Millboro*.[3]

While speaking at the same conference, I postulated that my first study of Civil War reenactors and my second on Dark Ages, Middle Ages, and Renaissance reenactors were fundamental attempts to understand what may guide our souls to return again and why we ultimately make the life choices we do.[4]

Like myself, other therapists had addressed the bitter cycle of war or persecution. Could such acts of inhumanity possibly be the balancing of positive and negative energies? Regardless, this cycle may never end until its participants recognize the soul behind their enemy's face.

Perhaps what was being revealed by these past-life therapists was a new way of healing that could assist in breaking the circle of negativity that is made manifest in war or in day-to-day relations where people hate because of differences: skin color, religion, gender, social class, political or social dogmas or body type.

Personal responsibility is the key ingredient in ending

these cycles. And personal responsibility may often mean the choice as a soul, to serve as a lesson for the rest of humanity, to prosper by, meanwhile perfecting, the ability to forgive and to love.

Transpersonal counselor and parapsychologist Dr. Hazel Denning finds accepting personal responsibility essential for obtaining results from past-life therapy. Cofounder and first president of APRT, Denning believes that when people realize that they are all on a soul journey and each experience is an opportunity for growth, they can then heal and transcend negativity.

Dr. Denning shared a private epiphany with me. Once, while showering, she told God that she wanted to know the "real" reason why she had a chronic health problem. Instantaneously, she experienced the vivid recollection of herself as a crusader. She was a male lying on a battlefield wearing a white tunic with a red cross, gauntlets on her hands, and a helmet. The crusader's right leg was flexed, and a spear had been driven through his kidney. His dying emotions had been of anger at being separated from his family, and horror and disgust at the abomination of war. Afterward, Denning said, she never had another kidney problem and the rage over injustice that had permeated her life for as long as she could recall was gone.

A similar tale of recovery was told by clinical psychologist Dr. Richard Levy. Under hypnosis, a female patient recalled a medieval lifetime in the British Isles in which she had been reduced to prostitution and stealing because of an illegitimate pregnancy. Her infant died of exposure, and the woman ultimately died of starvation. The sad story, however, has a happy ending. As a result of her regression therapy, Levy said that her high blood pressure normalized, chronic internal bleeding stopped, and she lost forty pounds.[5] Levy said that people often carry forward old negative patterns and lose their ability to identify them. Even if identified, however, they are unable to stop. Freud called this "repetition compulsion."

Personal empowerment results when the soul's energy is raised by understanding of ancient karmic events. This is what Dr. Bruce Goldberg has found and addressed in his book, *Soul Healing: An Alternative to Getting Physically, Mentally, and Spiritually Well Again.* Of Goldberg's clients who recall returning to medieval lifetimes, core issues surrounding relationships and victimization dominate. He has found that karmic ties are often uncovered with present lovers, family members, and friends. In his book *Past Lives—Future Lives*, Goldberg describes the case of a client who recalled being a soldier during the Middle Ages.[6] "Hans" wanted to usurp a castle after the death of the lord, but had to contend with the widow first. Hans organized a rebellion, but the widow amassed her own troops and crushed it. Hans was killed, and upon his death swore to get back at the widow. She was identified as the patient's current wife, with whom he had periodically struggled.

In more than one lifetime, hypnotherapist Henry Bolduc found himself a fighter in the Crusades. In one instance, it appeared to be an attractive way out of a little town. Fired with a passion to "save the world for Christ," Bolduc's past-life personalities were horrified to discover the betrayal of friends, greed, and other abominations committed in the name of religion. In one life, he had held a strong desire to see Jerusalem. Just as he came to the top of a hill and could see the city in the distance, he died. His fellow soldiers kicked him into a ditch and moved on.

Of Bolduc's clients who have recalled medieval lives, more of them recalled the Crusades. "Perhaps clients subconsciously select a therapist who has lived in similar civilizations or had dealt with similar themes," he mused. Some of his clients' medieval regressions touched on noble lifetimes, but most, he found, were laborers and homemakers in small, obscure towns.

Bolduc believes that experiencing past lives isn't just for cleaning up problems or merely to satisfy a curiosity. "It's also about learning more about the eternal self," he said. Psychic Edgar Cayce referred to this search for understanding as "the greater study of self." For this reason, Bolduc has called this work "past-life exploration." More people are coming to find out about their spiritual and personal life issues. The author of *Life Patterns: Soul Lessons and Forgiveness,* Bolduc teaches people to chart their past lives on a graph. As they cross-reference their good points and challenging points, they begin to see their soul patterns clearly laid out before them.[7]

Besides seeing effective, efficient, and permanent change in people's lives through eliminating symptoms and enhancing their lives, clinical psychologist Dr. Edith Fiore maintains that another result of past-life regressions is the overcoming of fears of death and the afterlife. Many of her patients recall lives, usually in the U.S., from 1930 to their current births. In her practice, Fiore has found that most past lives that cause problems are the immediate past life or fairly recent ones.

As therapists and their clients dig into the traumas of the past—whether their own or that of someone else from the collective unconscious—a healing of both individual pain and collective pain takes place.

"We're coming out of our bloodbaths and mopping up the historical residue," maintains Jungian psychotherapist Dr. Roger Woolger. The British-born author of *Other Lives, Other Selves* and *The Goddess Within* subscribes to the Hindu philosophy that we are completing a 5,000-year-old world cycle that's been dominated by warfare. "As we get closer to where things will change and maybe start again," he said, "it's as though all of history starts to repeat itself.[8]

"All we need to do is look at what's happening in Third World countries, to remember. Man does horrible things. There's the angelic and the dark side, as well as the shadow side of the glories and conquests written in history books." Woolger believes, as did writers of the *Vedanta*, that during these "end times" crude religious cultures and medieval conditions are arising in the Third World countries. Meanwhile, thousands of years of unresolved karmic mistakes are surfacing in individuals, in the psyche, and in the collective psyche of the time—more child abuse, divorce, etc. "It is as if we are all forced to be part of an enormous and unprecedented cleanup of the whole psychic history of our race," he said.

"Our hope is to transform our history from victims of a collective unconsciousness to new energies," Woolger emphasized.

"We each have a two million-year-old man we carry around," said Woolger. He said that some call this "residue" the collective unconscious; others the akashic records. The ability to access historical residues of history is in the "sacred time of the soul." This ability to move in time and space is not a modern concept. In support of this, Woolger references Taliesin, a Welsh bard in the ninth century who could do past-life remembering.

The psychologist himself, while lying on a sofa in a remote farmhouse in Vermont, recalled a lifetime as a crude peasant-turned-mercenary who found himself in the thick of some of the most hideous Cathar massacres, in which inhabitants of whole French cities were hacked into pieces and then burnt in huge pyres. In one melee, he was wounded and left for dead. The soldier, who never walked again, spent the remainder of his life in a village with the Cathars until he, too, was burned.[9]

Woolger believes that it is the role of the therapist to act almost as a shaman to compassionately listen to their clients' past lives with loving detachment in order to assist them in releasing, cleansing, and purifying the residue of negativity carried over from these times. Woolger encourages therapists to make the light brighter by working with the darkness within their clients, because by making the dark conscious and bringing the dualities together, this could affect our individual and planetary evolution into the next age.

In his work, Dr. Michael Newton moves beyond past-life experiences to a meaningful, immortal soul experience in the state between lives. He researches the activities of souls. Describing himself as a ruthless investigator who proceeds cautiously into the spirit world, he begins his process by taking his clients into a very deep state of hypnosis. In his book, *Journey of Souls: Case Studies of Life Between Lives,* he describes moving clients quickly into a past life and then into the spirit world where all memories are stored.[10] He calls the soul in this state the "immortal character." Here, the soul describes itself as a mass of pure energy which is guided by, in his words, a "Council of Elders." These higher beings help advise and explain the soul successes and failures and their choices for the future. Newton believes that this state is as close to God as we get and also that, with understanding and love, there is a place for all of us to evolve before our return to earth.

Upon reflection of the APRT presenters' and their clients' involvement in medieval lifetimes, I now had additional indicators that the medieval time period was an important historical marker that did indeed provide fertile soil for the growth and expansion of the soul in its journey through time and space.

With a historical perspective on healing and the tools of past-life therapy, I could hear the echoes of the residue of great medieval wars, civilizations, and cultures.

The fascinating past-life stories of the thirteen medieval and Renaissance reenactors range from lives of nobility to servants, the educated to the illiterate, and from peaceful to painful existences. Perhaps these riveting recollections collectively create a sumptuous tapestry of a deeper search into the psyche and soul.

3

Susan

"Souls of emperors and cobblers . . . "
—Michel Eyquem de Montaigne, *16th Century*

Describing herself as a "Renaissance woman," Susan Downs Reed is a historic costumer and graphic artist with an M.S. in textiles from the University of Maryland, College Park. Needless to say, the thirty-eight-year-old's talents are in demand among historical reenactors, who must either make their own garb or commission a seamstress, such as Susan, to make it for them. Susan has created costumes for many different time periods and purposes, including medieval en-

sembles for entire wedding parties. In addition, Susan
has hosted a monthly sewing circle, guiding her fellows
with historical and costuming information and practical assistance.

Susan looks at her longterm involvement in reenacting as a chance to exercise her academic achievements.
She not only takes authenticity seriously, but encourages
others to follow suit by making the endeavor enjoyable.

For her contributions to the SCA in the area of costuming, Susan was awarded the Order of the Laurel.
Throughout her sixteen years of membership, she has
also received the arts and sciences award, the Order of
the Pearl, for her work illustrating a newsletter, as well as
the Order of the Golden Dolphin for service. She teaches
other Scadians a wide range of courses that includes
"Fifteenth-Century Doublet-Making" and "Family and
Kinship in the Middle Ages and Renaissance," among
others.

In addition to studying historic costuming, Susan has
researched the domestic culture of the Middle Ages. She
is proficient in the art of High Table Service, attending to
the head table of presiding nobility at feasts and, in turn,
has others under her tutelage.

Another of Susan's interests is medieval religion. She
told me that she appreciates the predominant role of
spirituality in the Middle Ages, the mysticism, and the
symbolism of church art, stained glass, and religious
music.

The name of Susan's primary persona is Teleri Talgel-
lawg—a name inspired by the *Mabinogian*, a compila-
tion of ancient Welsh tales that includes one of the oldest
Arthurian legends. Teleri literally means "Cupbearer,
functionary, or butler." A more esoteric meaning might
be "Grail seeker" or "one who wields the elements of water and emotion."

The Welsh name, "Teleri," originated on an island

across the Irish Sea from Dublin, in the mid-1400s. However, Susan explained that she wears the fashions of different periods. She has carefully researched and crafted five subpersonas, whose lives range in time from 75 B.C. to A.D. 1700. Among them are an Italian lady-in-waiting of the 1470s, a sixteenth-century Portuguese widow of a sea captain, and an English Catholic woman who helped to settle Virginia in the seventeenth century. Preparing for her retirement from her role as a baroness in February 1996, she has developed the identity of a fifteenth-century Dutch woman who is retiring to the nunnery.

For nearly four years, Susan and her husband, Ken, have held the SCA-bestowed titles of Baron and Baroness of Ponte Alto. For two terms, they have acted as the personal representatives of the King and Queen of the Kingdom of Atlantia in the Barony of Ponte Alto, which includes parts of Northern Virginia. As the Crown's agents, they bear the royal arms, preside at all local events, hold court, and present awards. According to Susan, this enormous responsibility has taken its toll on the pair who have, at times, each put in twenty hours or more per week and at least two weekends per month in the service of the Crown.

Susan told me that she has found courtesy to be the glue of the SCA and believes that the members embody many traditional values no longer prevalent in modern society. The SCA, she told me, is an extended family that values altruism, hard work, and skill, and which honors the superlative achievements of its members, regardless of whether those achievements are tangible or intangible.

When we discussed her religious beliefs and the subject of the paranormal, Susan related to me that she has had déjà vu experiences suggestive of reincarnation memories. As a child, she recalled a square in a town in Germany during a different time period. As an adult, she once saw herself as a German soldier in the Thirty Years' War.

Susan also said that she felt convinced that reincarnation was possible—that conservation of spirit from one form to another just makes sense.

When it came time to regress her, we dimmed the lights in the usual fashion, and Susan stretched out on her couch. I then proceeded to relax her with visualization exercises that occupied her conscious mind as I guided her into the hypnotic state. Next, I directed her to a lifetime that correlated with her current interest in reenacting and asked her to describe what she saw, felt, or heard. After experiencing a sensation of spinning, as if she were riding a fast carousel, Susan began to see images.

"I see a village," she said. "The street is dirty. There are clam shells in the road as well as refuse and chickens. The road ends. There are two-story buildings, all shuttered and closed up. Most are brown with large wood beams, like wattle and daub. They're abandoned and wood-weathered.

"A front porch looks like a merchant's stall. Trees have serrated leaves. There's a person in a long, high-necked red gown, but it's not flowing. A man is dressed all in red. He has a tinge of brown hair and a short brown cap on his head. I feel scared in this village. It's so derelict." Susan was visibly uncomfortable.

"I'm wearing brown hose with leather soles. My feet are dusty. I feel like I've traveled a while. I'm wearing a tunic of sorts. The sleeves are pleated into the shoulders, and it's of medium-grade wool. The tunic could be an orange-russet color or be all dirt, it's so dusty. I feel there's a cap on my head. I have brown hair with a Prince Valiant cut.

"I'm a twenty-three-year-old male on my lord's business. I'm taking a message to an estate. I didn't know this small village was here. Death came through it and they all died. It's been abandoned for a long time. There's decay. I see an old black and white dog who's not fed. He has a spot over one eye. There are trees, old fields, a dirt road."

Susan was relieved to find that she had moved past the abandoned village and into a town that was much more lively.

"There are crowds, noise. It's market day and busy in a big town. I see cloth being draped, stalls opening, people shouting. One lady is selling fish. There's excitement. It's alive."

Susan forgot her former anxiety as she began observing the various personalities going about their business.

"I see a group of monks. Benedictines and Franciscans. I wonder if they will fight. They've been known to; they're not examples of true church charity."

Now, back on track with his mission, Susan's male personality headed for the church. "This is a good-sized town church. It's simple. I'm looking for Father Alford. I kneel before a statue of Our Lady. People are around the church; canons are readying for Mass. Someone takes me down a corridor to a room with a fireplace. Father Alford's sitting before a book. He nods. I hand him my packet. It's a leather pouch with an old, well-handled, large seal over the flap and chords hanging out of it. I was not told to wait for a message. He waves me away."

Done with his mission, the young man relaxes and remembers his hunger. "I'm looking for a vendor for meat pies. I'm very hungry and smell something good. It's a meat pie with spices." Savoring it, he told me, "It's sweet, with cinnamon, and also salty." Now that he was no longer famished, he once again focused on the people around him.

"The old woman who sold me the pie is short, arthritic, and bent over. She's got a white cloth around her head and is wearing something gray and shapeless. She's friendly.

"Some are more colorfully dressed, some aren't. There's a portly, muscular Henry VIII-type with a fur hat. He's wearing dark red and has several rings, one that looks like a sea moss agate. There's a man in blue with him. His clothing is a similar cut to mine, but more fashionable and his wool is finer.

"The cloth vendors are amazing. There's purple, blue, silver, and metal threads. A merchant gives me a sour look. He knows I can't afford it.

"A bunch of kids are playing tag. Most of them are ragged. A red-haired girl with a cap on is squealing. She runs under a stall and almost upsets the fishmonger. Another kid is rolling a hoop.

"I'm really tired. Church bells are ringing. Maybe the service is starting. I hear the sound of a horse. I see pots, pans, ribbons, horse shoes, a farrier, a blacksmith. I hear the sound of a hammer on an anvil. It's not on the street, but close to the village. Stalls are attached to the homes. The houses are two and three stories. They lean out, arching the roadway. They're white-washed with painted timbers and are a weathered brown-gray.

"A merchant with leather goods has the sign of St. Agatha over his shop. I see a nice white leather pouch. It's beyond my wages, although I'm not paid poorly for a groom. My lord is generous with his gifts."

Satisfied that the groom had finished his assignment, I directed him to return home.

"I mostly work in the kitchen and serve. But I want to be a steward. The steward keeps track of the estates and provisions, gives me my livery, hires and fires people, and knows more about my lord's business than he does.

"There are no windows in the kitchen and there's a fire going. I'm eating the leftovers. Bread, dried apples, frumenty—a thick stew with raisins—and hard cheese.

"There are visitors over. The butler hopes they'll go to bed so he will not have to wait on them tonight.

"A black-haired serving girl is washing dishes. Her sleeves are rolled up and her face is red-hot. I hear the clink of spoons as they are put away; the pottles [pots] are put in the cupboard. One of the cooks is falling asleep in the corner. There are three cooks and five servers in the room.

"Mostly, I serve, clean up, and put away napkins," he said. "I change the rushes in the hall, although I try to get a junior servant to do that."

The young man then reflected on his career. "Since I was fifteen, I worked as a manservant to a prosperous villager who holds much land. I was apprenticed to him to help him manage his property. But I wanted to work in my lord's house. I went with him to the moot and attracted the steward's eye.

"I'm ambitious. The butler is showing me how to fix the wine, set the table, and know where the guests should sit. A good carver has to know some of the sauces. When the Marshal of the Hall's not looking, I watch him. He thinks I'm an upstart. He's in his thirties and he reads. I know some. I learned from my mother and the man I worked for. Most of the others don't know how to read."

Next, I asked about his family. He became slightly nostalgic. "My family's more than a day's walk from here. I haven't seen them since I left the village. They do farming."

He brightened up as he continued to describe the household he was proud to be a part of. "My lord's place has a Great Hall with a large fireplace at the end. There are stone-carved arches, wall hangings with flowers, windows, and fresh rushes on the floor. Benches are along the wall, the tables are apart, and there's a passageway to the side of the fireplace. There are small chambers with beds, but most of us sleep in the hall on straw with a blanket on top. If I'm lucky, I get a spot next to the fireplace. The steward and marshal have their pick. The marshal has sent the hunting dogs back to their place.

"The kitchen is in another building," he continued. "It's a big room with tables in the middle. There's a large hearth, a bakery oven, cauldrons, tubs of water, barrels of dried carrots or parsnips, and locked cupboards. Only the marshal, steward, and the butler have keys to them.

"I like the scullery maid," he admitted suddenly. "Her name is Mary. Mine is William. She blushes when I tease her. She's from a poor family and is a day laborer from town."

After I questioned William about his location and the identity of his employer, he paused and then spoke, with a hint of reverence in his voice.

"It's York. He's the archbishop. He went to Oxford and he reads Latin. I don't know how to read Latin. It's the year of Edward IV, in the fourth year of his reign. I never address my lord. I only answer him, although he rarely speaks to his grooms. Only the steward or marshal tell us what to do.

"He's not spiritual, but he's pious and political. He arranges to get his friends positions in court. He advises the king and goes to London a lot. I'm not high enough to be privy to anything else. The chamberlain would know more, but he's probably too loyal to discuss his affairs. The chamberlain knows what's going on outside the country, although I don't."

Responding to my query as to whether he believed in the church, he answered vehemently, "Of course." He then moved on to describe his daily activities.

"The sun is rising. I'm inside the Great Hall. I stumble outside to the well and pour water over my face. Next, I go to the trunk to find a cleaner shirt and give the other one to the laundress. I comb my hair and clean my fingernails. The people in the hall are all starting to rise. The chamberlain is carrying water to my lord's chamber. Now, we're all gathering in the back of the chapel to hear Mass.

"My lord's going to London and we are helping to pack his bags. There are clothes, linen, and dishes. He's going to stay awhile. The marshal, butler, and steward are inventorying everything. Horses are brought from the stables, and chests are loaded on carts."

While the staff prepares for the archbishop's journey, William found himself on another errand.

"I'm sent to the apothecary to pick up a concoction. I have a letter. The streets are crowded as usual. It is not yet tierce. People are busy and booths are opening up. Doors are being unlocked and women are spinning. The apothecary shop has lots of drying plants, jars, and mortar. I hand the man my letter. He tells his wife to bring out different things which he puts in the mortar and grinds. She measures it on a scale and wraps it in a piece of parchment. I go back to the enclave and give the parcel to the marshal. He tallies it in a book to pay the apothecary later.

"There are errands to do. I'll be staying behind. When there's no work and just ourselves to take care of, I can go out with the other lads and hang out at the inn. I'm paid yearly twenty shillings," he said proudly. Temporarily relieved of his responsibilities, William became more boyish.

"I'm laughing in the courtyard with three other lads. It's fun. John is kind of stupid; he's a simpleton. One boy makes fun of him, but the older brother protects and watches out for him.

"Another one is John. There are lots of Johns. He's sometimes too daring for me. He sneaks a village girl into the hall. I want to keep my job. There are places to go for that type of thing. Most guys who go there are not married, so it's not a sin—not adultery, like when they do it and they're married."

I progressed William in age. Thoughts of girls and games had left his mind and he began to fixate on his career.

"I'm in my mid-to-late twenties. Guys of my station marry now, although rich men marry later. They don't inherit estates or find a rich widow until later. They need the inheritance to live as well as they did when they grew up. I'm saving my wages to be married, although I have no one in mind. My lord will arrange for someone for me—a woman who is a good manager, spins well, and has a good trade. Other than flirting with girls in the village and on trips, it's up to my lord.

"I don't have much spare time, except in the winter. My hobbies are dancing and playing a tune on a flute-like thing."

After again moving William forward in time, he experienced the sensation of floating in a dark, empty room. He described having tunnel vision and could only see a white wall with a wood carving in front of him. He then fixed his attention on the geometric patterns of a window that had small, clear glass panes. I realized that he was probably dying and that he was looking back on his life.

"It's light, so it must be daytime. There's a book in front of me. I'm reading and praying. I'm retired. I ran the household. I became the marshal and liked it. I got to meet many important people and traveled frequently. For me, London was a little too crowded and smelled much worse. And then there was the cheeky attitude of some servants, but usually they minded.

"Throughout the course of my life, I served two archbishops. I never married but stayed my lord's servant. It was lonely sometimes, but it was just as well. Some marshals married, while some didn't. I stayed in one of the church's houses. The bishopric properties were comfortable.

"I prepare for the life to come through reading, praying, and going to the priests for confession. I served my lord well and I feel proud. I was able to do things for my friends. Although I didn't see my family much, I was able to leave my nieces good dowries."

Now, as William began to feel the physical sensations of his death, I saw tears trickling down Susan's cheeks.

"My eyes are closed, and I'm grasping rosary beads. It's hard to breathe, and I can't move. I keep hoping for the chamberlain to come. I call for him. 'Mary, O Lady, help me.' I see streaks of blue. I ask God to forgive me. I can't summon a priest. Pray for me."

After Susan had roused herself from the regression, she said she felt groggy and later told me that she was surprised when, for more than four hours after the regression, she felt a "high-energy field" coating her body. This harmless but heightened sensitivity to her energy field was an indication that Susan's past-life regression was more than a purely intellectual experience.

She claimed no familiarity with some of the things she saw and admitted to an intensity of emotions that was startling. Even so, Susan questioned whether her current interest in fifteenth-century household management was the result of this past life or whether her knowledge had influenced what she had experienced. Still, Susan said she believed her memories were much more authentic than her reenacting activities.

To assuage our curiosity about whether Susan's prior knowledge "colored" her recalled past life, we set up another session, hoping to return to another medieval lifetime of which Susan would have no prior knowledge. Several weeks later, I returned to her home. Susan was now familiar with the procedure and gave me suggestions for assisting her into a more relaxed altered state.

Shortly, Susan found herself as a mother in her mid-twenties with two children. Wearing a blue and white tunic with diamond patterns around the hem, she was sitting on an evening hillside, dampened by dew, with a man dressed in woolen trousers and tunic. He had blond shaggy hair and a moustache, and was eating the joint of a pig. She heard laughter in the distance, smelled wood smoke and pigs roasting on spits, saw the light from torches coming over the hillside, and felt an air of excitement.

Soon, she joined others in the midst of a fall harvest festival. She saw apples, seeds, turnips, and root vegetables by the light of the full moon. Someone was playing a lyrelike harp and singing a song, while others joined in on the chorus.

"We're near a stand of alder trees," she said. "There are tall grooved sticks in the ground. Flashes of flames leap from the fire. I'm near the bright fire. I reach into a pouch, take a handful of something like the Viking runes, and throw it on the fire. The man announces that we will renew our marriage contract for seven years. There is much rejoicing."

She laughed and then, leaving the scene, moved to the last day of that lifetime. "We're in the foothills; mountains are off in the distance. Our home has a thatched roof and wooden fence. I'm inside. There are dried herbs everywhere. The hearth is in the center. Oil lanterns are nearby. I've been in great pain. I'm slipping away and I know it. Several people are there. I hear people crying. I smell apple blossoms and I'm gone. I'm about thirty."

Later, Susan explained that she'd had some of those memories recur while in a meditative state, but never so vividly or detailed. She felt that the lifetime was premedieval, probably before the year A.D. 1. She said she felt the location was the Danish peninsula, well before any Teutonic tribes migrated to the area.

We moved on to another life, one in which she had no prior knowledge.

"I see sandy buildings and a Middle Eastern bazaar. People are wearing colorful, striped, loose robes and turbans. There's activity like the fluttering of cloth and drapery. A tower with windows looms, partly in ruins, like it's sitting on top of the air.

"I'm a seventeen-year-old male and I'm Middle Eastern or Arabic. I'm learning tanning. It's a smelly job. I'm knee-deep in ashes. It's slimy. The boy knows what he's using. There are a pile of skins nearby."

Sensing agitation in those around him, the young man is distracted from his work.

"People are worried, anxious. They look like something may be happening that's not good. There's tension around. Two older men in a shop are talking anxiously. They tell me to keep working. It's a sunny, warm day. I hear the sound of a horn. Everything stops. We all kneel to pray."

Susan suddenly groaned, "Oh no, not another short life! Horses come in. A lot of people are in armored clothing and on black horses. They slaughter everyone in the bazaar. Here comes the sword for me."

We once again moved on. This time, Susan was a young girl in a cottage spinning wool, while an old woman told stories.

"There's a trestle table and wooden dishes over the hearth. A bed is against the opposite wall. There's a straw mattress on the floor. Shutters are on the windows, which are open. The door's open, too.

"My mother's gone to the river to do laundry," she continued. "There are five large vats inside the house to brew the ale. My mother's an alewife. We live in a fenced area with other houses nearby. The farmlands are farther away. Grain is being harvested. My older brothers have gone to help out.

"Life seems redundant. I'm cutting vegetables, getting the grain ready to be brewed, gathering eggs, milking cows, feeding chickens, day in and day out."

After this glimpse of her young, monotonous life, we moved forward to adulthood. "I've become the keeper of a tavern named 'Louis Malle.' It's near a well-traveled road, but not near a city or closely populated area. The landscape's flat. I'm in my forties, that's fairly old. My hair is wrapped in white veils. I have a mustard-colored gown on. It seems like the Netherlands.

"My husband's considerably older, in his sixties. He's wearing a dirty white and red coif, a skirted doublet, and pointed second-hand shoes from a vendor."

As an adult, she had a somewhat different outlook on her regular routine. "It's not drudgery, just ordinary tasks. We go to church on Sunday. The church is mostly white walls with brown or black beams. We're Calvinists. A bearded man is preaching with a black coif, Tudor cap, and long black robes. He's droning on and on."

Leaving the church scene, Susan returns to the tavern. "I'm holding a set of keys. I have the vague impression of a son. He seemed to work in the tavern. If there were other children, they moved out. The tavern is two stories. Half is timbered with a thatched roof, brown shutters, and open eaves. There are benches around the corner of the front. Serving maids work here." Then the scene began to recede. It got smaller until it was just a tiny beam of light and concentric rings.

When Susan came back to waking consciousness, she told me she was still a little skeptical of her recollections, but had definitely been given more food for thought. She told me later that after this regression it took her body two days to feel normal again, describing the sensation as like being in a duplicate tingling form outside of her own body. Partially due to Susan's strong sensitivity to changes in her energy field, the hypnotic experience affected her like a "psychic hangover" but faded naturally and safely. Perhaps some healing, integration or energy work had taken place in the process.

Because, in this life, Susan had studied household management and hierarchy in medieval homes as well as historic costuming, she questioned the origin of some of the more general information in her first recalled life as the archbishop's servant. However, that didn't explain the uncertainties, new information, and specific details—such as probable locations, dates, salaries, and her employer—which Susan and other historians began to research and confirm. These new confirmations allowed Susan to give her regression experiences more credence.

For instance, Susan said that she had never imagined anything like the plague town which she sensed was filled with ghosts. After the regression, Susan found old maps that indicated a medieval village near York, probably abandoned around the time of the plague.[1] In the *Guide to English Heritage Properties,* she also located an abandoned medieval village at Wharram Percy, about fifteen miles east-northeast of York. Susan speculated that a person heading to a number of known religious establishments or towns might have easily passed through there. Another deserted medieval village within range of York, though much farther away than Wharram Percy, is Gainsthorpe, about forty miles southeast of the city. The guide also notes that these places are but two of 3,000 identified medieval abandoned villages.[2]

One possibility for Fr. Alford's lively town is the oceanside city of Scarborough. Susan mentioned clam shells in the road, indicating an area close to the sea or an estuary. Shells have been commonly used for paving in oceanside areas as late as this century.

Although the plague, called the "Black Death," scourged Europe in the mid-1300s, killing nearly half the population in England alone, it continued to appear in small outbreaks for many years to come and its unmeasured effects still lingered in the 1460s. Diseases other than the Black Death also carried off large numbers of Europeans and potentially whole villages.

Death by small pox, the "sweating sickness," and other killer viruses were experienced every year, normally during the summer months. These outbreaks were so commonplace that many who could afford it regularly spent their summers in the country to avoid the cities in which the contagions thrived. Henry VIII, for example, was terrified of the plague, the pox, and the sweating sickness and moved his court regularly to avoid contact with the infected. He was so frightened of these diseases that, at the height of his infatuation, he ran from Anne Boleyn when the lady fell ill with the sweat.

As for the group of monks that the young man encountered, Susan discovered that a number of religious establishments had been based in Yorkshire: Cistercians (there are several remaining sites), Augustinians, Benedictines, and Carthusians. There were also a number of Franciscan establishments in Yorkshire. These were generally established in cities. Therefore, it would not be uncommon for Franciscans to have had business with the Archbishop of York or other church dignitaries. Few notable Franciscan or Dominican friaries survived.[3]

The Benedictines were founded in A.D. 530 while the Franciscan Order had come to England in 1224.[4] By 1524, the Franciscans were a huge, well-established order and active in the affairs of the country.[5]

Some commentators noted that a potential altercation between the Franciscans and Benedictines was not unthinkable.

Edward IV, the monarch in whose reign Susan placed her past incarnation, was king from 1461 to 1483. Dating the boy's journey to the fourth year of his reign should place it in 1465 or 1466. George Neville was the Archbishop of York during the reign of Edward IV. The Oxford graduate had a reputation as a patron of learning.

My experts verified that some highly expensive cloth of the era was woven, in part, with metallic threads—including gold. Food was indeed desiccated for storage. Also correct was Susan's placement of the farrier's shop off the main street because of the loud noise and the black, choking smoke it produced.

My historians agreed that the people of the time were used to covering great distances on foot and that "more than a day's walk" was not considered an excessive distance for the element of society whose duties included traveling. While it may be true that fewer than twenty percent of the people ever went farther than ten miles from their birthplace, it is also true that messengers on both foot and horseback regularly traversed the nation.

Professor Joann Moran described William's references to a deserted village, the liveries, and town as appropriate to the fifteenth century. She did note that canons— members of the chapter of a cathedral or collegiate church—would have been unusual in a town church such as Susan described, but not impossible if the church was run by the Augustinian Order.

Moran found no fault with the description of the hall or the life and work of the servants. She also verified that it was normal for men to marry in their mid-to-late twenties. It would not have been unusual for a butler to read, but Moran noted that it would have been unusual for this man, working in a kitchen, to have learned to read even a little from his mother. It would have been normal for the apothecary to read, to have wrapped the concoction in parchment, and for the marshal to have kept a book tally. Although William's annual salary was a bit high, Moran said that it was within an acceptable range. However, William's use of the word "moot" as an assembly was already archaic in the fifteenth century. In a final analysis, Moran thought that this marshal probably did not serve in the archbishop's house in York, but rather in one of his manor houses.

My clothing experts agreed that red, orange, and russet were standard colors for medieval clothing as the colors were easy to achieve in the natural dyeing process. Sleeves pleated into the shoulders and the Prince Valiant haircut were typical of the fifteenth century, also observing that the fine cloth and rich merchants indicated a wealthy town.

Susan was also correct about the outer sealing of the message that William had carried. Such a document would indeed have been fastened by a cord and the knot made untieable by encapsulating it in a sealing wax into which was stamped a personal or official image.

Susan also correctly placed the kitchen of the establishment in another building. Locked cupboards were indeed the norm, with each superior in charge of individual articles in chest drawers and cupboards for which they held a key.

The "wall hangings with flowers" Susan mentioned as part of the archbishop's decor were probably flowered tapestries. These were favored by all who could afford them, as they both cheered up a room and helped insulate it from outside cold and damp. Most great houses had small, clear glass panes set by leading into geometric patterns consistent with William's description. The flutelike instrument that William played was probably a recorder, a popular, common musical instrument of the age.

As a marshal, William recalled having difficulties with his staff, which would have contained a high percentage of adolescent boys. Books of the day still exist for training boys destined for domestic service. The volumes discuss such areas as correct dish placement and by what title to address the lord, his family, or other visitors; however, they also contained such general decencies as "don't spit or snot at the table."[6] Obviously, boys were boys both then and now.

William commented that his lord was more politically than spiritually minded. This was true of George Neville, who sustained his position throughout the turbulent reigns of Edward IV and Henry VII and was well known as a political schemer.

Moving to Susan's recalled life in a Muslim culture, Bruce Blackistone affirmed that ashes were used to help remove animal hair as part of the tanning process. The majority of my experts did not feel their knowledge of the medieval Middle East could do more than verify the likelihood of the chain of events Susan described.

When assessing the life of the ancient Danish woman, one of my experts confirmed that lyrelike harps were used by Vikings and Saxons. The Sutton Hoo exhibit at the British Museum displays a fine example of a recon-structed lyre. It was also postulated that the tall grooved sticks in the ground could describe a wooden palisade, a common defense structure of Saxon and Celtic hill forts, a precursor to the western fort. The clothing and the food, particularly turnips, were appropriate for Saxon Europe.

As for Susan's life as an ale maker, there was a long-standing tradition that women brewed ale, beer, and other fermented grain beverages. It fell into the realm of domestic duties, as water was rarely drunk when other choices were available. People had made a connection between bad water and sickness, and themselves par-ticipated in their own ruination by dumping trash, fe-ces, and dead animals into local rivers, lakes, and streams. It is also true that after A.D. 1200 the middle class first began its emergence, and women with expert skills, such as ale making, could participate with their husbands in building a family's better fortune.

The tavern "Louis Malle" was named after Louis Malle,

Count of Flanders in the mid-1400s, thus placing the date of the lifetime in the late fifteenth or sixteenth century. The clothing Susan described is consistent with western European clothing of the era.

Since Susan's waking knowledge of household management and certain other historical details was high, she remained suspicious of her regression process. At the same time, she was startled at the confirmation of the new, detailed information that her subconscious had brought forth, as well as the source of her emotional and physical reactions during and after the regression experiences—reactions completely outside her "living history" experiences.

The nature of hypnosis, the subconscious, and past-life regressions alone often make the participant feel as if he or she is "making up a story"—especially in light of the philosophical framework of our Western beliefs, which have not, for the most part, incorporated reincarnation. The subconscious is also apt to recall most readily what is most clearly etched on our souls—emotions and feelings. Given Susan's honest, conscientious nature, it would be natural for her historical knowledge to exacerbate these concerns.

Even so, Susan, like others, was able to look beyond the previously known elements—tempering her concerns by also focusing on what previously had been consciously unknown—individuals, vignettes, details, and especially lifelike emotions and sensations—her fear when she found herself in a deserted village, feelings of hunger and exhaustion while on a journey, pride in her job, or her tears at the hour of her death—that would have been difficult for her to have imagined.

4

Nick

"Leaving us the stars . . . "

—Anonymous

Nick Neville is a man of many talents. Once, in order to mint his own medieval coins, he created a wooden frame to hold the cumbersome metal pieces so that the die wouldn't double-strike and leave a blurred image. He described it as a "vibration damper." Later, he discovered "his" invention in a museum.

In his mundane life, Nick has one patent pending and twenty more inventions in the works. The thirty-six-year-old told me at our meeting in July 1995 that he is always creating and strives to be a "Jack of all trades and master of many."

When I asked him about the creation of the vibration damper, Nick replied that he was tapping into his ancestral memories. Nick believes he discovered these memories as a child, when he felt forced to turn inward after enduring early physical and emotional traumas.

Nick says he could read simple sentences by the age of three and told me he was reading the science fiction and fantasy novels of André Norton and Robert Heinlein when he was four. (His IQ was later determined to be 186). Particularly attracted to the myths of King Arthur and Hercules, he enjoyed research to discover if there was historical fact behind the tales.

Compared to King Arthur legends, Nick's youth was painful. Told that he would never walk again after being badly burned in a house fire, he worked to prove the doctors wrong. In college, he backpacked and took ballet and modern dance.

Nick told me that he had been interested in healing since his grandmother, a Pentecostal healer, had introduced him to the laying on of hands. She would visit the local hospital to attempt healing and he would accompany her. The youngster's short arms could barely reach the patients in their beds, but when contact was made, instantaneous healings would sometimes result. He believed that, together, the pair assisted in healing his mother's cancer.

This compassion for people inspired Nick to major in psychology at Eastern Kentucky University. Just credits short of earning his bachelor's degree, however, he joined the navy and served as a neuropsychological technician and hospital corpsman for six years.

Although he said that he was willing to fight to defend his homeland, Nick felt ambivalent about war. He explained that, on one hand, he was a pacifist who had practiced yoga for twenty-three years. On the other hand, he was drawn to the competition of battle. He had no interest in studying historical wars that occurred outside the medieval era.

Nick was intrigued when he first heard of the SCA. Six years after leaving the navy, he connected with Clan Cromlech, in the Barony of Ponte Alto, through the America Online computer service. After participating in his first medieval event, Nick felt as though he fit in. Shortly afterward, he was given the title of castellan, a male chatelain who holds the keys to the household and is the coordinator for newcomers, supplying them with loaner costumes.

His own reenacting persona, Micheal Gaidheal, or Michael the Highlander, reflects his love of the mountains. He dates his Gaelic persona to the mid-to-late 1400s.

Nick said he was currently being trained in the art of High Table Service. In the Middle Ages, young nobles would be assigned to serve the head table. This was thought to help them understand the concepts of gentility, service, honor, and chivalry. Servers formed a processional and presented the food with pomp and circumstance. Nick told me that the term "upper crust" originated from the actions of the *panter,* or keeper of the bread. He would cut off the crust, thought to be the best portion of the loaf, and ceremoniously present it to the highest lord.

An advocate of chivalry long before enrolling in the SCA, Nick fancied kissing a lady's hand. He also wore his hair long. According to Nick, who has Kentucky roots, the aristocracy of Kentucky carried on a tradition that originated in the Middle Ages, that of horse owners wearing their hair back in ponytails. According to family legend, one of his father's ancestors had been the High King of Ireland.

Nick's royal lineage may be more than genealogical.

He claims that his girlfriend Dori (see chapter 5) has psychic abilities and has seen glimpses of him in past lives both as a knight and as a Scottish highlander. He, in turn, has "seen" a flash of Dori in a medieval gown.

When asked about other paranormal experiences, Nick recalled for me his feeling of déjà vu the first time he put on a medieval leather jerkin. He has also felt a strange familiarity when hearing the methodical beats of drums and seeing the Pennsic War castles by the trembling light of torches. The fortresses touched a nerve, reminding him of his youthful desire to build a castle.

Nick mysteriously knew the steps to a medieval reel dance called "The Needle in the Hay," before he had ever seen it danced. He felt completely confident the first time he joined in.

Although he never had training in leatherwork, he fashioned a scabbard for a friend, which, upon further investigation, proved to be historically accurate for the particular medieval period. Also, he told me that making his own garb seemed effortless. Nick even purchased a sewing machine.

Comfortable in tights and a blousey shirt, Nick immediately felt himself a part of the medieval times. However, he claims to be extremely uncomfortable when dressed in a U.S. Civil War uniform. On one occasion, Nick accompanied Dori to a Civil War ball. He showed me a photo of himself looking stiff and uneasy. In contrast, a photo of him in his medieval garb showed a smiling, relaxed person.

Nick told me that he was most impressed with the well-adjusted children being raised by SCA parents. He observed that the SCA gives them a good foundation for learning self-discipline and industry in an environment that stresses honor, freedom, imagination, and reward.

Because he values the importance of early training, Nick is thinking of setting up a program for youngsters.

After all, at the age of seven, a boy in the Middle Ages would have left home and joined another knight's household to train as a page. By the age of fifteen, he would have begun five years of serving as a valet to the knight who was his master.

Nick admires spiritual principles and teaches seminars to Christian groups on the "Biblical Perspective on Love." Another course Nick teaches is on the mystical aspects of the Bible. Nick, who had a great-grandfather who was a Blackfoot Indian shaman, said that churches have forgotten about mysticism, which is prevalent in the Bible.

His spiritual background, training, and "ancestral memories" have allowed Nick to communicate with what he believes are other planes of existence. He believes that all ancestral memories are recorded in the energy field of the soul and are accessible. Although he doesn't believe that human souls necessarily reincarnate on earth, he thinks it's possible that our souls continue some form of internal soul progression after the soul essence moves onto another plane of being at death.

After we finished the interview portion of our session, he told me that he was prepared to go on a trip into the netherworld, into the minds of his ancestors, or wherever his subconscious would take him. He slipped quickly into a hypnotic state, and his first recollection was of falling. His tongue was thick and his head hurt on his left side. He felt people around and saw the stocky dark-brown legs and black-and-white hooves of horses.

"My body feels like raw wood," he began. "I can't get up. I don't want to be here. It's dark. No one can help me." Suddenly, he sounded alarmed. "I'm dead. Somebody lied and no one would tell me. I'm not supposed to be here. I didn't do anything. I'm angry that they lied.

"I see a face," he continued. "It's mine. It's Chinese. I'm spinning and twirling and then it's dark. The pain is on the left and starts at my neck where my migraines are. They killed my grandfather with a stick and he slumped over. They were afraid of him. I was real young, but I could walk and dress myself."

Realizing that he had gone directly to his death, I coaxed him backward in that lifetime, before his grandfather's death. "There's a forest around us," he began. "I have no idea the name of the place. It's close to a mountain. Something looks like a tent. It's like an upside-down basket, but it's darker inside. There's a fireplace in the floor with warm coals and gray ashes.

"My name means 'boy,' but I can't say it. I can't make out the sounds and tones. They mean something when you put them together. It sounds like humming, but it's more distinct.

"Grandfather is wearing britches and a gray robe with a big neck. It's just folds of cloth. He isn't big. He has pits on his face, although some of his skin is still soft and smooth. His hair is long and part of it falls to his shoulders. He's sitting cross-legged on a dirty gray blanket. There's no furniture.

"I'm the only one wearing red long pants and a shirt with no buttons or sleeves. I don't like sleeves because you can't see anything with them. I couldn't find the plants so good. We're always looking for plants. Sometimes my feet get so cold."

Restlessly moving his feet on the couch, he went on. "Grandfather is always picking plants like mint and 'ka.' I drink it and it makes my belly stop hurting. It hurts a lot. He gives it to others, too. Tea from red berries tastes good. It also makes me feel better. I'm too young to be sick, except that my body hurts.

"We eat birds, lots of plants, and lots of soup," he continued. "It's good. Sometimes it's too hot and burns my belly. Something in it would make it burn and then the mint would make it go away. He'd put the mint in my cup. The weeds would tickle my throat. Then, I'd wash it down with water.

"Sometimes he catches small animals with his hands. He has a funny-looking knife with jagged edges and broken pieces of white rock, but he doesn't use it except to clean the animals. We cook over a fire with a stick and we cook the soup in a heavy bag."

Now it was morning and the pair were outside taking bark off the trees to make "noodles" in the soup.

"The bark has a sharp taste. I was helping Grandfather and he was teaching me what I could eat. Bugs taste like candy. It's the only thing that tastes so sweet," Nick, as the boy, smiled happily.

"He hugged me a lot and told me that he was going away soon. I wanted to go with him, but he wouldn't answer. He'd laugh and talk of plants. Sometimes he'd talk and tell me stories. I didn't know what they meant.

"We slept during the day when it was too hot, but I'd get cold sometimes. He couldn't walk good. He'd have to sit down a lot. I was scared of him, but he was nice to me. Maybe I wasn't scared, but I didn't understand.

"Men would come and Grandfather would tell me to be quiet. They'd always ask me stuff. I'd look at a rock or the sky and tell them where they should hunt. They'd go there and find food. They never asked Grandfather.

"But he'd give them plants. Some tasted funny. I didn't like the smell and would hold my nose. They wouldn't stay in the tent. They wore shirts and something on top of the shirts. They wore shoes. I told Grandfather that I didn't like shoes because of the stinky feet. Grandfather laughed.

"But, I liked it when they came because they'd bring meat to eat. Grandfather liked a tea that would make him laugh. He drank the dark beer that the others brought. Why did he drink? It always stank," Nick said with disgust, "and he would spill some on the floor."

We moved on to another episode when the young child and Grandfather had a female visitor. "Once a woman came and stayed a while. She came from far away on a horse with muddy feet. The woman's feet hurt. The old man used a prickly nut that he ground up. Then her feet would stop hurting. I saw animals eat the prickly nuts, but he wouldn't let me near that tree. He said that it was dangerous and just to be used on human feet.

"She wore a dingy sheet. She had real long hair and she smelled good. Her toes would poke out of her shoes. She said I was cute. I laughed. She hugged me and said that she loved me. She was big and soft, and it felt good when she hugged me. I like hugs. I'd be scared if there was no one to hug me," he said in a whimper.

"She taught me how to make a basket," he told me smugly. "She showed me how to bend the shiny wood, put pieces on top, and tie it together. Mine always fell apart, but she'd just laugh.

"She told me stories about talking animals. That's silly. They didn't make sense. I didn't know what reading was. I don't remember seeing any reading," he said pensively.

"She also taught me to dig up big roots and throw them into the fire. They tasted good. The little roots were crunchy. Grandfather liked them in soup."

We now returned to the time of the boy's violent death where he had begun his description. This time, he understood that the men who killed both his grandfather and himself were angry because they did not get healed due to their lack of belief.

We moved on to his next remembered incarnation. Nick found himself a young man wearing tight pants, a yellow shirt with puffy sleeves, and boots.

"My name is Tadgh. I wanted to get married, but her daddy didn't like me. He was embarrassed by me because I wasn't rich like him," he said dejectedly. "I spent a lot of time in the garden with the plants. I've only been to that garden once, but saw her when she was visiting someone else. I was helping them with their garden. There were big mud puddles there.

"The women in the garden were dressed alike in big, wide dresses that fell straight down to the ankles and highlighted their big breasts. They wore flat, crowned hats. Her dress had stripes.

"The men wore pants and shiny or dark metallic sheets that would crinkle and rust when they went away. They would bend and squeeze the metal to fit. It would be a long time before they'd come back, more than one season. They weren't glad to go, but it was better than being bored doing gardening."

Now I suggested that Tadgh go to his own home. Complying, he moved on to another scene.

"I felt like I ran everywhere. Most people walked, although some had horses," he explained. "The homes are all close enough to see each other. They are all dirty homes of wood and dirt," he noticed. "Some have rocks on the bottom. The roofs are made of loose dirt."

Once inside his house, Tadgh saw a table and a couple of benches. "There are two men with my parents. We are all ready to go to bed. My parents are in the loft. The cloth on the straw is itchy. I sleep in my clothes. The two guys sleep with me. They are just visiting. One laughs a lot and is always friendly. They make me nervous. One wears the shiny stuff. They needed food and a place to stay."

Nick had been moving his legs and knees nervously ever since he began relating this scene.

"They ate soup, bread, and meat—what we normally ate. We didn't eat because there wasn't enough food for us. Mother prepared the food while I'd help with the fire. We'd carry water up from the river. It was usually muddy near the water.

"She was gone all day helping others. I took care of the garden. Dad didn't work but he'd help with the water. He drank a lot, something with oats in it.

"I'm scared all the time," he continued nervously. "Everybody's scared. Mother didn't like the guys. She'd serve them and then disappear. None of us liked it when they came. One would disappear with Mom. When they'd leave, she'd cry. Then Dad would drink again and leave."

At this point, I asked Tadgh if he could identify the country.

"I don't know the date or the country, but the town's name is Glenfadden," he responded. "It's near some small mountains and a river comes out of it. The language is guttural, like grunting. I hear it but can't say it. I could say it then though."

Nick progressed ahead in time. "They said I abused her," he stuttered in disbelief. "We had a chaperon. They lied. I couldn't believe that they said that. I didn't do it. It couldn't happen. I don't want to think about it.

"They killed me for it," he continued emotionally. "They put me on a table and cut off my head. The left side of my head hurts. Maybe one of those soldiers who stayed with us had assaulted my mother and also my girlfriend.

"The only time I was ever happy was when I'd see her. I don't remember after that. My head hurts. I want to kill him. I died too many times and remember violent deaths. People either love or hate me. Why do my stomach and head hurt? There's shooting pain in my left leg," he said grimacing.

After I helped him to calm down after recalling two violent deaths—both with damage to his head—Nick was prepared to go to another lifetime. This time he found himself a mercenary soldier.

"I fight a lot," he began. "I love to fight and I use an ax with drawings and lines on it. I wear a short dress and a leather coat, sometimes with a shirt underneath. It's itchy material.

"We have axes, swords, knives, and clubs. The shiny ones have shields," he continued matter of factly. "In battle, I grab them and hit around the shields, so that they will drop their weapons easily. I also hit their neck or arms because it's easier to cut them just above the hip. They are protected other places. If they aren't wearing metal shoes, I hit their shoes with an ax. Then, it's easier to kill them. But most of them wear metal shoes."

With maturity came a different attitude. "I hate fighting. It's stupid. When I got older, I was sick of fighting. Most of the men would die anyway. I'd go to battles and wouldn't fight," the soldier confessed.

"Later, when the fighters were hurt, they'd bring them to me. I'd give them herbs, and wash and wrap the wound. If they were hit in the stomach or the head, I'd give them herbs to sleep and they'd die. If they lived, they'd be in pain, so it's better to die," he determined. He spoke from experience.

"I was stuck in the stomach once. It burned all the time for the rest of my life. Sometimes eating helped for a while," he continued. "My left hand was wounded by an ax and I can never straighten it out anymore." I observed that Nick's left hand was clenched tightly into a fist.

"When it was too hard to go to war, I'd bring the wounded home. My house is round and made of rocks, plants, grass, and a lot of mud. I lived by myself.

"I had a wife, but she died young. She was sick. We were married for about four years and didn't have any children. I moved around a lot before I met my wife and again after her death. I can hear the town's name but I can't say it. Eventually, I went back home. I didn't see my family much because they were far away."

I was interested in hearing about the mercenary's wife, so I asked Nick to go back to the time when he met her.

"I met her when I went for a contest. Agnes was a cook.

The only time I ever talked to her was over a fire pit. I went to ask permission to court. Her father said no, but after my fighting, he asked if I was still interested. After that, I'd help her with chores.

"We married the old way, with no priest. An old man talked, then had us dance. He asked us our intentions, then we asked for approval, and he gave it. Then, he sent us into the woods for privacy. I love the woods. Afterwards, our neighbors came for a big party and then we went back into the woods. Everybody was happy. She moved into my house and didn't cook as a job anymore. When my wife was young, she'd make clothing by weaving designs on a stick. Only the rich people had looms. But she was proud that we had a metal pot.

"I worked for several weeks or longer to get that pot. I would work for whomever would pay me, as long as I got to fight. I was paid to fight for the guys in armor who could afford horses. When I was young, I'd always fight for respect or was treated like dirt. They called me 'the Bold,' and 'the Stupid' behind my back. I'd fight people I shouldn't have, but never backed down. How they saw me was more important than my name because they had to acknowledge my boldness. I did not feel safe until I was older and began to heal people."

Now, I asked Nick to move to another event that he had shared with his wife.

"We went to town for a big celebration," he carried on, sounding carefree. "We got a ride on a cart down a mud road that stank. There were lots of two-story buildings, bright colors, and lots of food. I got Agnes a belt of tanned leather with a bronze buckle. It was the most expensive thing we owned and she loved it. I won money from a wrestling match.

"When the crowd moved to the center of town to see the execution of a man who had stolen a horse, everyone thought it was fun but me. It made me feel angry and hurt inside. My wife said that that's why she loved me. She wouldn't go either."

Later, they returned home, and Nick's ancient personality talked about their more routine affairs.

"My wife attended the only church in the village. There were lots of priests there. I don't know the name of the village and I wasn't born there.

"Later, my wife got sick. She coughed and spit up blood. Even though she was sick, she still went to church. The priests called her illness 'God's punishment,'" he said bitterly. "Agnes was a healer who would touch people, hold them for a few seconds, and they'd get better. The priests called her a witch because she didn't pray first." His words sounding raw, he composed himself with difficulty.

"She never talked, but just listened to people's problems. She would heal without regard for recompense. Even the herbalists and priests came to her. After what the priests said, the people who had been healed were all scared.

"Before she died, she taught me to heal. Rich people came. Even the priests would come to me, but under cover of darkness. Some said that I cared too much.

"I missed my wife and was angry that I couldn't fight. My wife and fighting were the only things I wanted. I figured there was a God up there, but I was angry at the priests, so I'd go outside to worship God. "God doesn't live in a house anyway," he philosophized.

"I was so angry," he said with emotion. "It was hard to have friends until I was older and a healer. I'd go down to the inn and drink until I passed out. It was the only way to forget. My belly would hurt for the first few beers, then the pain would stop. I'd tell stories about my young fighting days. Eventually, my anger faded as I got older."

I asked him if he was aware of any political events of significance.

"I don't hear about the outside world," he replied. "I just take one day at a time." When I asked if he was literate, he told me that he didn't read, nor could he see any use for it. "Those squiggly lines just didn't make sense to me. But my wife could read some. Someone in her family taught her."

Now, I directed Nick's personality to the final hours of his life. The retired soldier was still angry with the Church.

"At my death, the room was dark and smoky. I smelled fire and the windows were shut. I had a lot of sickness. A few people were here with me. The priest prayed, but I didn't want their God. What kind of God would call my wife a witch?" he protested. "Is their God the devil? I didn't want their God. What kind of a God is it that makes others hurt? My stomach hurts. The priest gave me something for the pain and I finally died. It was a relief.

"My wife Agnes came to me and we left together. It was a happy thought when I found that Agnes was still alive, in heaven."

Relieved that his passing had ended positively, I brought him back to his normal conscious state. I noted that Nick's grandfather in his first recalled past life had been a healer, while "the Bold's" wife Agnes also did hands-on healing. In his present existence, Nick's great-grandfather was a Blackfoot Indian shaman while his grandmother, a Pentecostal healer, introduced Nick to the laying on of hands when he was a child.

When I saw Nick at an SCA event about a month after his regression, he told me that he had never known some of the fighting procedures he had described. He eventually checked with some Scadian knights who confirmed the practice of striking the enemy's feet.

Nick felt that his "Chinese" life could actually have been Mongolian, although he claimed to know nothing about Mongol history. One of my experts, Craig Greenbaum, who has studied the Mongol culture, agreed that it could have been Mongolian because of Nick's description of the wattle-and-daub, hogan-style hut with a hearth in the middle, the guttural language, and the low, almost subvocal humming. He said that the humming may possibly have been throat singing called "khoomei," which was also consistent with Mongolian culture.

As a youth in this life, Nick said that he had envisioned himself doing throat singing, although he had never heard of it. In addition, in his Mongol lifetime, Nick recalled hearing his grandfather whispering or chanting information. Craig reported that nomads had used a musical oral tradition. Although the boy had never heard of writing, Genghis Khan (A.D. 1162-1227) introduced it to the Mongols.

Other details that linked the life to the steppe nomads include the mention of a smelly drink, like beer, which the grandfather spilled on the floor. This could have been "kumys," a beverage made of fermented mare's milk. It was ceremoniously spilled in a ritual to the "Sky Father" and possessed a vile odor. Kumys was made in a heavy leather bag, probably an animal's stomach.

Also appropriate for a nomadic life in Eurasia from 2500 B.C. to the present are descriptions of the mountainous terrain, killing animals with bare hands like his grandfather, the instruction on cooking and using herbs, and the making of baskets. The Mongolian steppe ponies were short, shaggy, and stocky as described by the boy. As for the grandfather's clothing, the gray robe that was one piece of cloth could have been made of deer hide.

The only detail inconsistent with actual Mongolian life was the boy's deep red pants. These would not have been worn by Eurasian nomads, because they didn't dye their suede clothing.

Although he found Nick's description of the lodging to be more Eurasian than Amerindian, Bruce Blackistone noted that having beer would imply the growth of grain and an agriculture-based society. Amerindians drank a mild beer known as "chicha" and made tea from plants such as sassafras and wintergreen.

Additionally, he recalled that medieval Norwegians used bark in their bread, which was taken to be a sign of poverty. This would be in line with Professor Moran's suggestion that the life could have been placed in very early Europe. Also, honey ants were eaten by Aboriginal peoples and the consumption of insects is common to many cultures.

Nick's second recalled life, as Tadgh, was full of detail that my experts agreed place it in a Celtic country—probably Scotland. The reference to armor, metal shoes, and an inn could indicate a later medieval date.

"Tadgh" is a Celtic name, and certainly the village name Nick mentioned, "Glenfadden," has an undeniably Scottish ring. The village's location near small mountains and a river help little in identification, as the entire nation is covered in such small mountains. Rivers and streams are plentiful. Two candidates for the village could be Glenfeochan and Glenfinnanon in the west of Scotland.[1] However, it is highly likely that Glenfadden was a local place that did not withstand the winds of time. The "guttural" language Tadgh spoke certainly could have been Gaelic.

Tadgh's description of his home possessing a loft, a few benches, and a table could be true of all lower-class dwellings of the Dark and Middle Ages. The lofts were areas where children normally slept, while parents slept down below, close to the fire.

As Tadgh observed, homes of all classes were dirty. Most had dirt floors and paneless windows. Household objects and furniture were continuously covered with a fine powder of dirt, pollen, and dust. The very walls of homes were usually made of mud mixed with lime and other organic substances that flaked and crumbled constantly; houses made of stone were chinked with mud or covered on the exterior walls and roof by sod. This could have been what Tadgh was trying to describe when he said the roofs of the village were of "loose dirt."

One of my experts found an anachronism in Tadgh's comment that he slept with his clothes on, saying that folk of the era slept nude. However, said another, there are exceptions to every blanket statement, especially concerning the behavior of those living in cold climates such as in Scotland.

Tadgh's tight pants, or "trews," and yellow shirt, or "kine," can only loosely be dated to before 1600. His description of women's flat, crowned hats is correct, but less can be said about them having striped fabrics. It is, however, known that plaids were commonly used. Tadgh's reference to the visibility of the cleavage is indicative of Renaissance-era women's clothing featuring corsets that pushed up the bust.

It certainly seems as if the "shiny metal" the men dressed in was plate armor. It is possible that they were soldiers billeted at Tadgh's parents' home against the parents' will.

In assessing Nick's third recalled life as a mercenary soldier, my medieval warfare researchers thought that the combat described seemed realistic. Both Steve Hick and Bruce Blackistone referred to postmortem examinations of the war dead, showing that the foot, lower left leg, and head were among the first places to be wounded and were armored with external plates. But Bruce noted that head and abdominal wounds were more optimistically regarded than "the Bold" suggested, and although recovery may have been difficult, soldiers were usually given a chance to heal. In addition, paid mercenaries, or even paid soldiery, was characteristic by the eleventh century.

Another expert commented that "the Bold's" maneuver to hit his enemy's shoes would have been an effective method of distracting him from holding his shield. Although the "axes with the drawings" could have been knotwork inlay, she suggested that Nick could have been describing a zoomorphic animal common on axes of Scandinavian and Saxon origin. This, however, would date the mercenary's life to much earlier than the fourteenth century or later time period—proposed by Professor Moran because of the reference to his wife being a witch and the fact that she could read some.

According to Bruce, "drink-'til-you-drop"-type inns did not arise until the Middle Ages and only then in heavily traveled or well-settled areas.

Several commentators offered suggestions for what the mercenary meant when he said his wife weaved designs on sticks. One is that she was practicing an ancient weaving technique called "sprang" which results in a finished product looking much like netting or macrame. Another possibility is that the wife was using a backstrap loom, which was a very simple loom that could be constructed with a few sticks. Although it was a primitive loom normally found in early periods, it was not inconceivable that it might have been used well into the late Middle Ages among the poor.

The descriptives applied to the mercenary—"the Bold" and "the Stupid"—reflect the practice of identifying an individual by physical and mental attributes, deeds, parentage, place of residence, trade, and other qualifiers. These appellations would sometimes be used by the individual's children. The English royal house of Plantagenet, for example, is said to have gained its name from the wearing of a sprig, "planta genista" or broom, of the dynasty's founder, Geoffrey of Anjou.

This practice of narrowing down the individual by the use of a descriptive eventually led to the last names we use today. Unfortunately, many descriptives were based on unflattering aspects of a person or their circumstance. One example of this is the last name "Goldwater," which refers to urine, or Boyd, which comes from the Gaelic *buidhe*, meaning yellow or sickly.[2]

The issue of the wife's apparent reluctance to pray for those she tried to heal raised doubts in the minds of my historic commentators. Many pagan practices had been cloaked by Christianity since the days of religious conversion when St. Columba Christianized the Dalriada king and the king of the Picts in the late 500s. While it was true that people still observed pagan customs, it would have been highly unusual for those who "kept the old ways" to call calamity upon themselves by flaunting their nonconformity with the Church. The fact that people called his wife a "witch," again, indicates a fourteenth-century date or later.

Other interpretations are that "the Bold's" burning stomach could have been ulcerated, while the wife's illness may have been tuberculosis. The short dress or tunic with a leather coat, or "leine," would be considered in period, as well as the leather armor, linen, or wool—all of which feel itchy. Several commentators appreciated the description of the house and the stinky, muddy road. But they found it unusual that the wife could read, even a little.

Nick, who believes that he accessed ancestral memories, told me that his past-life regression experience was of an altogether different nature. He confided that, in opposition to the joy and fulfillment he experiences in reenacting, his recalled past lives were raw with strong emotions and pain.

With his regression long past, Nick claims that his longtime migraines and stomach problems have receded, perhaps by his discovering their root cause. If this is true, then experiencing these lives during the regression process has helped to put at least some of the past to rest—the painful experiences from long ago that continued to overshadow Nick's present life.

5

Dori

"Unhurt amidst the war of elements . . . "
—Joseph Addison, *17th Century*

While touring Scotland in 1993 with a girlfriend, Dori Clark visited Culloden Moor, site of the Battle of Culloden. This was where Prince Charles Stuart, the Scottish nation's beloved "Bonnie Prince Charlie," was defeated in his attempt to regain the British crown for the House of Stuart in the mid-eighteenth century. The defeat was not only a disaster for the prince, however, as the Highland Clans of Scotland were decimated, and those not killed were brutally repressed by the English.

During her preregression interview, Dori said that when she gazed across the battlefield, she saw her girlfriend transformed into a Scottish clansman dressed in a kilt and wearing an expression of fury and hatred toward her. At that moment, Dori, who claims to have been psychic since childhood, also saw herself as a Scottish Highlander.

Earlier, when she first arrived in Scotland, Dori said she was compelled to visit Duart Castle on the Isle of Mull, the ancient seat of clan MacLean. Later, the pair visited the Isle of Skye. Her friend loved the island, while Dori couldn't wait to leave.

Finally, Dori achieved a sense of peace when she visited an obscure castle in the Loch Ness district. Strangely, before her trip, she said that she had seen a vision of this same castle and a Scottish couple in love, sitting by the loch. She also sensed the presence of an older man, whom she had respected and for whom she would have given her life.

By the time she reached Culloden Moor, Dori was beginning to put the pieces of the puzzle together. She recognized that she had been of clan MacLean, while her companion had been of clan MacDonald and a Jacobite. Although Dori had held sympathies for the rebels, she had supported the Royalists loyal to the House of Hanover. Now, Dori realized that, because of the family into which she had married, she had been forced to fight against her own brothers, one of whom was her twentieth-century girlfriend.

Once aware of their past-life dynamics, Dori said she reached an understanding that allowed her to detach herself from the negative emotions the two women were feeling toward each other. At that moment, from Dori's perspective, the relationship was healed and she had resolution.

Dori related that, while on an excursion to another

Scottish castle, she envisioned herself as a cantankerous, black-haired knight who wore silver and black armor, drank ale, and rode his horse down the wide staircase. No sooner had she seen the image, than the guide referred to horse races that had actually taken place down the staircase.

Upon visiting the war memorial at Edinburgh Castle, Dori said she recognized a sword hanging on the wall as being "hers" and felt close to tears about leaving it behind. After her return to the United States, she attended the Pennsylvania Renaissance Faire and bought a similar reproduction sword. At home, she decided to sleep with it. Years later, she learned that it had not been uncommon for knights to sleep with their weapons.

Dori admitted that she was always fascinated with swords. Her special attraction was to sabers and to fencing weapons. After joining the SCA, she took up rapier, or Renaissance-style fencing.

The twenty-nine-year-old analyst for a government agency in Washington, D.C., had only been actively involved in reenacting for about a year at the time of our regression session in July 1995 and so had not been studying medieval history long. Previously, however, she had participated in Civil War reenactments with typically intense devotion.

Dori told me that she was a descendant of a family in Gettysburg whose roof was hit by a cannonball during Pickett's Charge. She could also list five great-uncles who fought in a Pennsylvania regiment. Once, Dori attended a Civil War era ball with Nick (see chapter 4). Flabbergasted that they danced the waltz flawlessly, she believes she caught the flicker of a Civil War lifetime in which the couple had danced together at a county fair.

Her recall of other details of her Civil War past life triggered a series of experiences which led to her eventual healing. In her dream state, Dori recalled being a Northern woman who attached herself to her Confederate boyfriend's unit. Later, in a déjà vu episode at Blackstone, Virginia, she felt a back pain from being bayoneted while witnessing her unit's ambush. Still later, she found a book which confirmed details of the skirmish.

After her conscious retrieval of these memories, she participated in the 125th anniversary of Appomattox and found herself in tears as the Confederates gave up their guns. But at the conclusion of the ceremony, Dori had a sense of closure. "It's done. I don't need to reenact the Civil War now. My interest in it has subsided," the seven-year veteran told me. "Perhaps when reenactors get 'Civil War burnout' and leave this time-consuming hobby, they have unwittingly resolved a past life," Dori speculated.

Since Dori not only remembered her own past lives and could often see those of others when they "locked eyes," I assumed that she would believe in reincarnation. But she told me that, although she used to believe wholeheartedly in the concept, she was now toying with the theories of alternate time lines and ancestral memory. However she chose to explain her memories, she was soon ready for her experience under hypnosis.

Expecting that Dori would slip easily into the deeply relaxed state, once hypnotized, she was strangely unable to effectively communicate what she was seeing. She would flash on a scene and forget that I couldn't see it, describing only its barest details. Each time I attempted to retrieve additional information of a particular life, she'd jump to the next life. Following Dori's regression was a little like riding a runaway horse. In the space of about two hours, she galloped through twelve lifetimes, including that of an eighteen-year-old Mayan boy running around a pyramid and a young girl who fell to her death from an upstairs window in an unknown era. Dori also flashed on her Civil War life as a twenty-three-year-old woman wearing a brown skirt and beige shirt. Her hair had fallen out of her bun and she was lying dead in a field. In another lifetime, during the 1600s in early America, Dori saw herself as a captain's mate adjusting to seasickness and polishing a sextant.

Dori's first medieval life, she later speculated, dated to the late 1400s or early 1500s in the British Isles. "I'm a twenty-year-old man wearing rawhide boots to the knee and charcoal-gray hose. I'm wearing a ripped shirt with a brown jerkin over it," she said as the young man. "We're in a pub with wooden benches and trenchers. The tavern's real dark and the candles are sputtering down. It's not fancy. A big burly man with a moustache and dark hair sits across from me drinking ale. A group has met in secret to smuggle a political leader to France. Something illegal's been going on. For some reason, I feel guilty about this. There's been a major brawl and I was accused of being called a traitor for something I didn't say.

"I was going out to the stall to get my horse when a large man started to struggle with me. 'You'll die for betraying him,' the man said. I was knifed in the stomach," Dori continued, "and I could feel the pain."

After this violent ending, Dori gravitated to an even more brutal death when tavern keepers gave a young noblewoman to an ugly, smelly, violent nobleman with bad teeth. He then slit her throat. Dori moved quickly to another life.

"We're knights marching down a road in dark armor with steel helmets with cones. Horses are pulling wagons holding big, heavy balls.

"We take the food of villagers," the soldier continued. "I'm mean. I don't care what happens to these peasants. I'm a warrior. I have no need of women. I get one from the village when I want. We're called Sambus. Our leader's name is Gullion. They call me Mouth."

Suddenly, Mouth abandons his cavalier attitude. "I'm

in my armor and can't move. Another soldier is laughing and leaves me to die."

Next, Dori found herself to be a young woman in love. "There's a man on horseback with jet-black hair, black boots, a moustache, and long black gloves. I give him a hair ribbon and he kisses me," she giggles. "It's a tourney on my dad's land and he fights for me amongst knights wearing blue and silver corduroy tunics. I see a triangle flag with the head of a lion. In the distance, there's a strange machine with four spheres that swing and posts that move.

"Now, we're shopping at a fair and he's buying me scented gloves," she continued pleasantly, and then moved to another scene. "I have honey-gold hair, and women are fixing it with ribbons. I'm wearing a chartreuse dress with thin, flowing sleeves. The bodice is cut down low with something white covering it. My mother has a cone hat with a veil. This man is wearing black pants and a dark blue cape with gold embroidery worn off to the side. My father is a big-chested man with gray hair. He's wearing burnt-orange trimmed in fur and weird pointy slippers. He announces our engagement. Mother pretends to swoon."

After the marriage, because of business, her husband had to leave his new bride.

"I don't want him to go. He goes to serve someone. I'm big with child. He tells me to take care of our son. He's still wearing my ribbon. I take my shoes off and walk in grass. I haven't heard from him," she said sounding lonely.

"I'm in labor," she said suddenly. "A woman from the village Pickney comes. She's old and comforting. I'm sweating and running a fever. The baby doesn't want to come out. Something's wrong," she said anxiously. "I don't have any more strength. I'm soaking wet. It's like I'm still pregnant, but the baby's gone. She puts a cool cloth on my head. My husband is holding my hand. The baby died," she said somberly.

"I was never the same after that," she said reflectively. "I couldn't have children and never forgave myself. I feel like I let him down and would sometimes cry. I lived to be forty, old for someone of my constitution. He taught me to walk again and he always kept my ribbon."

Later, Dori told me that she had been to see a recently released movie, *First Knight.* She was dumbfounded to see in the film several similarities to her last regression, including the colors of uniforms the knights wore at the tourney and the "weird machine," exactly as she had pictured it in her regression. Although Dori said she didn't remember seeing any previews of the movie, she questioned whether she could have unconsciously woven an unrecalled film promo into a vivid past life.

Susan Reed (see chapter 3), among others, would later comment that the clothing in the film *First Knight* was not historically accurate, nor were Dori's clothing descriptions consistently from one period. Susan, whose specialty is historic costuming, felt that Dori's reported experience had seeds of "reality" but was interlaced with fantasy. Most agreed that the description of the tournament, the mother's pointed "hennin," and the father's curly toed shoes ("poulaines") were reminiscent of the High Middle Ages, around A.D. 1350 to 1434.

Researcher Paula Peterka (see chapter 12) confirmed that the colors of the clothing mentioned were accurate, although Dori's description was not specific, and that the reference to black pants could have actually been to black leggings.

Medieval costume, dance, and cooking expert, Kathy Norvell, suggested that the dress Dori described was a cotehardie and surcote or cyclas, except that cotehardies usually had tight, low-cut bodices and long sleeves. Cloaks were frequently worn over one shoulder, she said, and Dori seemed to be wearing a "partlet," the medieval equivalent of the modern dickey. Kathy identified the period as the fifteenth century.

Recognizing Dori's "weird machine" as a "quintain" or "tilting machine" (a device used for jousting practice), Kathy mentioned that the post with "arms" sticking out of it would probably have had one arm with a board or shield and another with a sandbag to knock the rider off his horse. Steve Hick agreed that this could have been a tilting machine.

Ann Longmore-Etheridge, who reenacts as a Viking, identified the steel helmets with cones—described in Dori's life as a "Sambu"—as the helmets used by Normans or by some groups of Vikings. As for the mail or leather that a Saxon warrior would wear, Bruce, who also portrays a Viking, noted that a Saxon's fighting gear was fairly light and flexible and would not have pinned him to the ground. Referring to the primitive description of the heavy balls, he noted that early stone cannonballs tended to be hefty, many as large as thirty inches.

Regarding Dori's leader's name, both Ann and Kathy Norvell agreed that "Gullion" could have been an archaic French version of the name "William." Today's modern equivalent in French is "Guillaume."

After Dori's regression, I couldn't help but recall her claims of having had psychic awareness since childhood and the periodic glimpses of her own past or parallel lives as well as those of others. Perhaps because she was so sensitive, I theorized, she had woven bits and pieces from various sources, or even dredged the collective unconscious or ancestral memory, as she herself was beginning to believe.

Whatever the explanation, Dori told me that following the regressions, she felt better about her relationships, was more easily able to receive love and accept hugs. She also overcame an old fear—she was no longer afraid to have children. In addition, her friends noticed that she appeared markedly happier.

I recalled how Dori had felt a sense of closure about the Civil War and wondered how many more years she would continue her involvement with Middle Ages re-enacting.

6

Ann

"Tears, dried to Chance . . . "
—Vernon Watkins, *Welsh poet*

Ann Longmore-Etheridge is a thirty-three-year-old journalist who lives in rural Myersville, Maryland, and commutes sixty-five miles to and from her Arlington, Virginia, office each day. "I cover private security and law enforcement issues," she told me when we met in August of 1995. "That's pretty far from the history I love."

At the age of seven, Ann was captivated by a PBS drama her mother was watching on TV. "The Six Wives of

Henry VIII" presented sympathetic portraits of Great Harry's queens. Before our hypnosis session, Ann said that the wife who fascinated her the most, and who became a lifelong obsession, was the unlucky Anne Boleyn, the king's second wife, who was beheaded in 1536 on trumped-up charges of witchcraft, treason, and adultery.

Ann spent her childhood playing "the six-wives-of-Henry-VIII Barbies," re-creating the elaborate court gowns with her mother's scarves and jewelry. "I read everything I could get my hands on about the Tudors—books that were for adults and for scholars—way above my comprehension level. It didn't matter to me if I couldn't understand it all. I just had to know whatever I could know about that time."

As the years progressed, Ann says that she expanded her interest in the British Isles, increment by increment, until it widened to encompass the entire history of England and Scotland, including all ranks of society, from the king to the lowest commoner.

In her late twenties, Ann married a man with a deep interest in genealogy. Within a few years of research into her own family's past, Ann discovered that, through her mother's "Virginia gentry" ancestors, she was probably descended from many of the historical personages she loved best, including Eleanor of Aquitaine and the kings of Scotland. "Unfortunately," she quipped, "I don't carry a single Boleyn gene in my body."

During our preliminary interview Ann told me that, given her predilection for Tudor England, it was only natural that she should gravitate to the Maryland Renaissance Festival, an hour's drive from her childhood home of Annandale, Virginia. By the age of sixteen, she was already a "regular," and the festival seemed like a miracle world of costumes, clothing, and behavior that transported her back to the 1500s. "It was the highlight of my year," she told me. "The real Tudor England was as much like the 'Ren Faire' as actual twentieth-century life is like Disney World, but it came close enough to make me happy."

Eventually, Ann was hired to play Elizabeth, Countess of Shrewsbury, the redoubtable "Bess of Hardwick," as part of the festival's royal court. The shrewd countess, whose husband was the gentleman-jailer of Mary, Queen of Scots, was the wealthiest woman in the country, second only to Queen Elizabeth I—daughter of Anne Boleyn. "I ended up playing her as a bumbling evil foil to the queen, who always bested her, but in reality, Bess of Hardwick and Elizabeth were on good terms."

Eventually, Ann abandoned what she had come to understand was "pseudohistory," for the life that can be had in Markland's Viking Camp. She told me she'd been a member of Markland since the late 1970s, but it was not until the mid-1980s that the focus of the organization turned to serious living history. "That's what I wanted then," she explained. "A dose of reality. I wanted mud and muck and scrubbing iron pots with cold water on a chilly, wet morning while my campmates huddled around a fire pit eating dried berries and goat cheese. And it was more fun than anything I'd ever done before!"

Like the Scadians, Ann explained that many Marklanders have married fellow members and begun families together. Since her initial involvement, Ann has established her own family of Marklanders. Together with her husband, Mark, an archaeologist turned environmental analyst, their four-year-old son Nicholas, and good friend Teri, they portray a Viking merchant family, circa A.D. 950.

"My husband is Fordred—that's a good Anglo-Saxon name, and, of course, the Vikings settled heavily in northern England. There was a monier named Fordred in York. My son's name is Snorri, which is straight out of the Viking sagas, and my name is Sylvanna, which is not

Viking at all," she notes with embarrassment. "I used it for so many years in Markland that I couldn't bear to change it."

In the early 1990s, Ann became a Viking camp co-leader. "It has been an education in not only history, but in modern interpersonal relationships," she ruminated. "Recently, time constraints have made me step back from leadership."

Ann has traveled widely in England and Scotland. On her initial visit to the United Kingdom, she said she felt like she was home for the first time in her life. When she visited Edinburgh, she confessed that she had a terrible and intriguing sense that she had been there before.

"It's almost embarrassing to admit this," Ann was hesitant to further confide. "But I've always had a mild psychokinetic sense that allows me to sometimes read vibrations from the objects I touch and to see glimpses of what might be the previous owners of the item. This is also sometimes true of places."

While staying in a bed and breakfast in Inverness, Scotland, Ann says that she witnessed a bizarre apparition in her room. As time "shifted," she said she saw a man in an army uniform sitting at a desk that "existed in my own current physical position. The man was writing, and he looked up from his papers as a maid brought him tea." She said that at breakfast the following morning, she overheard the proprietor tell a guest that the house had been used as quarters for military officers during World War II.

As we prepared to begin her regression, Ann questioned the possible results of the hypnotic technique, wondering if what she might "remember" would be a confabulation built from her historical studies. She told me that she wanted to believe in reincarnation, but was, nevertheless, skeptical.

Ann had never been hypnotized before and she did

not go easily into a relaxed hypnotic state. Eventually, and after some difficulty, she found herself to be a young girl in the (postmedieval) 1690s.

Six-year-old "Martha" enjoyed life at the Underhill Manor—"a big gray house." Ann told me that Martha helped her mother to clean the manor house and tend the garden, while her father worked in the fields. The family lived on the grounds in a cottage with wattle-and-daub construction and reeds on the roof. On Sundays, she went with her mother to the small town of Westbrook in Surrey to sell eggs at a market cross outside a white clapboard church named St. Michael's. Meanwhile, her father scoffed at the church, calling the brand of religion preached inside "popery."

After Martha's nephew stole a cock to feed the family, they moved their belongings in a cart to a whitewashed house with exposed beams nestled in green hills. Their new lodging had a wood floor, fireplace and chimney, plain wood furniture, and a chair. The father was dressed in black knee-length pants and a black doublet, while the nephew wore rust-colored clothing and a wide-brimmed hat. Martha was dressed like her mother with black shoes and stockings, a white apron and cap, and a green- and creme-colored dress. Her mother also wore a strange cap with a big brim, and a green shawl covering it.

The child played happily with her handmade doll and top on the floor of the family home. At seven, she fell ill. Feeling fulfilled in her short life—saying she'd had plenty to eat, nice toys, and a new baby brother—she died peacefully.

After Martha's short existence, Ann revisited what appeared to be a medieval life.

"My mother's wearing a gray skirt, an apron, and a brown bodice. She's sweeping our home. It's a gray day in the close. People are workin', comin' in and out, cleanin', and bringin' in the food." I sat mesmerized as Ann now spoke in a thick Scottish brogue.

"I have short pants, a shirt, a vest, and naught on my feet. My black hair is a bit of a mess. It's sticking up. I'm a lad of eight years. Aye." She said that her name was Robert.

"We live off High Street. We're the first door at the end of the close. There are houses all around the square," Robert continued happily. "It's just one room with a fireplace, a table, chairs, and a bed. My brothers are older and sleep upstairs on the floor. I sleep with my mum. My father is dead. He perished; he was sick.

"Mum works for the people in the big house, in Andrew's Wind. She keeps their kitchen and cooks. They have other servants, too.

"She tells stories of ghosts, and ghouls, and specters. Death things and sylkies—things that take the place of babies. Says she's seen 'em. I don't believe her. She winks at me."

Now Ann, as Robert, smiled and sighed. "I'm thinking about what the king's doing. He's King James Stuart of Scotland. He has children up and down the road, and he's handsome. Mum wishes she were young. She talks about the sickly queen and says she's not likely to thrive because she drinks milk and doesn't eat. They had a boy who died, so they don't have any children.

"My mum talks about her family and jests that her mother was a harlot." Robert laughed. "That's the way she is. She talks about stupid things, especially when she plucks chickens.

"Most of the time, I'm with her. Sometimes, I go into the country and fish with the other lads," he explained. "The stream is a good day's walk . . . *Ta!* We don't catch anything big, but we eat what we catch. She likes it. She's a good mother.

"I like to eat, fish, play in the road, roll a hoop, chase

my friends, and tip over the hay cart. I don't go to school. Mother can't read. I want to read but don't know how. I don't think I'll learn unless a priest shows me," he said pragmatically. "He's one of the only ones who knows how.

"I'm Robert Murray. My mother is Catherine Murray. She works for Barrister MacDonald, who is an important man," he said proudly. "His children read. Aye.

"Now, we live in a dependency, a room that's built onto the house. My brothers are apprenticed, one with a smith, the other to a wheelmaker down the road. They like it. They work all day and come home at night."

Leaving his youth behind, Robert Murray then moved forward to his adulthood and later responsibilities.

"My wife's having our first baby. A midwife's with her. I'm nervous." Then, he breathed easy. "Before morning, the midwife tells me it's a girl. She's pretty. I'm glad everything's all right.

"My wife worked in another house. I met her there," he reminisced. "I was mending broken carts and wheels. I'm apprenticed. I'm seventeen and she's fifteen.

"We live upstairs in a house up the High Street, near mother's, and near St. Giles's, in the Grass Market. There's a garden with a wall behind it. It seems strange there, in the middle of the road. You go up the hill to the church. The street's brick.

"We live with her parents," he continued. "We've been married about a year. Her father makes barrels. He's got some money. In another year, I can make wheels on my own."

Curious, I asked Robert if he ever learned to read.

"I don't have to read. Whatever for?" he responded. "I'm too old to learn how to read now. I'm not a child anymore."

The next scene found Robert Murray the father of five, four of them boys. "I'm walking up the street. It's busy.

People are everywhere. I get hit by a wagon or horse."

Near death, he reflected on his life. "We still live in the same house with our in-laws. The father's still alive. My apprenticeship worked out. I would have wanted to have been a rich man, but we had enough. I'm sad to go," he said wistfully. "Seems too soon. I tried to be a good man. But now I just feel peace."

Until Robert Murray's last breath, he carried on his Scottish accent. When we moved to another life, however, Ann found herself once again in Scotland, this time as a woman. She identified the year as 1563, but she no longer spoke with an accent.

"I'm in the middle of a field. The hay stalks are piled up in bundles. I'm looking at my husband and he's looking back at me. I don't know what I'm going to do with him." She sounded distraught.

"He's been with my sister, Gowan. He loves her. I've always known. I wish he loved me, but he doesn't. My father arranged the marriage. You don't marry for love. We've just been married a few years and don't have any children, although we want them.

"He gives in to her. She's young, pretty, and always gets her way. There's nothing to do, but just go on. He's nice and kind, but I just wished he loved me," she said despondently.

"Gowan wants to be with me because we love each other. She's my best friend. I want us all to stay together. I've always taken care of her. That's the way it's always been. When we moved, she came. She doesn't want to marry."

The young wife collected herself. "We don't work in the field, but we spin, make cheese, cook, and run the house," she said practically. "It's my house. I got it from my mother when she died. It's in Dunblane," she said.

"The house is stone with mud or chink in the walls. The roof's thatched. There's another house or shed with sod growing on the roof. The first house has a big central room with a hearth and two rooms upstairs. It's nice. There are a few nice chairs. The shutters and doors are open all the time. It's like being outside. It's warm in the summer. In winter, we live in town.

"My name's Anne Langmore. My father's Andrew Langmore. He's a deacon and lives near the church across the road. I love my father. He's a good man." She continued philosophically, "He thought he arranged a good marriage. If he knew, he'd be angry. He'd make Gowan move back, but I don't want her to go.

"My husband, James, lived in Edinburgh, where my mother's family used to live. Maybe he's a cousin . . . ? He raises and trades horses. He lives off my income from the farm and the horses," she said and paused. "Six men work the farm. We grow oats and barley. The cattle have horns and spots.

"I'm wearing a dress with a green skirt and bodice, and a hat," she diverted her attention from the issue at hand. "I can read the Bible a little. James tries to read, but doesn't do very well."

At this point, the unsatisfactory domestic situation deteriorated even more.

"I killed her," Anne admitted softly. "I was trying to help her get rid of the baby. She begged me to, so I did. Now I have to pay. She's dead. It's dead. She wasn't very far along.

"My husband's going to run away and leave me to take the blame. He doesn't want to, but there's nothing he can do. It's not worth both of us dying. My father knows about the baby. He says he can't help me.

"I go before the magistrate," she said. "It's not easy to think about. They cut off my head outside the house. My father arranged it so it was private. I'm resigned and feel like I was betrayed. It doesn't matter, because it's not worth living. Will I ever see my sister again?"

When Ann returned from the hypnotic state, she told me that the only details that genuinely took her aback were the descriptions of clothing and buildings in Martha's lifetime. She had no idea from where that information had originated, nor was she knowledgeable of the culture or period.

As for Robert Murray, Ann said that his character, complete with his humor, gentleness, and stoicism, was reminiscent of a Scottish personality that she had created for a novel that she was writing. In addition, she said, she has a proclivity to mimic accents. She told me that the hypnotic experience had been very different from what she expected: that she felt both totally in control, yet, at the same time, completely out of it. She also felt that she may have been answering some questions in order to please me.

Later, in a letter, she wrote to me about Robert Murray, "What we have here is a case of 'which came first, the chicken or the egg?' Did I imbue the book character with those traits because I subconsciously remembered Robert? Or was Robert a reconfigurement of the book character?"

Ann felt that she couldn't adequately judge her experience, unless she could visit another lifetime about which she knew nothing. Consequently, she returned for another session with me. This time, the state of hypnotic relaxation came more easily, and she soon began describing a post-Renaissance life that she had lived in Germany or Switzerland. She began to tell a story about which she had been completely unaware. Ann found herself to be a woman whose name sounded like "Clayo."

She described her life in a peaceful mountainous village named Albertfurt, which appeared to have outer walls. Clayo and her husband lived in an upstairs room of a private house. She worked in a tavern and was somehow kin to the proprietor. Dazed after her young husband died, Clayo moved in with the tavern owner and his wife. Later, she remarried, this time to a brother of the tavern keeper—a merchant who, with her help, became successful. She recalled herself working over financial books in a room much fancier than where she had lived with her first husband, and that the work consumed her. Her special hobby was breeding sheep. She lived a long life and eventually died an old woman, attended by her granddaughter.

After her second regression, Ann was now intrigued because she had not known the information she recalled under hypnosis. She was also struck by the feelings of being dazed that she had experienced after her first husband died. In addition, she was surprised that some of the details she had not known going into her first sessions had received positive feedback from the historical commentators. Although Ann had visited the British Isles and been to St. Giles, she had never heard of Westbrook, Dunblane, or Andrew's Wind. Still, some locations could not be traced.

In spite of her analytical, scientific orientation, this new information positively influenced her perception of the regression process, giving more weight to her first regressions and the possibility that her novel could have been inspired by the memory of her life as Robert. She even anticipated regression sessions at a future date that could explore more details about the life of young Martha as well as whether a current-day friend may have been her Scottish sister Gowan.

In checking the facts of Ann's recalled lives, research by my experts and me revealed that there is a "Westbrook" in Berkshire, England, although none on a map of Surrey. Westbrook is in a hilly region on the Lambourne River. Many homesteads in the British Isles were originally named for natural locations. "Underhill" meant, perhaps unsurprisingly, "a place at the base of the hills."[1]

Several of my experts commented that the clothing of Martha and her family was indicative of the time of the Puritan movement. Bruce Blackistone also suggested that the father's religious dissent and the mother's selling goods on Sunday may have contributed to the family's being ostracized. All agreed that the houses inhabited by the family were of a correct construction for what appears to be a life in the mid-to-late 1600s.

Regarding Ann's life as Robert Murray, the youngster referred to the man his mother worked for as a "barrister." However, in Scotland, lawyers were called "advocates," even though they practice the same legal work as the barristers of England.

As for the Grass Market, it was a grassy meadow just outside Edinburgh's city walls, which had been built up as a commercial area after the Battle of Flodden (1513). It was a place where people went to buy and sell animals. This information should date the life of Robert Murray to the reign of James V (1512-1542).

The young Robert mentioned a king and his queen, who was sickly and not likely to "thrive," and that they had no children. James V was married to Princess Madeleine of France, who died childless in 1537, and then to Marie de Guise, who bore him a daughter, Mary (Queen of Scots), as he lay on his deathbed after the calamitous battle of Solway Moss (1542). Either of these wives could have been the queen that Robert's mother gossiped about. Also, King James V had a son who died in infancy. His extramarital affairs were legendary, and several illegitimate children resulted, including James, Earl of Moray.[2] These, then, are the likely years of Robert's boyhood.

Robert's representation of the literacy of the population is entirely believable, as was the description of Robert's childhood home. Although the fact that the Murray's had chairs should indicate that they must have had some wealth, it is possible that the chairs could have been hand-me-downs from the man who employed his mother.

Several experts agreed that smiths, wheelwrights or wheelmakers, and barrelwrights were legitimate and necessary occupations in the Renaissance world. They believed it would have been unusual for Robert to have married before he finished his apprenticeship. However, after a year of marriage, Robert's comment that he would soon be able to make wheels on his own, indicates that he may already have been a journeyman at that time. (To become a master, the journeyman had to pass an examination or make a product that would be judged a "masterpiece" by the masters in his guild.)

According to Professor Moran, the life seemed to be authentically detailed. Other experts also found it plausible that Robert Murray could have lived with his in-laws, have never learned to read, and been killed by a horse. They were particularly impressed with the emotion, as well as the idioms and expressions in this regression.

Moving on to Ann's life in Dunblane, in which she identified herself as having an almost identical name (Anne Langmore), several experts felt that the story was plausible and that Anne's pragmatic attitude was correctly premodern. However, they also felt, instead of beheading, that Anne was more likely hung, wheeled, pressed, or exposed. Ann's later research, however, indicated that beheading was a common capital punishment in Scotland at that time. It is true that women were tried as witches for helping other women abort their babies. Mike Worling, of Old College University of Edinburgh, noted that the year Ann recalled, 1563, was the same year that the Witchcraft Act surfaced. He wondered whether Ann's could have been one of the first witchcraft trials in Scotland for helping her sister with an abortion.

Anne described her father, Andrew, as a "deacon" or layman, who had duties similar to those of a ruling elder in the Presbyterian Church. He must have had a fair amount of influence to have been able to arrange a private execution.

Dunblane is a modern town with ancient roots, close to the Highland line. Anne also correctly described the cattle in Scotland as spotted, not the shaggy Highland cattle seen today.

Finally, in Ann's postregression research, she stumbled across "Gowan," the name of Anne Langmore's sister, in *The Concise Scots Dictionary.* Gowan has two meanings in Broad Scots, a Lowland Scottish dialect still heard today. It means either a buttercup or a daisy. Ann says she wonders if Gowan may have been a nickname for the beloved sister, daughter, and lover who brought such tragedy to the Langmore family.[3]

Several months after Ann's regression sessions, we met in a Metro train station in Rosslyn, Virginia, on our way to the "Military Through the Ages" historical competition in Jamestown. As I approached Ann, she held out for me the front page of the *Washington Post.* The lead story concerned the massacre of school children in Dunblane, Scotland. I couldn't help but recall Ann's own untimely death in Dunblane, four centuries before.

7

Eric

"Shall he live again?"
—Old Testament, Job 14:14

When Eric was six years old, his parents took him to the Metropolitan Museum of Art in New York City. There, he remembered crying because he couldn't have a suit of armor. He also recalled hating school, except when the class was studying the Middle Ages. Then, he did not want to miss it.

When I met Eric in July 1995, he told me that he felt entirely at home as an armorer—an expert in the creation of chain mail. According to Eric, mail is the mesh of interlocking steel rings invented by the Celts around 300 B.C., later copied by the Romans and used as the armor of choice for 1,200 years.

Eric is also an enthusiastic SCA fighter. His gear includes steel leggings, gauntlets, a French-style helmet, greatsword, and shield. For his SCA fighting endeavors, as well as for achievement in science competitions, he has earned the title "Lord." He has also held the office of Shire Archer Marshall, responsible for safety at the archery range.

His interest in swords harkens back to childhood when he used tomato stakes from his backyard as fencing foils. He instinctively knew the stances, a decade before enrolling in a college fencing class.

In the Middle Ages, he told me, it was harder to kill people. "You needed to get in their faces and hit them over their heads. War was up close and personal. These days," he winced, "it's a smart bomb in the bunker."

The twenty-six-year-old with streaming red hair told me that he had attended five Pennsic Wars, the tumultuous two-week gathering that takes place each August in Pennsylvania. In fact, he added, that's how he and many other Scadians mark the number of years they have been involved in the SCA.

To his Scadian friends, Eric is Lord Fergus of Hanua. His twelfth-century Scottish persona was taken, in part, from his ancestors, the Scottish Hanua clan. He says that wearing a kilt is a great conversation opener.

Currently, as a member of the House of Colderwile in the Shire of Highland Foorde, in Frederick County, Maryland, he participates in medieval melees as well as in bardic circles where he sings bawdy songs and is a storyteller. In his spare time, he backpacks, rock climbs, absorbs science fiction, and plays role games.

When I asked him about paranormal experiences, Eric confided that he has had so many déjà vu experiences that he considers them minor annoyances. They happen about once a month, he explained, and usually occur during normal activities like driving or watching television. When I asked him his thoughts on reincarnation, he told me that he considered himself an agnostic. He claimed to be skeptical of reincarnation although he was open to the possibility of its reality.

Now, I prepared Eric for an adventure in time travel.

"I'm alone in a forest of trees with needles," he said, after entering the hypnotic state and moving backward in time. "It's cloudy. Smoky smells are coming from the chimney. The house is made of stones mortared together, and has a thatched roof, and a small, square window with glass in it. Stones from the riverbed surround it. Smells of the ocean come from a distance.

"Somebody is walking up the dry stream bed," he continued smoothly. "This man with long blond hair is wearing a chain-mail shirt and a brown helmet with a nasal. His pants are made of leather. He has a blond beard and broad shoulders. He's very big. He's coming closer. The stream bed is off to the side of the forest now."

Eric's eyes fluttered and he became agitated and shaky, as he continued. "I'm a barefoot child. I don't know if I'm a boy or girl. I'm watching this man walk by. I don't know him. I don't know if he's coming or going from war. I'd think he'd be coming back, but he's too clean. There's a port or bay not far away.

"I saw a rabbit run through the trees," he carried on. "I have a long, brown tunic on. The sleeves are too long and frayed at the bottom. It's a hand-me-down. I see my feet. I'm standing in the mud. I like it squishing between my toes. It's springtime. I smell the pollen in the air. I think the man was smiling, but I can't tell. He had a round shield. He's a Viking."

Eric began to cry. "I'm afraid," he whimpered and began to tremble. "Vikings kill people, but I don't know who they are. There's no one else around."

Suddenly, Eric calmed. "I just realized who he was. He smiled at me and just walked by. I'm clenching something."

Now that the danger had passed, he began to observe his surroundings. "There's a thatched roof barn with lots of hay, but no animals. In the barn, the thing you put over the horse's head is hung up. I don't see a stall though. There's a smithy. I see a broadax and a stump. A hammer is leaning against a support post. It's a 'three-pund' (pound) hammer, which is thin for modern days.

"The house where I live is behind me. It's still muddy at the bottom of the hill. The forest covers the hill. There's a dried-up creek bed by the house with just a trickle running through."

I asked Eric to shift to the next scene. "This is much later," he continued. "I'm holding the hammer and lifting it against the hot metal anvil. I love watching the sparks fly and the metal being shaped. I'm making a sword. I've done this before—heating it up and pounding the shape out of a pound of metal.

"I'm late teens or early twenties. I'm wearing a glove of cow or sheep hide. It's a big leather one wrapped around steel. The '300-pund' anvil is huge. The forge is round and two feet by two-and-one-half feet across. Large bellows are hooked up and go slowly. There's not much coal, but it's burning hot. It's deeper than it looks. A barrel of water is nearby to quench the blade. It smells like charcoal. Bread is baking in the stone oven."

With that, he switched to another life. "I'm on a grassy plain now," he said. "A man on a horse is dressed in the armor of a samurai. He's holding a *yari*, a long spear with a six-foot shaft and ten-inch curved blade, slashing people on the ground. He has a tall bow across his back. The quivers are on the horse. The bamboo arrows have brown feathers and are over three feet long.

"I'm carrying something. I'm a retainer, running behind him. His armor is trimmed in gold. He's riding his
horse. The others behind me are busy running over a big
grassy hill. He's stopping. 'Kagi-yari' comes to mind, but
I don't know what it means.

"In front of me across the creek, 1,000 men in armor
are in line across the plain. They are all wearing black
with flags on their backs. I have a white or green flag, a
coat of arms, a breastplate with lacquered skirting, black
leggings, and armor. I'm holding a spear.

"People are singing. It's a challenge to our soldiers who
are dressed like me, carrying spears. We're trying to cross
the stream, to charge down and kill them. They're not
taking the bait. They're turning and leaving.

"Our army's turning to the north, near a temple. I'm
running behind my master. His spear is propped against
his hip, held high. Everyone's falling in behind him."

Now, the scene faded away. I suggested that he move
forward again. "I'm much older. I'm drinking *sake*. My
wife is wearing a kimono of blue, silver, and gold tied in
back in a red bun. Her black hair has two chopsticks in
it. She's smiling at me. I'm talking to a friend and drinking. She walked in and out, not on her knees. He must be
familiar to her. She brought us warm sake. My friend has
a thin moustache and is wearing a silly black hat with
flat sides."

Then Eric moved on. Now, he was wearing a loin cloth,
was wading in water, and holding a torch in one hand as
he pulled a small boat with the other. He noticed a leech
on his leg and sensed crocodiles nearby.

He next found himself to be a Chinese man dressed in
thick boots, a bulky Chinese jacket, and a fur hat. His hair
fell in a long braid, and he criticized a fat man who appeared useless and was wearing paper clothing.

His next incarnation was as an Aztec in Mexico. Eric
won a javelin-throwing competition and was honored by

being sacrificed with an obsidian knife plunged into his heart. The ceremony insured that the sun would rise. At death, the athlete felt euphoric, perhaps having been drugged.

Finally, after hopscotching all over the globe, Eric remembered a medieval life as a French crusader.

"It's desertland. I see a Muslim on horseback," he began. "I saw my arrow fly into him. He and his horse are lying on the ground. I go over to him and strip the body.

"There's a separate image of the same place on a hilltop looking down," he continued. "There's a city with a wall around it. It's close to the ocean. We're going to sack it and kill every person in there. They're not Christians, so they deserve to die.

"We use catapults, throw burning pitch into the city, and use a battering ram to take out the gate. In the siege, the tower hits the wall. There's screaming as we charge in.

"I don't remember the battle, but there's blood caked on my body. We're cutting the bodies open to see if they swallowed anything. The blood is wonderful. They needed to die. I feel sorry for the women and children who were in our way, but I look on the dead men with disgust. They weren't Christians.

"I think it's Israel," he contemplated. "We came from France. I don't know the date. I'm a member of the peasant's unit. A group of knights is with us. We've been ridiculing them for riding on oxen. The Moors were so startled, they almost dropped their weapons. It's so funny," he laughed. "The city begins with an 'A.' It's north of Israel. It's not Alexandria, even though there's a library there. We don't care. I chisel a cross into a rock wall or column.

"Oh damn," he exclaimed. "I've been hit in the chest with an arrow. I heard the thud, and now I'm dying, but it's not that bad. No pain, just a thump. Guess I'll never reach Jerusalem," he sighed.

Eric left fighting behind as he next became a seventeen-year-old female maid in eighteenth-century Chambrean, France. She was pinning and sewing trim onto a green dress, tightening the corset, arranging the petticoats, and flattening the breasts of her employer. The young woman was more interested in her boyfriend, the stablehand, than the vanities of the mistress of the household.

His female lifetime was just a respite from war. Eric was again heavily clad and on campaign. "I'm marching through the forest wearing a steel lamella and carrying a big shield. We're north of Gaul. We have to kill some German barbarians. My hat looks like Marvin the Martian's. It's red and bristly, and the hair is sticking straight out. It's a Roman helmet with a brush down the center that ends in a forked tail. I'm wearing a bright cloak. My armor's better than the others. Some are wearing loricas. We've hiked through the mountains into Germany or Gaul. Someone said something about elephants down the road, but it's too steep. They would fall down and get killed. I don't know the year.

"We're part of a column," he continued. "We see some Gauls on horseback with spears and short swords, but no saddles or armor. They're no threat to us. They don't want to fight us and they're marching away.

"There are chariots. It's hard because we have to carry them. Why don't they make them lighter?"

Proceeding to the next scene, Eric seemed to have landed in Britain with his company only to meet face to face with a strange civilization. "Some are the same, others are different," he noticed. "I see kilts. They're not dressed well. They're savages with their faces painted blue.

"My shield is resting on the ground. It's almost a game. They charge and we spear them. They have no armor. They are barely human. They're Celts. Both men and women attack us, yell and scream. Their charges aren't well organized. Their first attack disturbs us, but we overcome it. Our auxiliary company is not doing its work. They get their faces smashed. The Celts are slinging stones with long slings. We slam across the river and have them surrounded."

Next, Eric targeted yet another war-torn lifetime. "I'm in Templar's armor riding a big horse covered by cloth with markings. I'm wearing chain mail and a crest with a cross on top of my helmet. I have a fifteen-foot-long heavy lance with a barge point on the end.

"A bunch of knights are charging at a gallop. It sounds like an earthquake rolling across the land. Each one's helmet is a little different. Their shields are long and their horses are big. No one could stand against these men. We're invincible. We fight for the Order. I don't know the country, but I see us in France heading across Germany into Poland.

"Other men are Asian or Mongolian and much smaller," he went on boastfully. "The enemy are cowards. They're running away. Wait. Something's wrong," he said anxiously. "Arrows are bouncing off our shields. I know this is a trap. We shouldn't be charging. They're all around us, thousands of them. We're being slaughtered. We shouldn't have charged."

Next, picking up threads of a life as part of a hunting expedition, Eric held the trunk of a friendly Asian elephant which was transporting a prominent personage in a fancy carriage. While a trainer held the leashes of two panting cheetahs that had been trained for hunting, they playfully rubbed up against his leg.

Ricocheting to another life, Eric found himself preparing for battle with a long spear and small shield. He didn't have armor, although other men did. "Our leader's name is Philip of Macedonia," he said. "He's got a son who thinks he knows everything. He's a kid, but he's harsh on the men. I'll see the look on his face when I put my spear into his back," he glowered.

Next, involved in the military strategy of attacking a walled city, possibly Troy, Eric and other soldiers design a siege tower on wheels and cover it with the hides of dead horses. Jokingly, someone finishes it off with a horse's head. They burn the grass and level the ground nearby with dirt to make the siege tower the right height. Then the men go up over the wall. Eric's memory fades, probably because he was mortally wounded.

In his subsequent recalled past life, it was a chilly day off the coast of Ireland as Eric raised up a fishing net. The sea was choppy and the bottom of the boat was covered with fish with big eyes. Eric whistled as he pulled his hat over his ears.

Flashing on yet another life, this time Eric found himself in a cave in what he thought was France. He was holding a torch. "Three torches are strapped to my back pouch along with a flint, knife, tinder, and sheath. I hear the sound of dripping water. Water soaks through my leather boots. It's muddy. The bottom is gravel. It's a very long deep passage. Someone dared me. I'm standing by the bottom of a natural chimney in the cave. There's a lot of stalactites and flotsam along the wall. Big stalagmites look like stone columns. I spend hours looking around. I hurt my ankle, but I'm not worried. I drop one torch, but light another one. I have to turn back. Wish I could have explored the whole thing.

"It's colder outside than inside," he continued. "I'm covered with mud. No one's around. I'm disappointed. I throw the rest of the torch into the cave and walk back to the village. People look and say, 'I did it.' Some laugh and say, 'That's great.'

"They are wearing tunics, leggings, and leather shoes with boots. There's a tall church in the village. Most of the buildings are low and ramshackle. There are wood houses with boards, and some are stone, while the roofs are all thatched. I don't know the name of the village or if I can read, but I'm very proud of myself as I walk through the street. People notice me. Some say, 'Congratulations.' Most look like, 'Boy, is he muddy.' I'm walking barefoot with my boots slung over my shoulder."

In his next recollection, Eric was rowing a boat along with a lot of other men. "The boat is fairly long and low to the water. It's a *drakken,* a Viking longship. We've got a weapon on board, a battering ram made of pine that's hidden under the water line. When we pull on the ropes, the ram will drop off the ship. It never comes above the water and it's designed to break off, so we don't have to dislodge it. We're going to another boat and punch a hole in its side. It'll sink immediately. We're looking for anyone. It's what we do. I see a small fishing boat. They're afraid of us, but they're not worth attacking. It's upsetting. We have a great weapon, but no one to use it on," he sighed in resignation. "I think we're in the English Channel, west or south of Dover."

Focusing in on another lifetime on water, this time from the vantage of an English vessel, Eric spied what he thought was a Spanish tallship through the fog. "I see a tall ship with a big square sail. It's so tall, it's top heavy. The ship has a lot of cannons. I don't think it's carrying cargo. It's sitting high in the water. They don't know we're here. We're trying to sneak past them. I hope she hits a storm and sinks. The ship goes its way and we go ours."

Now, Eric summoned up another Chinese life, this time as a practitioner of martial arts. Then, he returned for his second life as a female—a little girl who was possibly killed by an asp while playing with it.

After exploring snatches of eighteen lifetimes, I decided to end the session and bring Eric back to full waking consciousness. Eric was shocked at how he had cried and shaken violently in his first recalled life. He told me that he had never felt the terror that he recalled as a little child when he initially noticed the Viking, then mused if there could be a connection between this memory and his discomfort around Scadian friends who had chosen Viking personas.

My experts on the Dark Ages agreed that Eric's description of a Viking was accurate in every detail. One anachronism, they pointed out, was the mention of glass windows in an era when glass was a precious commodity. A general date for this life, probably located along the Irish Sea or English Channel coastal areas, could be A.D. 800 to 1000.

Bruce Blackistone, who is a part-time blacksmith, agreed with Steve Hick that the anvil seemed too heavy and large. Medieval hammers were small because of the scarcity of metal. Indicating that medieval hammers tended to be light by modern standards, he suggested that perhaps Eric was describing a short sledge intended for the smith to use either one- or two-handed without an assistant. He also found the mention of a circular forge most unusual, as Europeans used a side-blast *tuyere* (air inlet). Blackistone said that with all the dust, scale, and ash in the forge, baking bread there hardly seemed a good idea. Nor do hay and a smithy go together, he added. The mix would have created perfect conditions for a conflagration.

Those commentators who have studied medieval Oriental warfare agreed that songs were used by samurai warriors to insult the enemy and identified the black and red warriors' flags as popular medieval colors. A samurai sickle spear would have indicated a fairly early period, while "Kagi-yari," a term used by Eric without his understanding of the meaning, was the correct term for an early polearm. Also, it was not inconceivable for the samurai to learn bow and sword because cross training was not uncommon.

As for the Asian lifetime in which Eric depicted a Chinese man wearing paper clothing, my commentators told me that paper clothing was worn by mandarins to show that they didn't have to work. The individual mentioned with long braided hair, however, appeared to be more of a merchant or townsman. Meanwhile, a fur hat could indicate an Asian steppe culture.

Alexandria, Antioch, and Acre are all candidates for a town beginning with "A" that Eric recalled from his crusader lifetime, although Alexandria is west of Israel—not north as Eric had indicated. A well-known massacre occurred at Acre during the Crusades that probably included unremorsefully cutting open Muslim bodies in search of plunder.

Several commentators, however, found it hard to believe that a European peasant would have been aware of a library in a Middle Eastern city. Others were troubled by Eric's use of the name Israel, which did not exist as a state until this century. It should be noted that Eric told me he translated the geographical information he recalled into modern terms.

Others felt that for a peasant to ridicule a knight was extremely dangerous, but that it was likely done. The term "peasant unit" was also troubling. Peasant levies would have been part of a landholder's retinue and not their own unit. Also, a longbow was most likely English since the French preferred the crossbow. The practicality of the knight as a horse archer was in question.

Although the lifetime of the French chambermaid fell outside the medieval and Renaissance periods, it provided accurate costuming details and an air of honest simplicity.

The military experts concurred that the equipment mentioned was unusual for an ordinary legionary, although the Romans made extensive use of auxiliary troops and the term in Eric's life as a Roman soldier was based in fact. "Lorica" was simply a generic term for Roman armor, while "lamella" was a metal armor plate. The description seemed, to the commentators, to be that of an officer in the late Empire period. They also noted that the horsetail crest was rare on Roman helmets and usually found in earlier Greek depictions, but agreed that European saddles and stirrups had not yet been introduced.

Several commentators speculated that Eric was part of the XX Legion, which was sent to Britain, and may have clashed with blue-painted Picts. (The Picts were a Celtic tribe from northern Britain and Scotland.) These Celts used "woad," a psychoactive drug, to dye their skin blue and draw designs on their bodies. Their women were usually behind the fighting lines, for encouragement. However, the reference to elephants could tie the lifetime to Hannibal's crossing of the Alps in 183 B.C.

This possible reference to Hannibal as well as lives that appeared to be connected to Alexander the Great, the Spanish Armada, the making of the Trojan horse, the Knights Templar, and the Mongol hordes cast an air of suspicion on Eric's regression experience.

Even so, experts indicated that the Mongols' military maneuvers and description of the horses in the Templar life appeared accurate. Additionally, the chain mail could have been worn by a Teutonic knight around the fourteenth century.

Although they found Eric's participation in the sacking of Troy contrived, they regarded the siege tower covered with horsehides a possible protection from burning pitch and an interesting interpretation of the legend of the Trojan horse.

Turning to Eric's French cave experience, it was determined that limestone caves abound in southern France, particularly Burgundy. Medieval French expert, Lisa Steele, noted that timber and stone houses with thatched roofs suggest northern France where caves are less common.

Discussing Eric's life as a Viking on a longship, Bruce Blackistone, captain of the longship *Fyrdracia*, was emphatic that a battering ram was totally unworkable and could not be carried under the water because the pine it was made of would float. If it were fixed to the bow on a longship, he added, the stemport would crack.

In looking at Eric's recalled past lives overall, several commentators suggested that Eric was a well-read person with a deep interest in martial studies who could have confabulated these lifetimes from his reading. However, it is important to remember that because some past lives may appear to have been partially confabulated, this does not mean that they are. Eric's recollection of the terror of a child faced with a killer or a bored, high-sexed chambermaid ring as true as others may ring false.

∿ Mavens of Medieval Times ∿

The reenactors pictured here are dedicated to reliving the feasts, romance, and life of medieval society. They perform at Renaissance festivals, "living history" events, and functions sponsored by The Society for Creative Anachronism, Inc. (SCA). Many of those pictured participated in the author's past-life regression study. Their chosen reenactment personas follow their real names. (All photographs are by David H. Morse unless otherwise noted.)

Viking Life

Left: Ann Longmore-Etheridge (Sylvanna, co-leader of the Viking Camp) in Viking garb including a linen cap copied from one found at York, England. She wears a silk-linen blend dress and linen Viking apron. Visible jewelry is a bronze stick pin copied from an original artifact, a necklace of glass beads, and genuine 1,000-year-old Islamic coins. (Photo by Mark Etheridge.)

Right: Historical commentator Bruce Blackistone (Atli) in Viking garb. Bruce founded the Markland Medieval Mercenary Militia, and was its first "Warlord." He is also a seasoned Viking longship captain. (Photo by Mark Etheridge.)

Early Renaissance

Nick Neville (Micheal Gaidheal) wears a commoner's leather jerkin (c.1400-1600), forester boots, hose, and a bag to carry wine, food, and feast gear. (Photo provided by Nick Neville.)

1

Above: Living history interpreters, Larry and Paula Peterka, wear clothes that are historically accurate for the first half of the sixteenth century.

Below: Paula portrays Her Royal Highness, Princess Anna of Cleves, wearing a dress reproduced from Hans Holbein's portrait of Anna now hanging in the Louvre. The dress has been slightly modified to be worn over a Spanish farthingale, or hoop skirt, which Anna adopted while living in England.

Above: Many medieval reenactors enjoy history for the fun of it. Genevieve Horst (left), who does not subscribe to the theory of past lives, portrays King Henry VIII's eldest daughter, Princess Mary. Ashley E. Davis plays the role of Princess Elizabeth. Ashley, fourteen, wears a reproduction of an actual dress that the princess wore at that age.

Above: Larry Peterka (Dr. Heinrich Olisleger) wears a white linen shirt trimmed in gold lace, a white velvet jerkin, a black velvet basecoat, a dark green velvet schaube or surcoat, and a velvet flatcap. He wears a chain of office to denote his positions as Chancellor to Her Royal Highness and as special envoy from Cleves.

Above: Eric Knibb (Lord Fergus of Hanua) holds a Scottish claymore greatsword and a hector shield (used from the thirteenth century). He is wearing homemade chain mail (the primary armor used for 1,000 years until the 1200s) and various pieces of armor.

Above: Here, Eric is dressed in a great kilt and kilt shirt, typical of a Highland Scot, c. twelfth-thirteenth centuries.

Above: Eric is joined by Richard Weissler (Razmus the Innocent) who wears a tabard over his armor.

Above: Richard and Eric practice for a medieval melee. Eric (left) wears a French-style helmet, gauntlets, arm and leg armor. Richard wears a barrel or great helmet (eleventh-twelfth century). Both fighters made most of their own gear.

3

∾ See You at "Ren Fest!" ∾

At the 1996 Maryland Renaissance Festival, held annually near Annapolis, Maryland, the king and his entourage enjoy the antics of a fellow performer. Renaissance festivals have become popular all over the United States.

Below: Musician Felicia Eberling (Felicity Flutabec) portrays a simple Elizabethan landowner. Her green underskirt, brown overskirt, and boned bodice are all handmade and are typical of the Renaissance during the sixteenth and seventeenth centuries.

Top Right: Here, Felicia plays the recorder with Celtic harpist, Lee Davenport. At her side is a doumbek, a goblet-shaped medieval Middle Eastern drum.

Bottom Left: Actor Thomas Earl "Tee" Morris enjoys his persona as an inventor named Quinton Edmund Devonshire. His colors are rustic forest green and brown. In the top of the bag hat is a "pencil holder" and book. "An inventor must always have his notes upon his person and quickly within reach."

Left: Here, Tee plays the part of a Renaissance fop.

⌒ Studies in Contrast ⌒

Left: Susan Downs Reed, formerly the S.C.A.'s "Baroness of Ponte Alto," now reenacts as the fifteenth-century Sister Marguerite, "retiring to a nunnery." A professional seamstress and costume designer, she wears a fifteenth-century black wool kirtle (gown), a white wimple, and black hood.

Left: Karen Beary portrays a fourteenth-century French persona named Ysabeau Madeleine de Gascogne. She wears a parti-colored blue-and-purple cote-hardie with jeweled hip-belt and her hair in a black snood.

Right: As her belly-dancer persona, "Is'Dihara al-Hakima," Karen wears a hip-length yelek with harem pants and tassel belt. She uses predominantly Afghani tribal dowry jewelry.

Right: Tony Guida (right) caricatures a medieval cleric, "Cardinal Sinnius Lascivious Vice." He has been known to perform marriages on the spot. He maintains that his character is based on genuine Dark Ages clerical personas. To his left is "Winifred, the King's Cook," portrayed by Judith S. Smith.

6

Top Left: Craig chats with Katharine Bradley (Lìadain Nì'Bhrollachaìn), who wears an Italian Renaissance sixteenth-century raw silk skirt, velvet bodice in black with silk trim, white cotton chemise, and white silk veil.

Top Right: Craig Greenbaum (Corun McAnndra) holds the office of Baron of Storvik. Here, he wears a tenth-century hand-embroidered tunic, slit for riding. It is embroidered in the Celtic interlace pattern of the period.

Left: Two noblemen confer about court affairs. Timothy Vert (left) is "Sir Anthony Denny, Head of the Privy Chamber," who runs King Henry VIII's private affairs. He is a member of the cabinet and "Keeper of the Dry Seal." With him is Larry Peterka (Dr. Heinrich Olisleger). Both men wear velvet jerkins, gold brocade basecoats, and velvet surcoats lined in fur with matching flatcaps.

∾ Landsknechts and Camp Followers ∾

Right: Robert Taggert (Lars Holtzclaw) wears a "bishop's mantle" of mail around the shoulders. He is a German soldier, or *Landsknecht,* and is a member of King Henry VIII's royal guard. His helmet is called a *sallet.*

Left: Jennifer Lease (right) and Kellie Hendley reenact as Landsknecht camp followers, "Johanna Bauer" and "Danica." They wear white linen chemises, striped, mismatched hose, banded underskirts, and square-necked overdresses slashed in a variety of colors. They often carry stout walking staves and wear valuable jewelry that they have "looted from the battlefield."

8

Katharine

"Where souls do couch flowers . . . "
—William Shakespeare, *1564-1616*

Katharine Bradley grew up near Valley Forge, Pennsylvania, where her family could often be found in co-
lonial dress manning a log cabin farmhouse where
George Washington once headquartered. At the age of
five, Katharine remembers spending her weekends
drawing on a slate board, while her two sisters used drop
spindles to spin raw wool into yarn. Meanwhile, her
mother demonstrated the cooking of period dishes.

Even with this family focus on the Revolutionary War,

Katharine found herself drawn to the Elizabethan era after her introduction in high school to the works of Shakespeare. Gradually, she found that her interest in the period broadened.

At the age of fourteen, Katharine's mother took her to the Pennsylvania Renaissance Festival. Four years later, it was a natural progression for Katharine to participate as a "camp follower" in a Scottish regiment.

Later, while attending college in Kutztown, Pennsylvania, Katharine joined with her college crowd in becoming a Scadian. In nearby Allentown, Isenal College had an active medieval group who became Katharine's "playmates."

While still in college, Katharine—nicknamed "Lindi"—became a lady-in-waiting to the queen. For two years, she attended to her mistress's needs before, during, and after each royal court event. These duties took up anywhere from one to five hours a day and included tasks such as embroidering gifts for the queen to distribute. Her attendance was also required at functions each weekend, often for the entire weekend.

Since her retirement from royal service, Lindi has not been complacent. The twenty-four-year-old nanny has resided in Northern Virginia as a member of the Barony of Ponte Alto in the Kingdom of Atlantia. In her first year in Ponte Alto, she earned an Award of Arms, a Kingdom-level commendation for setting up public demonstrations of SCA life and serving as liaison with diverse groups ranging from the Boy Scouts of America to the Smithsonian Institution. She has also received Baronial "Veneral beads," which she describes as "attaboys," for helping to staff local events and has been inducted into the Baronial Order of the Garland.

Katharine has made her own embroidery patterns, does cross-stitch, and is researching the medieval period with hopes of starting a massage guild since finding out that Queen Elizabeth's physician prescribed massage for the overstressed ruler.

But Katharine has not limited herself to more traditionally feminine pursuits. She spent three months training in heavy weapons until her doctor ordered her to cease and desist. Next, she tried fencing—until her finger was broken by her fencing instructor.

Identifying her fellow Scadians as hailing from almost every walk of life, she says she's rubbed medieval shoulders with lawyers and politicians, firemen, policemen, and a preponderance of computer people. To her, the hobby is a great equalizer.

Many new members are shy people, she explains, who, because of the welcome attitude and fanciful aspects of the SCA, quickly blossom. "Portraying someone else, it's much easier to flirt," she told me with a smile.

Katharine, who is heavy set, was amazed to find that many Scadian men are attracted to large women. She says the attitude is a medieval one. Statuesque bellies and breeder hips were a visual indicator of the possibility of progeny as well as large dowries, for surely stout forms did not have to scramble for scraps of food.

Originally a bar wench, Katharine now places her Scottish character, Lìadain Nì'Bhrollachaìn (which means daughter of Bradley), in the 1580s. Lindi's father was a sailor. After her father was killed at sea, Lindi found herself shipped out of Scotland to live in Europe with her grandparents. Lindi created this scenario to allow herself to wear a variety of different clothing styles. She admits that she's more comfortable in medieval garments than in twentieth-century clothes. In relation to her accoutrements, her emphasis is on comfort. "If they had had it, they would have used it," she stresses.

In preparation for her regression, I asked Katharine about any paranormal experiences that may have occurred in her past. She replied that she has felt a strange familiarity with some reenacting experiences although she can't explain it. Nor can she explain her fascination with Scotland, except that she may have experienced several flashbacks to a former life lived there.

As for reincarnation, Katharine said that she was open to the possibility. She categorized herself as slightly skeptical, but, nevertheless, eager to undergo the regression experience.

Wrapping up the interview, we began the next phase—that of relaxation that would quiet the conscious mind enough to unlock past-life memories. We were not disappointed.

"It's daytime. I'm outside, alone," she said. "I'm wearing sandals and a loose dress to my ankles. I'm a teenager with long, blondish-strawberry hair. I'm waiting for my brother to come home.

"There are hills and a farm that's not too well kept. It hadn't been used in a while. There's a run-down house with a thatched roof," she continued. "Leaves are turning green and just starting to bud. It's early summer. There aren't many trees, just a couple near the house. The house is made of wood, like a log house. I'm standing in a small garden near the front."

Now, I asked her to go into the house.

"It's one room and smells musky, moldy, wet. A fireplace is in one corner and a loft on the opposite side is filled with straw. In the middle of the room is a table. There aren't many things around, just a couple of plants drying near the window. Herbs, pots, pans. A sheepdog named Brandy is sleeping in the corner near the ladder to the loft. I'm Cassandra.

"Everyone is gone. I have a strong sense of the loss of my parents. There's a hill out back with my parents' gravesites. I never knew my mom. She died when I was born. Dad's death is more recent—a painful accident.

"There are neighbors, but not close by," she continued. "The town is far away. My brother's there. He left me to watch the sheep. I find it boring. He went to sell some wool and vegetables from the garden, so we can get by. We don't have much income left, but my brother refuses to leave the farm. Since he's older, I listen to him."

At this point, I asked for the name of the town. "Edinburgh? I'm not sure," she replied falteringly. "I don't have much schooling. I only know what my brother tells me, and he doesn't tell me much. He'd been to school before father died, but then he came home. He can read and write his name, too. I can't write my name yet, but he's teaching me when he has time.

"Most girls don't know how to read or write. They say it's not important, but I wouldn't mind learning. I think it would be good."

Her thoughts turned to more pressing issues. "What if my brother dies?" she asked. "He's trying to find me a husband, but it's not working. We don't have much to offer. Usually it's land, money, or something substantial. With just me and him, we can't offer the farm. It's his, not mine. Besides, it's not up to his standards."

Once again, she focused in on her isolated lifestyle. "I don't get to see many people. A girl over the hill is nice. We get together by where the sheep graze. Her name's Margaret. Her family's well-off in comparison to me. They have more sheep, and she still has parents. We talk and watch the sheep, run in the woods, and play in the meadow.

"She goes to town and says it's crowded with people living close together. There's a lot of noise and lots of boys. Yeah. We like boys," the teen giggled. "I'd like to go and see more. She's got a little brother, but he's not old enough.

"Sometimes, I'll go to her house and we'll sew. She shows me things her father brought from town. We help each other do chores. We ride her horses up and down the pasture. We only have one, and my brother doesn't let me ride it often, though I'd like to someday."

The girl now centered her attention on her relationship with what seemed to be her only living relative. "My brother shelters me too much. He never lets me go anywhere or meet anyone. When I ask him, he changes the subject. He says he knows what's best for me. He's three or four years older.

"No one seems to want the farm," she continued. "I guess we can keep it. We keep it well enough, but he would rather live in town and make better money. He feels obligated to keep the farm. He doesn't talk to me about it. He'd probably worry if I was in town. I don't know many skills to work in town. He's not bad at blacksmithing—shoeing a horse and making things. He could be an apprentice. He's very good at learning. I bet he could learn anything."

At this point, I thought I'd try to get a specific date from Katharine, now Cassandra. "I don't know what year it is, but they will be having a festival soon. It's a 'Welcome to Spring.' There's dancing and games. Guys show how tough they are and wrestle. They also dance with us. And there's lots of food. At least my brother lets me go. It's the only time I go into town.

"I'm usually pretty shy. I don't know many people," she said quietly. "My brother likes this one girl. She's snobbish. Maybe she has money, though. He acts silly and clumsy around her. She treats him okay and acts like she likes him. Then she plays hard to get. She doesn't strike me as the type to live on a farm. Her parents are merchants. She's pushing Richard to move into town. Maybe she'd like him more."

A detailed description of her brother's girlfriend's dress came next. "She has a full-length dress on. It's tight to the body and sky-blue, but darker like the winter sky. It laces up the back and is trimmed with a collar and sleeves. It's a full, complete dress with a chemise. It's very different than the blouses and skirts I wear on the farm. I wear a shirt and wrap cloth around my waist and belt it. Her clothes were made. Most of our clothes came from Mom and Dad. I don't fit into Mom's clothes yet. They are packed away. My brother fits into Dad's stuff. He's much bigger than I am."

Now, Cassandra turned her attention to the festival food. "We eat game, fruits, meat, deer. We will eat all day, as we feel it's necessary. Everybody brings a little something. Those who are well-off bring more. It's a time when everyone is treated the same. It doesn't happen very often."

I directed Cassandra to go to the end of her life. She found herself now between sixteen and eighteen years old. "My brother and I are inside the house. It's very hot." This was interesting, as the air conditioner in my office was on full blast.

Her voice started to rise. "The house is on fire. I can't get out. I can't see him. It's too smoky. He's yelling. I can't understand him. It's very painful. The walls are falling in on me. He could be yelling from outside. I'm confused—disoriented. There's fire everywhere. A beam falls from the loft and pins me. There's lots of pain, then darkness. It's all gone. I don't know what happened to my brother."

After reflecting on her experience, Katharine said she realized that Cassandra's brother was her good friend Steve, who she currently feels treats her like a little sister. She also related that she had jumped out of Cassandra's body before the beam fell on her.

After a short rest, I sent Katharine back into another lifetime. She recalled being a "pale-faced" woman who had apparently been found as a youngster by Native Americans. Her abode was of dome-shaped straw or thin wood, with animals hanging by their feet near the front entrance, and baskets and deerskins on the floor. Later, she found herself ostracized from certain ceremonies, social gatherings, and marriage because of her different ethnicity. Because this appeared to be post-A.D. 1650, I decided to move Katharine further back in time.

"I'm inside a large home, visiting," she began. "Several of us are sitting around, talking, sewing, and doing needlepoint. A few guys are playing board games and talking nearby.

"The men are wearing houppelandes, big blousy things to the knees with fancy sleeves. We're wearing them, too. Ours are longer, down to the floor. They're all different colors. Mine's a nice red. Two other women have off-white and blue, both made from nice fabrics. One guy's matches my dress. The other one's in black. We're all the same age, around fourteen or fifteen.

"It's a manor home and belongs to the woman in blue," she continued gaily. "I came with Stephen, the one in red. He's my fiancé. We're to be married next year. He's introducing me to his friends. They're kind of boring, not well educated, but nice."

I was grateful that Katharine wasn't leading another life of isolation.

"I have an education," she continued proudly. "My father taught me at home. I read a little and write a little German. I can speak a little French. It's hard enough to read German. Father told me not to show off. Stephen is sometimes nervous because I know some things other women don't know."

Curious, I asked where she lived.

"Around Denmark," she replied. "That's where Stephen went to school. He met my father who is a teacher at the university. Father would bring him home. He brought lots of students home, but I liked him best.

"When we go back home, we'll live with father," she continued. "He has a house for us on his grounds. He has plenty of money and he's comfortable. Dad says we'll switch houses when we get older. Dad's not ready to give up his house for us yet. He'll give us land and a couple of horses. He's happy for us.

"My fiancé's nice," she smiled. "Not bad looking. Blond hair, blue eyes, broad shoulders. I have blonde hair. He says he likes my spiritedness and talking to me about the world and books. He's finishing school.

"Meanwhile, I don't do much," she told me. "I read, go out, ride, or go to town and look around by myself. Dad's working and Stephen's in school. I meet him for lunch. I don't have any chores. We have servants for that. Mother got ill and passed away. Father raised me, kind of like a boy."

She was now beginning to recall more specifics. "My name's Martha. It's the 1490s. We live outside a city in Denmark, on the edge of town. It's nice there. You can't have a garden and stables inside town because there's not much room there.

"My father's house is slightly smaller than this one. There's a great big stairway by the entrance and a winding staircase from my bedroom down the back of the house. My bed has a canopy with curtains. When I was little, I used to pretend it was a cave. Now, it just looks pretty. Everything else is pretty normal—chairs, tables, mostly of wood or stone, some are carved."

Martha now mused about her future in-laws. "His father knows my father. He collects money; he's an accountant, or does taxes. Stephen doesn't talk about his dad. They don't get along, although he gets along with his mother. She hangs out in town picking out things for the house, which has only five rooms upstairs. But they're still well-to-do and they have vineyards."

Now, I asked Martha to describe her own activities. "I don't like embroidery. It's boring. I'd rather be outside, riding, playing, gardening, even walking. We see each other in the summer, when he's in school, on the weekends, in between classes. I go to the university to bug father and him."

I asked her about church. "We're both Catholic and go to church often," she replied. "I try to get out as much as possible. It's boring with lots of talking and sitting. I don't agree with everything. Some things sound harsh, like being damned if you don't go to church. I don't think it's true. If God listened, He'd listen wherever you are. Stephen likes church. He reads Latin, but I can't very well.

"Father doesn't want to educate me too well. A woman is supposed to provide children, be a good wife, and take care of the affairs of the house. As the mistress of the house you are to be a lady, and greet and cater to guests. I learned from my aunt how to keep the servants in line so everything's ready when Dad comes home. She takes the firm attitude. She's strict. I like to treat them like human beings and talk to them. If you're good to them, they'll be good to you."

Sensing that she was ready to move on, I suggested she go to the last day of her life. She found herself in her bedroom surrounded by her family.

"Stephen is there. Our three children are older than toddlers. Our son goes to school while the daughters stay home with me. My father has passed away."

I asked her to look back over her life's highlights. She reflected on her outdoor wedding with flowers in bloom and described the experience of giving birth as painful, but wonderful. She recalled holding her children and watching them grow up. As for Stephen, he became an academian and taught at the university. Her father had been instrumental in getting him the job.

"I'm in my canopy bed. My body aches all over. It's like I'm giving up," she sighed. "I've been sick a while. It eats away at you, making you weaker. The doctor says there's nothing you can do. It wasn't bad at first, but now I can barely move."

And then Martha was gone.

When Katharine roused herself, she said she'd found a vast difference between her reenacting and regression experiences. In reenacting, she said, she could only speculate as to what medieval life was like, while in her regression, she knew it. Also, while Martha enjoyed reading and gardening, Katharine dislikes these activities. Furthermore, she maintained that she had known very little of the information that was forthcoming in the regressions. She was also able to draw sketches of what she saw while hypnotized, including her house and clothing in her first life as Cassandra.

Several of my experts agreed that Cassandra's house appeared to be a simple peasant dwelling from the late Middle Ages or early Renaissance. It was unusual, however, for it to be the log cabin type in a wood-scarce environment such as Scotland, where crofter homes were normally built of stones. This type of building is much more common in heavily forested nations such as Scandinavia, where churches from the Dark Ages and Middle Ages yet survive. In spite of the fact that the names Katharine mentioned were English or Scottish, Professor Joann Moran speculated that this lifetime could have been spent in Scandinavia or Russia.

Most agreed that Cassandra's descriptions of her clothes appeared to indicate medieval Scotland in the thirteenth to fifteenth centuries. Although several questioned the wearing of sandals, all agreed that clothing being left to children by their parents was a common occurrence.

Upon Professor Joann Moran's review of Katharine's first regression, she agreed that the comments Cassandra made about her illiteracy were accurate. Also accurate was ignorance of the year, which was often measured in years of the reigns of kings. Unfortunately, Moran found the teen's life too isolated to glean much more.

Several of my experts questioned the modern ring of the names Brandy and Cassandra. Assuming that the name Brandy derives from the drink brandywine, it must date after A.D. 1600. However, it is possible that the name was derived from a Lowland Scots or Gaelic root.

Bruce Blackistone noticed that Cassandra said her diet included deer and felt that this fact could be a mark against the validity of the incarnation. According to Blackistone, the killing of deer was usually the right of nobility and was considered "poaching," a serious offense in England and Scotland. However, judicial records indicate that poaching was carried out frequently and surely not all poachers were caught, especially in the desolation of sparsely populated medieval or Renaissance Scotland. It must also be noted that Cassandra said she ate venison at the springtime festival, where everyone was an equal for one day. Perhaps the venison was a donation by members of the local nobility for the special occasion.

Blackistone also pointed out that Cassandra said they "owned" their own farm, a highly unusual situation in the Scotland of the era. It is possible that Cassandra's family had a freehold on the farm and that it had been passed down through the family to Cassandra's brother, although the land was the actual property of someone else. It was also possible for Cassandra's brother to attend a town or village school, which was common.

Another conundrum was Katharine's drawing of the dress worn by her brother's girlfriend, which appeared to be of a much earlier date than the clothing Cassandra had worn. Two-piece outfits generally dated from A.D. 1500 on. In Cassandra's defense, if her memory had been of Scotland, then it was appropriate for her to wear an underdress with a kilted (or wrapped) piece of material that could serve as both a skirt and cloak.

Cassandra also mentions riding her friend's horses.

Horses were expensive status symbols far beyond the means of Scottish crofters. Worn-out nags used as plough horses would be slightly more tenable, although probably still a rarity. Most crofters would have used oxen to pull their plows.

When assessing Katharine's third recalled lifetime as Martha, the experts dated the wearing of the blousy houppelandes to the late fourteenth or early fifteenth centuries. These were made of elaborate, heavy material with massive sleeves, usually worn with a large, heavy overrobe.

It is also correct that many homes in Denmark and neighboring states had vegetable gardens in the back. Even today, Danes still grow much of their own produce, even in town settings.

Also feasible is that a family of Martha's station might have had stables. However, Bruce Blackistone questioned whether Martha's father's profession could have been lucrative enough to support such an extravagant lifestyle.

Others questioned why an unmarried girl of Martha's rank would have been allowed to go to town alone, let alone that a respectable woman would not likely have been found visiting in university precincts. Several also questioned Martha's mention of meeting Stephen for lunch. Lunchtime meetings and gatherings are a modern convention, as was Martha's mother-in-law's shopping. In medieval times, Susan Reed indicated that men did most of the shopping.

Martha's identifying herself as Catholic was also from a present-day perspective. In the Europe of 1490, they told me, no Christians would have yet begun to call themselves "Catholic." In fairness, however, we must keep in mind that my subjects all spoke as visitors to a foreign time. None consistently used archaic language, which is rare in regressions. Even when a memory is valid, it is still being processed by a living brain that filters the recollection through a modern "data base."

Susan Reed was also speculative. "I get the impression that if the subjects are really accessing past lives, they are unable to fully become those people again," she said. "They may feel the feelings, but are unable to take on the mentalities." She said that twentieth-century ideas or translations of actions and attitudes often encroach on a subject's account. If a subject lacks knowledge of the period and the period mind-set, wouldn't they substitute modern equivalents for something they are perceiving but not understanding?

"For example," Susan continued, "Kathy Bradley related an incident where she met her boyfriend for lunch when 'lunch' is a fairly modern meal. Do we discount this as "made up," or was she experiencing some such act as meeting her boyfriend in town on a market day, buying a snack at a food vendor, and translating this into a modern equivalent, such as meeting someone for lunch?"

Professor Moran confirmed that it would not have been unusual for a girl from that area to learn to read a little German and Latin or speak a little French. Writing was less common for girls but was taught to them sometimes through home instruction.

In my own research, I found that the University of Copenhagen was the oldest and largest university in Denmark, founded in 1479. By 1500, nearly eighty universities had been founded in Europe. Interestingly, the model for the majority of universities in northern Europe was the University of Paris, which developed from a teacher's guild at the cathedral of Notre Dame. The universities that developed from these guilds were run by corporations of teachers. Some southern European universities began as students' guilds in those cases where most students were mature, professional people.

During the Middle Ages, university students were not required to have completed primary and secondary education. A fourteen-year-old might have begun attending universities, wandering from one to another for years until he reached adulthood. Students were generally taught orally and books became more available from the twelfth century onward. Writing was a more specialized skill. This was before the age of the printing press, and books were still painstakingly copied by hand. They were becoming more common by the fifteenth century.

In the Middle Ages, these scholars were taught, either by local parish priests in a bishop's household or through monastery or cathedral schools. Some children were taught by schoolmasters attached to guilds.

Education, or the lack of it, was a common thread through Katharine's recalled past lives. First, she hungered for intellectual tidbits from her brother; later, she was surrounded by academia, yet could not receive its fullest benefits. Her quest for knowledge continues in her current life. Could this indicate that the talents and learning we desire will be eventually achieved—even if it is in another lifetime?

9

Rich

"No hurt, no aches, no sore . . . "
—Anonymous, My Happy Home, *16th-Century Jerusalem*

On the day I met Richard Weissler, I opened my door to find a young man with shoulder-length brown hair and chiseled features, who looked as if he had just stepped off the movie set of *Camelot.* As the twenty-five-year-old entered my office to participate in my study, we settled on the couch to talk. I was startled by his quiet demeanor and calm, almost otherworldly presence.

The soft-spoken Scadian assured me that he was very much a product of the modern world. He holds a bachelor of science degree in economics and another in management science, and an MBA. A computer specialist who broadcasts messages to and from satellites, Rich explained that, to him, computers are engaging tools in which the user starts with nothing, and yet, in the end, expresses his or her own creativity, much in the way of an artist. He said he had always found it interesting that many Scadians made their mundane livings by, or were extreme enthusiasts of, the computer.

As a member of the SCA, Rich portrays a fighting knight and counts a broadsword and pole ax among his weapons. Before each battle, Rich explained, he reminds himself that he is committed to honor and chivalry, and that his first priority is not to hurt another or be hurt himself.

Rich said he feels more comfortable in his fighting gear than in modern clothes, preferring, instead, a replica of imported Italian armor, chain mail that he created from steel wire, and other hand-sewn and embroidered garments. The six-foot-one-inch Scadian says he catches himself "standing straighter" in his garb.

He became animated as he told me how he enjoys these moments stolen from the twentieth century. Reenacting, like the computer, he said, affords him the opportunity to create something out of nothing.

In August 1995 Rich first immersed himself in the medieval experience. At the time of our session, he had only been involved in the SCA for fourteen months, but he had already won awards for brewing and was victorious in a mead-making contest. Rich told me he now allocates between twenty and forty hours a week to reenacting activities.

His interest in the Middle Ages, however, was sparked much earlier. Rich, who was born in Ottawa, Ontario, Canada, said that family legend held a genealogical connection between his mother and Mary, Queen of Scots, which fascinated him as a child.

Then, as an eleven-year-old Boy Scout, he was introduced to Dungeons and Dragons, a fantasy, role-playing game which encompasses history, science, astronomy, and science fiction. This game of imagination pulled Rich squarely into the Middle Ages, hooking him on history and reading, resulting in his placement on the dean's list of his Newport News, Virginia, high school.

Later, while still on the dean's list at Virginia Polytechnic Institute and State University, in Blacksburg, Rich first saw SCA demos displaying medieval armor, fighting, and clothing. Everything, including the feudal system, appealed to him. Almost immediately, he joined the Barony of the Black Diamond. After college, he relocated to Martinsburg, West Virginia, and later to Frederick, Maryland, where it took Rich eight months and the assistance of the Internet to find a new home, the Shire of Highland Foorde. Once connected, he quickly climbed the ranks to become the Shire's Deputy Seneschal (or vice president).

From Rich's perspective, the Middle Ages were a low point in the history of civilization that produced a quality of life somewhat akin to that of the modern-day Kurds in Iraq, Iran, or Turkey. In the Middle Ages, Rich explained, a typical French peasant had to contend with heavy taxation, marauding armies, and the Black Plague. He described life as rough and short, and only pleasurable (at least to his modern eyes) for the nobles. His hope for humankind is that we learn not to repeat war, which he characterized as a strategic game that is generally unjustified and almost always economically driven.

Rich told me that he has spent significant time researching the Middle Ages and was beginning to learn such crafts as calligraphy, medieval cooking, and handstitching. He sewed his own forty-pound, red wool, furtrimmed cloak. Nevertheless, he didn't describe himself as an authenticity enthusiast. It is important to him, he told me, to be authentic within the confines of a budget, adding that it is not uncommon for him to spend between $100 and $250 a month on his hobby. The expenditure can climb to as much as $1,000 for shopping during the annual Pennsic War event.

Aside from his love of medieval history, Rich said he appreciates the camaraderie that exists among SCA members, describing the sense of community like a church group in which its members could be trusted. He described his fellow Scadians as being scholarly and brighter than the general population. Besides friendship, Rich has relished the acceptance, recognition, and infinite possibilities for the learning and creative expression he finds in the SCA.

Rich told me the story of how he came by his reenacting persona. While hearing a bawdy song at a feast, Rich turned bright red, threw a cloak over his head, and shook. Thus was he dubbed Razmus the Innocent (Raz for short) by his companions, with "innocent" being interpreted as "bereft of thought or clueless." Since then, Rich has embellished his new personality, deciding that he began as a Flemish monk who was excommunicated, then became a soldier of fortune who marched across France.

Now, we moved on from his persona to more esoteric concepts. As I had with all my participants, I asked Rich his thoughts on life after death. Rich theorized that the soul doesn't disappear at death, postulating that the remaining ghostlike spirit may influence the psyche of a new person. In addition, he told me that he believed in karma and the ripple effect of good deeds eventually being rewarded.

Eager to discover where the regression experience would take us, we wrapped up the interview. He stretched out on the couch and I began the relaxation process. As I directed him back into any previous past life he might have lived, he had to squeeze his eyes tight against ancient sunlight.

"It must be daytime. I see white," he said. "I feel the wind and warmth on my leg. I don't see or hear anyone. I'm sitting at a table by myself. It's a heavy, thick table. No, it's a beam," he corrected himself as things became clearer.

Now, Rich's breathing became labored. "The beam's solid. It's on top of me!" he gasped. "I can't feel my left leg. I can feel the wind against my right leg. It feels wet. I must have fallen down. It's very dark now. I can't see anything. My arms are numb."

The strained, heavy breathing ceased. I believed him to be dead, but after a moment he winced and continued."The weight of the beam is on my body. I feel dizzy. I feel wind on my left hand, which is under my right hand. I can't feel the beam now. I can't move. I have pain in my left leg—a sharp pain in the foot."

In spite of the pain, he was aware of his surroundings. "It feels like a church. I remember stained glass. There's large pieces of color, a little red and lots of blue. The stained glass has been removed by raiders or townspeople who moved on. The church is rough wood. The floor's dirt. The pews are logs cut in half. I can't tell how they are sitting up. The church is empty. The roof looks intact, but I can't tell what the roof's made of. I don't see any beams. The walls are mud or clay, not brick. The windows are paneless. It's very dry inside and out. The church is on a small hill. An area around the church is cleared of trees; there's a path that leads down the hill. There are no other buildings around. There's no one around, no one outside. It's silent."

He winced again and continued. "I feel dizzy. I'm tumbling—like my feet are overhead and then flipped back the other way. I don't know why I can't move. There's something across my middle and left leg. The left leg is numb except the foot and it hurts.

"I think I'm meant to die," he sounded anguished. "I don't have a weapon. I think of wolves. I have the image of a wolf on hind legs like a man's. Part of me says a werewolf, but I have no knowledge of that. Perhaps this is what I fear.

"The church is abandoned," he continued. "He said they'd come. I've never seen them."

Now, Richard said that the pain had stopped and he could see himself. I realized he had probably left his body.

"I'm trapped under a pew. It's very heavy. My nose is broken and bleeding. I've never seen a nose pushed to the side like that. It's almost sideways. It itches.

"I think I'm male," he observed. "My brown robe is pulled away from my right leg. My leg's a mess. There are long gashes from the knee down. Rat bites pulled away skin from the knee. My hair is long and short at the same time; not cut, but hacked into no shape. My hair's been cut by a dull knife to keep it out of my face. I can't make out the color.

"I'm young—just a man. I had hair growing on my face . . . Something is wrong with my stomach. I feel weight there, but don't feel anything. It's a belt or a rope, a lighter color than the robe. The rope got tighter when I fell.

"Oh God, my hands are numb and bloody and covered with insects," he gasped. "Oh, something's writhing in my gut." He cringed. "Maggots! It doesn't so much hurt as writhes just below the rib cage. I can't feel the wind on my leg anymore."

He utters a horrible gasp. "That shouldn't be alive! It's me, covered with bugs. I feel numb and cold. Something is in my right hand. It's soft and firm. It's a dead rat or a cat. I killed it when I could still move my arms. It was getting too close.

"Something's eating my left thumb. It doesn't hurt so much as it is uncomfortable. The skin is peeled away from my left thumb and my throat . . . "

Now, Rich moved away from his own decaying corpse. "It's spring. Outside, the grass is new green. There are red and purple flowers on the nob of the hill. I can't tell if the church was ransacked. Only one stained glass window is gone. Little else was disturbed."

Rich had trouble moving out of this lifetime. After a few moments, I directed him back into the imaginary, peaceful garden where I ask my subjects to sit at the beginning of their regressions. Here, I told him to rest and heal.

After he seemed refreshed and renewed, I decided to direct him to go to any pleasant lifetime he might recall. This time he found himself in a stable.

"It's daybreak. A page is tending the horses. I'm getting ready for a ride. I have a message to deliver," he said. "I'm checking the saddle and the hooves. It's a good horse, so I'll make good time. I'm not usually a messenger, but I'm riding today for the lord with an important message: 'My half-brother's getting married.' I'm delivering the message to his wife's father.

"My father's the lord," said Rich. "He has another title like 'duke.' My half-brother will be heir to a duchy. It's strange thinking of him like that. Even though I'm a bastard, he loves me. We fought well together. He's seen sixteen or seventeen winters. His wife will be older than he, in her twenties," he reported and then became emotional. "I'm overcome with the importance of it. I'm getting ready to go. The language seems strange to my ears . . . similar to Germanic, but I don't recognize it."

Final preparations having been made, Rich mounted his horse and began the ride to his destination.

"I feel wind against my chest. I'm riding a dark brown horse and I'm by myself. The page is not as good a horseman as I am. If I ride well, I should be able to make it in a day. I'd better, since I don't have supplies for more than that. But the land is cleared and the road is good.

"I ride almost hugging the horse's neck. There's no horn on the saddle and the weight of the saddle's behind me. I can stay in the stirrups. I'm making good time. I'm numb, from holding the reins."

Rich begins to breathe deeply. "I don't hear anything other than the horse and the clank of the sword against the saddle. It's a light sword, a gentleman's sword . . . a thin one-inch-wide blade with a thin hilt that's wire and leather wrapped. I've killed with it before.

"I have problems keeping in the reins. It makes me numb to hold on. The horse is slowing to a trot. I drink some water. It's acidic and there's some dry wine in it. The wine is imported from the rivers. Large gray, rusty, metal-bound casks of wine—too heavy for me to lift—are floated down the river.

"My goal is to make it before sunset. The gray, leather pouch is over my shoulder. I am wearing leather riding breeches and fine clothes of blue and red. My legs are sore from riding."

His hand tightened and balled. "The inside of my right hand is tight from a scar from fighting. It was a puncture wound on the outside of my hand. It was dressed well by my lord's own physician. Oh, but it hurts. I dumped mother-of-wine on it. It stung! It healed clean, but it cramps. The muscles never seemed to hold up right again, but I can still hold a sword.

"My mother wouldn't be happy about that. She's dead. She was killed when I was born. I was not noble born. I used to be beat up for that. My brother took me into the manor and my lord said he saw something of himself in me.

"I have three sisters. One's by a fourteen-year-old girl in town. Another illegitimate sister's still alive. She's fairly homely and older now. My legitimate sister's four. I only know because I backed up the seasons since she was born.

"My father's, the lord's, mistress is very pretty. She has a husband. He doesn't know the homely girl is not his. The girl is blonde, while her husband has dark hair as has all his family. He's from a Germanic people, but Germanic feels strange in my mouth. He's more solidly built than most of the village."

His musing stops as he refocuses on his journey. His right hand is now seriously curled up on its side.

"Riding's stiff work. My hands are cramped. I'm tying the reins to my arms so as not to have to hold them. I know my father worked a good trade on the wine. I'm continuing along a river that flows north."

As it approaches evening, a village comes into view. "There are single-story, low buildings. Grass roofs have bits of wood sticking out from the edges. The wood's only dark when oiled. There are seven or eight small buildings. People are working and milling about, not taking much notice of me. One elderly person is unhooking a nag of a horse from a plow.

"A little girl is jumping up and down on sacks of wheat or grain. It's good to see that her hair's covered in a bonnet or coif. She's wearing an untied, simple shirt of the same material as the bonnet. It comes down to her knees, there are no cuffs on the sleeves, and something is clenching the shirt in folds. The old man is wearing something similar. He's got tight socks on and very simple undyed pants on underneath. A youngster is looking out of a window."

Rich's hand was still awkwardly curled, so I suggested that it relax. As it began to go limp and flat, he continued. "I'm going to make it back to the manor so I don't have to ride hard. I give the horse its head. He'll get us there. I live in the manor. The title 'Duke of Krasstein' comes to mind."

When I asked him his name, "Donovitch" was the answer.

"I don't know how to reference what year it is," he continued, "but there is no king. The grounds are a little rocky here. It makes no sense, but the sun's setting to the north of the duke's manor."

Finally, the young man had reached his destination. "I'm at the manor. It's after dark. The walls look white. They're lit with torches. Inside is a courtyard; stables are to the right. The boys have taken the horse. I'm just a poor bastard child. The duke's man takes the satchel and tells me he'll have a return message in the morning.

"They will assign me a place to sleep and give me something to eat. I missed dinner, so I get dried meal and bread; water, no wine. The food's very salty. Now, I'm supposed to sleep in the stables. Great! Oh well, I'll make the best out of it. At least it's dry."

Confident that Rich had fulfilled his mission and knowing that our twentieth-century time was growing short, I suggested that he move forward to the last day of that life.

"I'm on a battlefield. I've had a better life than most. I have a beard and a young pregnant wife. My stepbrother loves me. I have tried to serve him well. I tended to his land and he has prospered. I lived in the manor and administrated his fields, insuring he got what was coming to him." He smiles. "My nephew has my nose. He will grow up to be strong.

"There are hundreds on the battlefield. I don't even know why we're fighting. I'm on horseback, wearing a coat of plates—a large number of steel plates, and my sword. There are some crossbows and long spears. We're riding forward to meet the enemy. It's sparsely wooded and slightly rocky.

"I fall face-first and hit the ground. There's pain under my left armpit towards the back. There's lots of screaming; the horses are screaming the loudest. My brother was behind me. I don't see him. He was in the last third of the mounted men."

With the bastard son of the duke lying dead in battle, I wrapped up the regression and brought Rich to full waking consciousness. We were both grateful that the second regression was more uplifting than the first, which had, in truth, unnerved us both. Later, Richard would tell me that for the next week he had felt physically exhausted and had decided to forgo his normal reenacting activities, including fighter practice. He said he wondered if his mind was trying to heal. Meanwhile, I was haunted by his description of the maggots writhing in his stomach and the rats ripping open his throat as he lay dying on the church floor.

After reviewing the transcripts of his gruesome demise, my experts tried to date the life, agreeing that it was probably High Middle Ages to post-Renaissance. The church that Rich described as being surrounded by open lands could have been possible during the High Middle Ages, after which some villages disappeared, leaving semiactive churches in the middle of nowhere.

Pews were also not used in churches until well past the Renaissance. Medieval churchgoers stood or brought their own chairs or knee pads. Susan Reed and others thought that perhaps a beam had fallen on the young man and he interpreted it as a pew. She said that if Rich's tragic end had occurred during the Reformation in a Protestant, Puritan, or Calvinist area, his formerly Catholic church might well have been stripped of its valuables and some of its materials, such as windows and floors. This was especially true in England, where monasteries and nunneries, closed by Henry VIII, were systematically removed of all items of value to the crown. Rich's former self would have thought of this stripping process as stealing.

Several of my experts, however, felt that the church as described did not sound stripped, but crude. They found the description of the rough church with the dirt floor inconsistent with the stained glass, a precious commodity. It should be added, however, that stained glass of the Dark Ages consisted of very small, simple panels. Although it appears childlike against the stained glass windows of the High Middle Ages, these little windows were the pride of the religious establishment. It is possible that the crude church possessed several, small primitive panels, and these are what Rich remembered. Also, staining or enameling techniques developed in the 1300s brought prices down.

Some of my experts thought that, because Rich described himself as dressed in a brown robe and lighter-colored belt, his face clean-shaven, and his hair self-cut, Rich may have been a monk, friar, or lay brother in that life.

Sensory images, strong feelings, and vivid details of death gripped many of the experts who reviewed the transcript. Ann Longmore-Etheridge was fascinated with the soul clinging to the body even after it began to decay. "The man seemed to be convinced he was not meant to be dead," she told me. "I think this is reminiscent of what we believe we know about some forms of haunting—that souls with unfinished business refuse to leave until they are convinced that they have been listened to and understood. Others seem not to be aware of their passing and stay put, trying to figure out what happened—as if they are in some sort of deep state of denial.

"I have read accounts of departed entities who are still attached to their former bodies," she continued, "and supposedly visit the decaying matter—just not able to leave it behind and go on. All of this is consistent with Rich's recollections."

Looking at Rich's second remembered incarnation, it appeared clear that the location was a Slavic territory united in a large Lithuanian-Polish empire or Bohemia. Germany was not a united country until the nineteenth century, and people identified themselves as coming from a number of small kingdoms and duchies rather than calling themselves "Germanic." (One example is the Duchy of Cleves, home of Henry VIII's fourth wife, Anna.)

Several experts were surprised by the young man's relegation to a bed in the stables. As a rule, bastards were barred from inheritance, but did not suffer bad treatment because of their illegitimacy. Many fathers were fond of their bastard children and often treated them as well as their legitimate children. Richard described himself in that life as being well-dressed and a trusted member of the family. This makes it less likely that he would have been treated as a common messenger unless the duke on the receiving end of the message had been unaware of his status or was simply deliberately cruel.

Rich's assessment of age by "winters" or other season counts, as well as his reference to "from daybreak to dusk" as an expression of time, are correct for the era.

Professor Moran affirmed that according to northern European demographic patterns, it would not have been unusual for a man to marry a woman a few years older than himself. But, for a man to marry at sixteen or seventeen would have been early and only common among aristocracy. And although Rich may have meant that his mother died in childbirth when he said she was "killed," the idea that his mother was murdered for bearing an illegitimate child was not inconceivable. Such killings did take place, usually by a member of the mother's own family.

My experts agreed that it was common practice to add clean water to wine, although water by itself was not commonly drunk. All water came from rivers, springs, lakes, ponds, rain barrels, or wells with no cleansing process as we have today, other than perhaps the screening out of organic matter. Although the mechanisms of contagion were unknown, a mental connection had been made to dangers of stagnant and impure water.

Professor Moran surmised that "the river running north" might have been somewhere between the Elbe and the Oder, going into the Baltic Sea, yet near enough to where wine was being manufactured. This, then, would probably have been closer to Germany than Russia. Bruce Blackistone also noted that the Rhine, Ems, Wesser, and the Oder all flow north through at least part of their length.

Blackistone also identified mother-of-wine as either a brandy or alcohol distillate that would make a good antiseptic, but said there was no knowledge of germ contamination and no surviving evidence of this particular practice.

It should be noted, however, that the discovery of the beautifully preserved Bronze Age "Ice Man" in the Italian Alps earlier this decade included the discovery of a ball of fungus on a leather thong. Current speculation is that Bronze Age people knew this fungus had antiseptic properties. In their minds, it just helped make a wound better and was therefore carried by the Ice Man as part of a primitive first aid kit. Pouring mother-of-wine on a wound could easily have been a "home cure" taught to Rich's former self millennia after the Ice Man died. As for the final attack, Bruce indicated that the screams and wounds were accurate for a flank attack.

Other details rang both true and false for my experts. Plows were generally pulled by oxen because horses were expensive. The use of a horse behind the plow would suggest thirteenth century or later. Meanwhile, armor expert Stephen Hick noted that the "coat of plates" armor which Rich described appears to be from an earlier time period, while his gentleman's sword could date post-1550. Nevertheless, Hick was impressed with the messenger's deep level of sensitivity—from the exhaustion of the ride to the physical complications from an old injury.

Despite a few apparently anachronistic details, several of my experts agreed with me that Rich's regressions stand out as unique. Although the notion of being a bastard son of a duke might initially have sounded "romantic," the cramping of Rich's hands and difficulty he experienced riding his horse was by no means glamorous. Later, after reflection, Rich told me he felt that this personality had been mentally dull—perhaps retarded. It was hard for me to conceive of this bright, educated computer specialist, who quickly grasped new subjects and won awards in new fields of endeavor, as ever having been retarded. It was equally as hard to rid myself of reminders of the broken body of a young monk whose only company at death were rats and maggots.

10

Karen

"The soul secur'd, smiles . . . "
—Joseph Addison, *17th Century*

In the third grade, Karen Beary's class undertook a three-week study of the French language. When it ended, Karen felt bereft, as if her newly expanded world had suddenly shrunk back to the confines of her one-room school in western Pennsylvania.

From that time on, unlike the rest of her family, Karen lived for her next taste of French. Five years seemed like an eternity, but finally, as an eighth grader, Karen resumed her study of the language. She says it quickly became her consuming passion. In college, Karen earned her bachelor's degree in French literature with a 3.95 grade-point average, while never cracking a book. Simultaneously, she earned a bachelor of science in communications/journalism.

Her continuing passion for the language prompted her to travel to Quebec, Canada, for an eight-week summer language immersion program. While studying there, she related an incident to her teacher in which a string of unknown French words spontaneously escaped her mouth. Her teacher was stunned and refused to tell her the meaning of what she'd said, calling it a French "black curse." To this day, she has no idea what she said or where it originated.

Her penchant for French eventually led Karen to choose a fourteenth-century French reenacting persona, Ysabeau Madeleine de Gascogne. Karen says she admires the women of medieval southern France for having been free thinkers and more independent than their medieval counterparts elsewhere. "The women of the Languedoc region made decisions and didn't take garbage from anyone," she explained to me in our interview. "Besides that, the clothing of the period suited my body type. What a vain way to pick a country!"

When we met on a hot summer day in August 1995, the thirty-year-old vivacious redhead, who earns her living as a computer purchasing agent for *USA Today,* had been a member of the SCA for three years. She had grown up, she explained, in a small town, never leaving a twenty-five-mile radius of her own backyard.

Born eight seconds apart from her sister Karla, the pair shared a close relationship. Her fraternal twin was the first to get involved in the SCA. She also gave Karen a recorder as a Twelfth Night gift, which prompted Karen to join a recorder ensemble.

Karen said she had a few rocky moments as a newcomer to the SCA. During her first introduction to Queen Garlanda of the Midrealm, Karen spilled melted gourmet chocolate on Her Majesty's royal red silk cotehardie.

After relocating to the Washington, D.C., area, she arrived at an after-work SCA meeting wearing a business suit and makeup. But she says she wasn't approved until she matched the look of the group. (Laughingly, she told me she decided to take off her makeup and wear her hair straight.)

Since then, Karen has become a member of a family in Clan Cromlech (in the Barony of Ponte Alto) and has made a wide circle of genuine friends. This optimistic woman has retained a childlike appreciation of life, believing that laughter is the best medicine. Despite her early sour experiences, she described the SCA events she now attends as "instant rejoicing."

"It's Halloween 365 days a year," she grinned at me. "It's freeing; it makes me feel that I'm a different person whether I'm dressed in my 'Gates of Hell' surcote or my belly dancing outfit."

Our conversation turned to her feelings about reincarnation. Karen remarked that the theory fascinated her, although she was generally a skeptic of the paranormal. Not sure if she could actually be regressed, she was nevertheless ready to try. Once in the hypnotic state, Karen began to receive fragmentary images. Gradually, the impressions became clearer.

"There's a gray haze," she began slowly. "I smell the ocean and see myself looking out over a wide space. It's not a fully sunny day. I think it's morning. The sun's just coming up; it's yellow-orange. The sky has some misty bits of clouds. It doesn't feel warm, but it's comfortable. I don't think anyone's around. I'm standing higher than the beach, maybe on a cliff. It's high, but not rocky. Now, I hear the ocean. I want to take a deep breath. My feet feel lighter—like I want to run."

Karen told me that her arms felt heavy. That was a good indication of an acceptable level of hypnosis. We continued.

"People are down the road. A man and a boy are up ahead, away from me. I don't know them. The boy has dark hair. His father is holding his hand. The man is wearing a white shirt with long sleeves, a vest, and dirty gray pants—nothing special. The little boy has brown pants and no shoes or shirt. The road is brown dirt with stones along the side and brownish-green scrubby grass."

Abruptly, Karen no longer felt the open air, but instead felt closed in. She felt heavy and hot above her heart and her legs twitched. Suddenly, what she saw got brighter, as if she were in the sun. I wondered if she had experienced her death. In either case, she had shifted by herself into a new scene.

"I have bare feet and a skirt to the ankles that's of a nubby, brown fabric. It's rough, but not scratchy. I have long brown, wavy hair, and brown skin like a tan. I think I'm pretty. It's a different face, different cheeks, full lips. I'm about twenty-three. My long, puffy light-colored sleeves don't bind me at the wrist. I'm glad," she confided. "I don't like that. I'm turning and skipping. I feel good and want to smile.

"The houses are one-story. There's stuff on the outside but not shutters. The roof's not steep," she observed.

"Now, it's dark and I'm inside. I see my hand on the back rung of a chair. I have short nails and long fingers. There's a shelf with a grayish pot that's stone or clay. Under that is a tiny fireplace. Nothing's burning on it. It feels empty and dark. It's not my place. I don't know why I'm here. Where's the door to the outside? I feel better.

"Now, I'm walking in a dusty, unpaved, small street. I can hear scuffling. 'Scuff, scuff.' There are no sidewalks or trees, but just one structure that has a thatched roof. I just keep walking. I feel things, but don't feel connected."

Since she felt a little disoriented, I suggested to Karen that she arrive at her destination.

"It's night," she told me. "I see a door. A man with dark curly hair answered and let me in. I don't have a cloak. He asks, 'Where's your cloak?'

"There's a soup bowl on the table. I'm hungry. I sit down. There's a spoon and bowl. The hot stew smells good. It doesn't smell like it has meat in it, but vegetables, carrots, and turnips. I like it. It's good.

"He sits down, too. I love him. He's handsome with bright green eyes. His shirt is open at the collar. He has big hands. He touches my arm. I'm home. This is where I need to be.

"There's candlelight. I see candles on the table. The table and bench are wooden. On the other side are two chairs that have straight sides with a peg across the top. There are beams along the ceiling, but they're not connected to the ceiling. They're partially round. It's one big room with a table in the center off the side of the door. There's a stalk hanging, herbs drying, twigs and leaves. They don't smell. There's no bats or birds. That's good. There are no stairs, but there's another room, probably with a bed."

Karen moved on to another scene. "It's daytime. I'm outside, washing clothes of linen fabric with another woman. She's got an apron on, she's older, rounder, and has a glint in her eye. She's smiling. She's doing most of the work. 'Scrub, scrub.' We're wet up to our elbows. It's a wooden tub. We're picking up clothes and socializing. The little girl running around belongs to my next-door neighbor. I don't have any children, but I want them. It's a sunny day. The air smells good and clean."

Excitement distracts the women from their chores.

"What's going on? I gotta watch. Groups of people are milling around like a carnival. The girl ran over. Kids are playing, chasing each other.

"I have to go see the juggler. He has a brown shirt with a hole in the elbow. His elbow's sticking out. He's short. The juggler is tossing two things in the air and behind his back. Everybody's watching. He's throwing and catching them. I'm curious. I've seen his cone-shaped hat. It's funny."

As Karen leaves the juggler and moves to another event, she holds her hands up in the air. "I feel something," she told me. "It's stone or wood, and it's flat. It keeps going. I have the impression it's like the side of a house or a wall. My hands are on it. It's a tall stone wall. It curves. I'm walking alone. It's colder. There's something in my right hand. A walking cane? It's round. My hand is on top. I take the stairs down. They're not smooth. They're cold and chilly. At the bottom I can't see. It's curious. It's not strange, but new. There's a breeze. It's like the ground is cut.

"I'm walking around. There's no danger or no purpose. There's pressure on my forehead. Now, my head is face down. There's pain in my head. I'm crouched down. My arms are out to the side. I can look and see that my body's lifting up—standing upright, but not floating.

"I'm breathing fast and running," she continued, leaving me wondering if she had died, but was now going to backtrack. "I'm taking in air fast. I have to go fast. I feel a grip on me. My chest is tight. I have to run. I don't feel like I'm in danger, but I'm not going because I want to. I sense the wind. My hair is going back. The wind is against my face and clothes. I'm running through the woods. I must be careful; I don't want to trip. If I trip, it's going to get me. I don't have to race. There are trees and knee-high scrub. I can't hide behind it, but at least I can dodge.

"At this spot, I can stay here and look out. I'm behind a tree; my hand is on the bark. I see the moon. It's not full, but fairly bright. It's not a happy situation. I feel like they'll get me. I don't have to run; I'll just stay here. There's an open area beyond the trees. I can't tell if someone is coming towards me. This is serious; not a game. I feel warm and sticky from running—like my shirt is sticking to me.

"I see a little house beyond the opening. The light's on, the door's open. If I leave this place, I don't know what will happen. If they catch me . . . I don't want to think about it. I'm anxious. I'm going to that house. The house is bigger. I don't want to look in. Why? It's brighter. I can't see anything. There's something on my head. I had to get it off. I'm nervous. I'm surrounded by light; like candlelight, only bigger.

"I'm not there and I'm not anxious. What is this? I sense a door frame. I feel very warm. There's an ache in my head, like I'm thinking too hard. I have to work it out.

"It's brighter inside," Karen went on. "I see cups and things stacked. I see flashes." Now, Karen wrinkled her forehead. "Uh-oh. Something's not right. I can't stay. Maybe I have to find somebody here. There's urgency. Ow! There's a pain in my head.

"It's daylight now. I see better. A familiar woman is with me. I don't want to be alone." She winced. "Another ache in my head. The person's older and seated, not wanting to leave. I leave and go back to the hiding place. I notice a pouch on my back and my things.

"I have to keep going, but it's hard to leave. She's my grandma, but I can't go back. I'm torn. I must get her out. She's got to come with me. She's standing up and having a hard time. She can't move fast. 'Grandma, we have to go.' We're outside. People are crowding around us, closing in. I'm having a hard time breathing."

Now, that life seemed over, and Karen flashed on a hand running a big comb through blonde hair. Karen said she looked down and saw a wooden cross below her head, thinking that perhaps she was the one wearing it.

I redirected her back to the last scene. "I'm here. Grandma's not here with me. She's gone. She's collapsed and is lying flat on the ground. My head hurts. The pain's sharpened. Something hit me. It's not clear. I don't want to know. There's a crowd of people here. My head aches.

"I feel light, but the pain hurts. I see light. I can see myself from above. I look okay. It's the same me with long, brown hair below my shoulders. I'm bigger and older. I'm just lying there. I don't want to know what happened.

"I was running from a man who beat me. The man was someone I knew. He was going to hurt my grandmother. She was all that I had left. I don't know the reason."

I asked her if she could recall the geographical area or time frame. "The French countryside; 1561 when I died," she responded.

"Where are the blue specks coming from?" she asked me distressed. To calm her, I directed her to move to the light and then converse with any spiritual beings she might encounter. She relaxed, telling me that her "council" was there to confer with her about her lessons and purpose in that lifetime. "It's going to be all right. You shouldn't worry. It was just an accident," was the message. She also received a reminder for her current incarnation. "I have to find my path again," she explained. "It's a question of love. It's spiritual. Where's my spirit going?"

After some moments of quiet reflection and healing, Karen returned to normal consciousness. In the weeks that followed, Karen discovered that the regression experience had affected her immensely. She told me her confidence, capabilities, and self-esteem had all expanded dramatically.

In discussing her recalled past life, Karen said she believed the bronze-skinned woman with wavy hair and almond eyes could have been Syrian. She also identified the intense pains in her head as having come from a head wound and her husband as the cause of her death.

Karen sincerely believed in the validity of her experience and acknowledged that she couldn't have known the historical details beforehand, describing her knowledge of history as "terrible."

My experts agreed that Karen's description held little datable detail, but they also held no troubling anachronisms, save one. Karen had mentioned candles on the table of the typical lower-class cottage to which she had returned. The lower and even emerging middle class used tallow and rush lights for interior lighting. Once again, we cannot be sure that Karen was not describing the rush light of a hand-formed tallow candle, since tallow is made like candles.

A balance to the possibly anachronistic candle was a sketch Karen made of the juggler's hat. A modern person might describe it as a "Smurf hat." Its distinctive shape was identified by my experts as a Phrygian cap worn extensively during the Dark Ages.

That historians could find nothing out of place with her experience surprised Karen, who claimed, unlike some of my other subjects, to have little knowledge of history. What startled her even more, she told me, was that reincarnation, something she had so little faith in, had affected her so profoundly.

11

Felicia

"No rest in that which perishes . . . "
—Michelangelo, *1475-1564*

Shortly after World War I, Felicia Eberling's mother, Elizabeth, then age six, stood on a chair and sang for homesick occupation officers in the German restaurant where her father worked. Her mother was eventually trained as a piano teacher at the Potthof-Zimmermann Conservatory of Music in Wuppertal.

Later, in a Germany controlled by Adolph Hitler, the young music student would play popular tunes in beer gardens. Local patrons, wearing their only set of finery, including shined shoes and black-market silk stockings, would dance to her upbeat tunes with the same conviction of the merrymakers, who, half a millennium earlier, danced to forget the destruction and fear caused by the Bubonic Plague.

Elizabeth's father and grandfather had also played in beer gardens with their village dance band. Each time Elizabeth's grandfather, who conducted the band, was shorthanded, one of his six sons would make a trip to a pawn shop, buy the needed instrument, and teach himself to play it for the next performance.

Stateside, in the 1940s and 1950s, Elizabeth was a pioneer in bringing recorders to public consciousness, hosting recorder-playing sessions in her home and occasionally giving presentations of what was then an exotic and arcane instrument.

As a youngster, Felicia Eberling followed in the footsteps of her mother's family. She was singing in parts from the time she could talk and is self-taught on many instruments—including the recorder, which she learned in seventh grade. She apparently inherited this ability to teach herself.

Although Felicia wasn't drawn to Renaissance history, she was drawn to its music. As she listened to it, she told me she would conjure up pictures of incense-filled neo-Gothic churches adorned with jewel-like stained glass. Drawn into the shimmering shadings and intensities of sight and sound, she would seem to float in a bath of swirling colors, with a heightened awareness of each musical note.

But that's not the only type of music Felicia relished. On her walks home from school through a rough Baltimore neighborhood, she would absorb and move to the vibrancy of African drumming, the Chinese dragon dance, Cuban, Italian, even Gypsy ethnic music. At home, her mother taught classical-method piano. As a small child, Felicia would cuddle under the piano near the pedals while her mother practiced for hours at a stretch. Meanwhile, her father, whose speech betrayed a hint of his mother's Irish brogue, was a stonecutter by day who could dance up a storm after hours.

With such parents, it was little wonder that Felicia would be eager to dance everything from ballet, tap, and ballroom, to salsa, Irish, and international folk dancing.

In high school, Felicia sang in a madrigal club. She also teamed up with a fellow lifeguard to play Early Baroque duets. Later, at a music library, the pair stumbled across a recording of Elizabethan lute music. The lute instantly became Felicia's favorite instrument.

While playing or listening to lute music, Felicia would envision her dream house with its Elizabethan decor, leaded-glass windows, ornate woodwork, and courtyard with a fountain.

In college, Felicia says she teamed up with another friend to create their own medieval/Renaissance ensemble called Vox Ventii. Felicia's alto voice was perfect for that era's vocal pieces, and she said that she instinctively knew that thirteenth-, fourteenth-, and fifteenth-century music was sung in a clear, nontremulous manner. She remains fascinated with re-creating music as it would have sounded in the past, in the various acoustically charged environments where it would have been performed.

At the time of our meeting, Felicia, wearing period-researched clothes, worked part-time for the Maryland Renaissance Festival as "Felicity Flutabec," a street musician, and also performed in Markland's historical dance and music troupe Thrir Venstri Foetr (Three Left Feet).

Felicia told me that she had first attended the festival with a friend and was immediately thrilled by the ambiance. Felicia auditioned the following year. She created the character of Felicity, who slips away from "the family ragweed farm" to spend the faire day doing what she loves to do: play her flute-a-bec (recorder) with no bratty brothers, sisters, or stray pigs to deal with. Her basic Felicity Flutabec character is now part of the festival's persona pool, available for use by other festival performers when she's not present.

When interacting with patrons, especially the very young and old, Felicia explained that she has sometimes felt as if they were sharing a "timeless enchanted fantasy bubble," with the gentle Tudor tunes and the natural sweetness of the wooden recorders as the captivating vehicle.

Besides the sound of woodwind magic, Felicia's delight at the Renaissance Festival has always been to jam with other musicians. Her eyes welled with tears as she spoke softly of those times when she slips through the here-and-now and forgets that the actors are costumed and the cottages are props. Particularly at sunrise or twilight, the smell of the campfires, the bustle of merchants and blacksmiths setting up shop, and glimpses of friendly exchanges peppered among the trees, make her catch her breath. Exuberant about music, Felicia views the Maryland Renaissance Festival as a "portal to personal magic."

Felicia eventually joined the SCA, which reaps the benefit of Felicia's talent when she performs on late-medieval and Renaissance woodwinds (recorders, shawm, cornamuse, and krummhorn), strings (bass viola da gamba), and percussion instruments (framedrum and doumbek). She has pulled together "period" ensembles for "medieval" gatherings, taught several workshops, and organized the SCA *ad hoc* Renaissance dance band, "Demo Fodder." For her service, she has been recognized by the King and Queen of Atlantia with the Award of Arms.

At the time of our meeting in mid-August 1995, Felicia had spent about six years with the SCA in the Baronies of Storvik and Ponte Alto, and ten or more years at the Renaissance Festival. The red-haired forty-two-year-old technical writer from Silver Spring, Maryland, holds a master of arts in French literature and is a former French and German teacher.

Always on a quest for adventure, Felicia told me that she pursues grants and scholarships to study foreign languages. These have taken her to Laval University in Quebec, to the Goethe Institute in Germany, and to an independent writing project in Paris. While in Germany, she was charmed by its remaining medieval architecture and old, narrow village streets. Felicia told me that she felt more at home there than in Maryland. Wherever she travels, Felicia said she takes her recorder and finds herself connecting with other musicians.

Felicia's passion bubbles over into sewing, reading, writing, and canoeing; and from computers and cooking to an interest in tarot and kabbalah.

When we discussed her spiritual life, Felicia told me that, through meditation, she's learned receptiveness, focus, and how to break down her inner and outer barriers. She believes this has led to her growth as a musician.

"Lightning seems to jump when I perform well or reach a patron, and especially when I team up with others and we hit that good vibration," she assured me. Through the years, Felicia has spent thousands of dollars on musical instruments, sheet music, books, and fabric for her costumes. She feels more graceful in her hoop skirts than in twentieth-century clothing, noticing that she changes her body language and takes smaller steps.

I asked her opinion on the possibility that she had been reincarnated, perhaps from the Renaissance era. She replied that she wasn't convinced about reincarnation, although she was convinced of the continuity of souls. She said she also believes in different temporal dimensions. In fact, she related, on one occasion, just prior to an electrical storm, she saw the brief apparition of a man dressed in Renaissance attire. He appeared to be in a study, reading and writing, and was also startled by her intrusion. "It felt so real," she confided.

Another time, once again prior to a storm, Felicia was strolling past century-old townhouses that looked onto Mount Royal Terrace, which was once a sumptuous estate and park in Baltimore. She was unnerved when a good-looking man, seemingly disoriented, "appeared out of nowhere" and hurried past her up the nearby promenade path. He had chestnut-colored hair and wore mutton-chop sideburns. His gray coat was nipped in at the waist and his tight trousers reminded her of stirrup pants. In an instant, he was gone.

When we were ready to begin, I banished my inquisitive cat, Finnegan, and we got underway with the regression experience. "I see a room that has paneling and black leather on the chairs," she told me. "I'm looking at myself. I have a nice dress on. It's a Tudor outfit with lots of dark velvet, while the inner part is damask."

She seemed confused and she questioned whether the person, who didn't resemble the twentieth-century Felicia, was "she" or someone else. In a moment, she seemed satisfied that it was she. "I'm wearing a headpiece. I have brown hair, a nice complexion, and am in my late teens to twenty-five. I'm in the garden, focused on how it feels to wear the clothes. My hair is up. It's weird . . . I remind myself of Paula Peterka!" (Felicia knew Paula from the Maryland Renaissance Festival. Paula is the subject featured in the next chapter.)

She described her surroundings for me. "There's a high fireplace going into a chimney surrounded by pillars. I see dining room chairs and a big, rectangular oak wood table. The arches are vaulted.

"Superimposed on a fireplace is a bas-relief of a swan swimming. The bank of the pond is in the upper left-hand corner. I have a hand on the back of the chair. My back is to the fireplace and I'm looking at the table."

Nervously, Felicia disclosed that her arm didn't feel attached and she couldn't feel her hand. She twitched her finger to make sure that it was still there, then returned to her description.

"On the right is a windowsill and a white wall. The window, surrounded by paneling, opens like a door and there's ivy on the other side. It's not clear glass, so I can't see through it too well. The window panes are diamond-shaped. A cat is lying on a windowsill on its tummy. It's a cute tabby pattern with white on the chin, bib, tummy, ears, and black and gray booties. Its tail is curled.

"Past the windows is an atrium with a fountain. There's a wall, pillars with arches, herbs and flowers. Sun is coming from everywhere. Huge doors open onto this garden colonnade. This must be a palazzo."

Realizing that she has been describing a country home, perhaps in Renaissance Italy, she paused to question whether atria were popular then. She also told me that the clothes felt like Italian Renaissance when she moved in them.

"It's very hot. The garden has shrubs with green leaves but no roses. The granite fountain is simple with a round, layered base. Water collects in a square goldfish pond and cascades down through three layered bowls.

"The garden tiles are black, gray, and white with a neat design. The floor in the passageway is covered with terra cotta bricks, with bright blue-and-green-glazed pieces of tile in a pretty pyramid pattern. Also, there's red and yellow tiles that are cheerful and bright. In contrast to the newer courtyard, the passageway is older and not gussied up.

"Maybe the passage runs between the main house and the stables or kitchen, to the right of the fireplace. There's other property to the right. This must be an older house that was built onto. It still has an original Roman atrium. The doorways are fancy Renaissance woodworking, while the passage windows look Tudor or late medieval."

Felicia was now seeing herself, at thirty, in the garden in an Elizabethan outfit.

"I'm wearing a yellow brocade outfit. There's a ruff around my neck, a piece down the back, Elizabethan sleeves, and a pointed corset. Simple pearls are sewn into the bodice and sleeves. I have a tiara of pearls and my hair is up. It's the same color. The bodice looks straight with a narrow hoopskirt that is too simple to be full Elizabethan. It could be an Italian or Spanish dress. It's comfortable. Maybe I'm wearing a corset that fits," she wondered aloud.

"I'm not fat or skinny, and have fair coloring. I'm past the blush of first youth, no longer a young girl. I'm the lady of the house; the adult in charge. This is my home and I like it here.

"Now, I'm in the dining room. A cabinet on the wall holds linens on the bottom, dishes and heavy glass on the top. The big dishes are on the sideboard. It's a cozy atmosphere. There's a well-mannered, sleek, black hunting dog by the fireplace.

"A man in a chair has his back to the fireplace," she continued. "He's wearing light-colored Tudor or Elizabethan clothes. His pants are fat and baggy with hosen cut off at the thighs. His shirt is white. On the outer layer, there's a fur-lined piece falling down the back. It doesn't match. He has a light brown doublet, a short cape, and light-colored comfortable shoes for pattering around the house.

"His little round Tudor hat has a pin in it and a white

plume. It's very strange. He has dark black hair with chestnut highlights, well-defined eyebrows, animated, black, French-Italian eyes, fair skin, and finely chiseled bones. He's a bit of the bawdy type, not really fit. Maybe he's northern Italian.

"He's about my age, in his twenties or thirties. We're lower nobility; well-off, but not ostentatiously wealthy. There are servants."

Felicia's mood shifted from peace to agitation. "I went to the atrium to collect myself. There's some kind of major life change. Could it involve losing it all . . . ? There's some problem with this man. I don't have a close feeling. I look at him and wonder what mood he's in. I'm trying to find some way to be comfortable with him. Is it an estrangement?" she asks herself.

"We're not on the same agenda," she continued. "There's something important to him at home that's radically different to me and my security, something that affects others. Ours could be a business arrangement. He's not repulsive but there's no spark. I'm definitely running the household.

"A girl with a forest-green dress lives here. She's part of the establishment. Does she belong? Maybe she's related to him, not me. She's on her way somewhere. She's about to go into the kitchen.

"She looks Italian or Spanish with an oval face and black hair. Her personality's defined, not pastel. This could be a marriage settlement and she's about to leave the house. She's torn. Maybe she'll have to leave the country."

I wondered whether the other woman could have been the source of her anxiety. Felicia indicated that she felt fear and panic at the thought of pursuing issues related to the dark-haired woman. I moved her forward in time to get some perspective on the issue. She went to the last day of her life.

"I'm late middle-aged and I'm in bed. It's cold, but I'm all right. He's dead and I'm ready to go. The angels are coming. It's bright and sunshiny. I don't worry about the pain. There are other things to concentrate on."

Before she passed over, I asked her what had happened with the other woman. "There was an understanding with her. It was good that she went because maybe he was interested in her. Things got better with my husband afterwards. There were good feelings and some affection between us. It was a comfortable partnership. Although there were no children, the house was okay because there were other relatives to step in."

Digging for more details, I asked her how the childless couple had spent their time. She gravitated to an activity they both shared.

"We both liked to dance. As a dance partner, he was a pleasure, not a noodle. There was a spark when we danced. He played the flute and the treble gamba, a stringed instrument, by ear and did fairly well for fun. Music was therapeutic for him. I enjoyed his playing, too. He was a dreamer and spent a lot of time in the library poring over tomes filled with philosophy and metaphysics.

"He can read Latin," she went on. "He had a medieval or Renaissance education. He writes poems. I listen out of accommodation, not out of interest. I don't care.

"He has a head for diplomacy. We have a nice estate and he's a good land person. He goes around in person, so his peasants know him by sight. That's unusual in Italy. They look at him as a god.

"I do well with other's children. They talk to me," she continued. "I take care of the day-to-day running of the household," she spoke proudly. "I'm business-minded and have a head for business, more than fun. I'm pragmatic. I keep the household humming and the linens changed. I can read respectably for practical reasons, but not scholarly. I'm like a steward, an empowered person. I don't write, but do the accounting.

"Our marriage was like a business arrangement. We're like roommates. We weren't in love, but there was some affection."

In her more relaxed moments, Felicia told me that she had gardened and walked. Now, I asked her the role religion played in their lives.

"We're Catholic, but not terribly serious. It's a built-in part of our daily routine, like lacing up a corset. We do it without thinking about it; like cleaning our teeth. We have Mass in our little chapel, and the chaplain visits. Although we're aristocrats, we are low nobles and don't have our own chaplain or house musician."

Curious about her view of politics, I prompted her. "I worry about Spain and France," she replied. "There's always intrigue. Our allegiance is to the Duke of Ferrara. Whatever the duke does, we support him. My husband, Frederico, dabbles in politics and scholarly endeavors. My name is Bianca."

These were the last details that Bianca recalled of that earthly life. But there was more, and it was unearthly in nature.

"It's cloudy and dreary," said Felicia unexpectedly. "It's the same place, but it looks like it's deserted. It's 100 years later. Either the plants have died or it's autumn. There's no activity; no one lives here. Maybe the household lost people through misfortune or war. Perhaps someone never came back. The household is gone. Our things are gone—plates, dishes, the big candlestick that sat on the floor and held several big candles. There's no water in the fountain. The property has gone to the dogs.

"I see a black-and-white painting of the clean-shaven caretaker with a hawk nose, blue eyes, and white hair."

What Felicia said next astonished me. "I feel like a ghost wandering through this place." Had Bianca's ghostly self returned to visit the now-abandoned household?

When I moved Felicia to another lifetime, she again appeared to find herself in the same house which had undergone major renovations. Could she have been drawn back to a home, much like others are drawn back to people or circumstances?

Now, its style was eighteenth-century rococo, and it boasted a grand foyer, white marble floor, glass doors, higher ceilings, and a gracious stairway with a banister. This time, however, Felicia was a man of the leisured class in his early twenties.

A "fop" dressed in a powdered wig, powder-blue coat, white hosen, tricorn hat, and wearing a beauty patch, he showed contempt for himself and his opulent lifestyle after he failed to follow his personal inclination to go adventuring by purchasing a commission in the army. Feeling trapped by duty to his family and the familial seat, he set off on a destructive course. Drunk and filled with rage, he impetuously rushed to the pleasure ponds and suffered a fatal fall.

After returning to waking consciousness, Felicia said that the regression experience allowed her to be able to see another aspect of herself, rather than an external event that may have affected her. She regarded the regression episode as a reality, in contrast to reenacting or living history events.

Felicia was startled to know that the Duchy of Ferrara was an Italian dukedom that became part of the Papal States in 1598. For five centuries prior, many of the dukes of Ferrara had come from the Este family.

None of my experts, including a university professor of early modern Italian history, found anything historically out of place in Felicia's account of the daily life, clothing, and music in Renaissance northern Italy.

All agreed that the paneling and furnishings—including the chimney, window glass, and velvet—suggested a wealthy person with an expensive Renaissance home. They found the distinctive layout style of the house with an inner courtyard reminiscent of the architecture around Renaissance Florence and Venice. Frescoes were common, as were center courtyard colonnades, kitchens in a separate outbuilding, and the rebuilding of old Roman sites.

They also agreed on the authenticity of the clothing, including Frederico's baggy pants and small Elizabethan bowler hat. Bianca's dress in a later scene could have been a Spanish-style farthingale, which was worn until about 1590.

Both Frederico and Bianca were plausible Renaissance names. Bianca's use of the word "noodle" was an affectionate epithet for a fool.

It was also appropriate for Bianca to be fairly well-educated, run the household, and keep the accounts. There were many pragmatic businesswomen of the age who amassed fortunes for their families by their shrewd judgment.

For Felicia, her girlhood "dream house," inspired by the music, now took on a new interpretation. Had Felicia recalled the Italian household that Bianca had managed? Or was Bianca's home merely an imaginary extension of the dream house Felicia had envisioned as a child?

12

Paula

"Here below all is incomprehensible . . . "
—Martin Luther, *1483-1546*

Paula Peterka and her husband Larry spent part of
their honeymoon at the Long Beach, California, Renaissance Faire. The pair had met three years earlier at a
lecture in Fresno in preparation for a festival in central
California in which Larry portrayed the Captain of the
Guards of Henry VIII. Both had worked at various Renaissance Festivals in the state without having encountered each other before.

Several years later, Paula played the German princess,

Anna of Cleves, the fourth wife of Henry VIII, at the 1994 Maryland Renaissance Festival. Paula said that she regards Anna of Cleves as having had the best life of Henry's six wives.

Henry and Anna's first impressions of each other were unfavorable. Anna was tall and thin, while Henry preferred voluptuous women; Henry was older than the portrait she had seen; Anna was seasick when they met; and the cultural and educational differences between them were enormous. The marriage, therefore, was never consummated.

Unlike Catherine of Aragon, Henry's first wife, whose intractability prolonged the king's royal divorce by ten years, Anna agreed to an annulment after only six months of marriage. Her obedience earned her Henry's lasting affection. He retitled his ex-wife "the King's Sister" and gave her 5,000 pounds a year and extensive manors, many of which had been forfeited by Thomas Cromwell, who was executed for his part in arranging the marriage.[1]

When we met in mid-August 1995, Paula was preparing for her second year portraying Princess Anna. She had spent three Renaissance festival seasons in Maryland and, before that, four years in California, serving in the Court of Henry VIII and as Mistress of Protocol.

But the twenty-nine-year-old hadn't always played royalty at the festivals. While at the University of California, Los Angeles (UCLA), her roommate suggested that Paula take a job at a flower booth at the faire in Agoura. In her booth, Paula dressed as an English peasant and was able to watch a troop of German military reenactors practicing and performing. They intrigued her and she joined them to practice her German.

As an official Renaissance festival participant in California, Paula received a stipend of food coupons and wore her own costumes. Years later at the Maryland Renaissance Festival, Paula was reimbursed two hundred dollars for making her own gown for Anna of Cleves. She also received a small salary.

Paula shared with me her observation that, in general, Renaissance festival workers on the West Coast are composed largely of Renaissance hobbyists, while in Maryland many are professional actors.

Aside from working various Renaissance festivals for nearly ten years, Paula and Larry have been a vital part of a sixteenth-century, living-history German troop, the Landsknechts or "servants of the land." Paula and Larry were drawn to the Renaissance German mercenary troops prior to knowing each other. In 1991, the pair moved to Alexandria, Virginia, leaving their troop behind. Three years later, they had recruited soldiers to start their own local unit, Das TeufelsAlpdrücken Fähnlein (the Devil's Nightmare Regiment). The name came from an old French saying, which translates to, "the landsquenet thrown out of Paradise cannot get into hell, for he would make the Devil afraid."

These troops of German foot soldiers were originally established by Maximilian I to rescue Mary of Burgundy, the woman he was planning to marry, and fortify her property in the Netherlands. He placed units of 500 men shoulder-to-shoulder with sixteen-foot spears and found that they could break a cavalry's charge. This was the beginning of the modern infantry.

Paula explained to me that the newfangled infantry was never short of recruits. One advantage to becoming a Landsknecht was that in five years or less, if he survived, a soldier could retire as a wealthy man. The lowest pay grade was four gold marks or guilders a month—a sizable salary in those days.

In all eras, dress has been a way to identify one's social betters. At the time of the Landsknechts, wealthy merchants had begun to outdress nobles and sumptuary laws were created to reinforce the social hierarchy. These laws dictated the wearing of clothing designs, fabrics, and colors—such as "cloth of gold" and "clothe of purpalle"—by rank. Because of their important role in society, the soldiers received immunity from sumptuary laws and the Landsknechts, whose love of fancy dress became legendary, were given leave to wear silk, velvet, lace, and clothing designs of their preference that took the form of brightly colored balloon trousers and sleeves, slashed with opposing hues beneath. The soldiers' gold chains and jewelry were a portable means of wealth and, if necessary, could be used to ransom oneself.

Their wives, also absolved from sumptuary laws, dressed just as lavishly as they followed their husbands into battle, to cook, sew, and care for their wounds as a way of maintaining the family unit. Each man could bring only one woman with him. This rule was enforced both by the military organizational structure and also by the wives themselves. Any woman who was perceived as a threat would be beaten, have her hair cut off, be run out of camp, or killed by the wives.

"These women were pragmatic, practical, and lived continuously in survival mode," Paula told me. "They looked death in the face on a regular basis." During battle, they would follow behind their men, slitting the throats of the wounded enemy, picking up discarded weapons, and scavenging the belongings on the bodies of the dead.

"But they got to travel," she went on. "They got to live beyond their station in life and escape the boredom of being behind a plow every day."

Paula's Landsknecht persona, Anjabeth Blöde, is a Bavarian campfollower wife with skills that include making beer and cheese from heavy cream, spinning wool, embroidering, singing, and playing period songs on a recorder and dulcimer. As "Hauptfrau" or "head camp-follower," she's been elected to be in charge of all non-combatants. As Hauptfrau, she keeps the couple's tent in order, cooks stews and pottages, and roasts meats over an open fire. She also runs the bureaucratic aspects of camp, directs the preparation of all the meals, and ensures authenticity at events. She seldom breaks character and converses with a heavy German accent.

Between running the Landsknecht unit and the couple's yearly participation in the Maryland Renaissance Festivals, Paula says the Peterkas have less than fifteen uncommitted weekends per year. Paula admitted that the couple has spent most every waking moment, and $15,000 or more, on their decade-long avocation.

But Paula told me she thinks the money and effort have been worth it. Aside from thriving on the tribal interdependency and mutual support among the group's members, she honestly enjoys informing the public. "Perhaps if people understood history, they would comprehend the human condition, which hasn't changed much," she said earnestly.

"I like to make people think, to appreciate 'the now.' In order to survive into the future, we must understand the present; in order to create a healthier present, we must know what happened before. I like to make history come alive for others."

Paula, who believes in conflict resolution through peaceful means whenever possible, hopes that through the graphic portrayal of Renaissance-era warfare and brutality, the message will be clear—war means that people die. Although she believes in war as a last resort, she does not believe in glorifying war or violence. "Perhaps when our better virtues of honor, valor, and courage are not tied into war, we can rid ourselves of it," she reasoned.

Our conversation turned to her thoughts on life after

death. Paula told me that she was raised by parents who were a traditional Southern Baptist and a Methodist. Considering herself a Christian, she said she nevertheless thought it might be more just and positive to allow a soul to return again to "get its lessons right." She maintained the viewpoint that "anything's possible" and that to be closed-minded was a "sign of arrogance."

The cheerful, vibrant, down-to-earth woman who, as a youngster had loved tales of castles, had wanted to be Robin Hood or Little John, and had performed since she was three, was now ready to try a new adventure. As a living historian, during events with a high level of authenticity, she had occasionally received glimpses of the past as she momentarily would lose her twentieth-century identity. But what she was about to experience in past-life hypnosis was entirely different.

After Paula reached the hypnotic state, she told me that she saw a winter sky, tall evergreens, and flat countryside. There was a bearded man staring down at her as her heavy, lifeless body was dragged to a cart and taken away.

In the next moment, Paula became a six-year-old girl who was wearing an apron. She giggled as she eyed the flowered design on the church ceiling, the fluttering fabric against the walls, and the carving of a strange creature with a big mouth. She admired the black velvet dress of a wealthy parishioner who admonished her not to stare or dawdle. The little girl's life came to a sad end after looking into the snarling face of a dog and hearing a man's laughter.

After two frightening deaths, she moved into what seemed to be a more pleasant lifetime.

"I see a brick path," she told me now, "green bushes, arches in a walkway. It's a garden. Inside, there's a large white room with high rounded windows. It's a homey place with detail over a big fireplace. There are pointed arches on one side and a balcony on the right.

"I'm in the hall. I'm spinning and having too much fun to be working," she said gaily. "There are people everywhere. It's a party. We're all about fourteen or sixteen [years old].

"Now, we're playing a game and I can't see anybody. I'm blindfolded." She laughed. "They tickle you and before you grab them, they're gone again. I'm stomping my feet. I know they're there. I reach out. Someone grabs me by the hand. I'm not letting go of him. Everybody's laughing.

"Tom, you silly thing!" she said suddenly. "I'm upset. My gold French hood with pearls is off. I'm wearing a fashionable, tight-cut gold gown that flares out and has big, hanging fur sleeves. Mary says I have to kiss Tom before I get my hat back. I like him, but I don't want him to know. I grab my hat and storm out. A girl follows me and says he's very comely. I say I don't care, but I know I should act more grown up. There's a long hallway with paintings and figures with suits of armor.

"I'm trying to find a place to fix my hat," she continued. "The girl grabs both hands and asks me earnestly, 'Please tell me you'll come.' She has a rounded face, pretty eyes, wisps of hair, and she's sweet. Now, we're both giggling. I'm trying to get my hat on straight. I wonder where my mother is. She always gets it on straight.

"Now, we're in the middle of the hallway in the great hall and she looks coyly back at me. One of the boys is out in the front hall. Bowing low, he says, 'Ladies, we so missed your presence.' She walks forward, sniffs at him, and we walk past him, arm in arm. Wish I had something to throw at him."

It appears that the party is now winding down. "It's late. They're cleaning up. The musicians are gone. They were up in the balcony. It's only us left and the servants who are cleaning up.

"My pretty friend is wearing a red dress similar to mine. Mary's in white and gold. Nan is in blue. We like Nan. We should get back or a grumpy-faced dowager will deal with us," Paula said hurriedly.

"We've made our farewells. The poor boys looked so dejected. It's proper they should look like that when we leave though they probably don't mean it.

"It's a Twelfth Night party. They go on for weeks from before Christmas to after Epiphany. It's so nice here in London. I wish I could stay here," she said wistfully. "Home's a long way from here, to the northeast, in the country. I'm not allowed to come here by myself. This is so much fun. I just want to dance, stay up late, have a good time."

The festivities over, the young woman returned to the country where life was unexciting. "At home, I sit and look out my window. There's cleared land around the house. Mamma wants a formal garden, but she probably won't get it.

"I listen to the master drone on forever about the most boring things. My sister and I stay upstairs for lessons. Then we get to do needlework with mother. That's fun. We embroider Spanish work on shirts.

"Father goes out a lot," she continued. "It's nice when he comes home, stomping through the front room. He has a great booming voice. Papa's wonderful. He used to pick us up when we were young," she reminisced.

"Our home has dark wood paneling inside. It's smooth to the touch. It's nice and warm with tall windows, a carpet over wood floors, and a couple of rounded chairs. Books are over to the left. Windows have a dappled effect; they're mullioned. I like this room. Father's in here a lot. He's the wealthiest man in the area." Her mood shifted. "He makes us giggle," she laughed.

"My sister Catherine is two years younger and smarter, but not as pretty as me. She always understands Master

Hawkins's lessons. I know how to read, but the Matins (morning prayers) are very difficult. No one sees them but the priest, so I don't have a need for it. Master Hawkins has dark hair and a crooked nose, like a bird. I'd rather be out writing or playing than listening to him drone on.

"Clara, Sarah, and Sally are the servants," she went on. "Sally looks after Cat and me. Mama has ladies looking after her and a manservant to cook. They address her as 'Madam' and father as 'Sir.'"

The young girl continued to describe her home and lifestyle.

"Cat and I share a bed with a platform, and a pretty wood carving hanging on it. If we get up early before Sarah is there, we brush each other's hair. Every day we go downstairs and out to the chapel to prayers, although I'd much rather sleep.

"Sometimes I'm with Mama, sometimes the music teacher, or Papa takes us out riding. Our midday repast is dinner. On a plain day it's nice, but when guests come, it's grand.

"Then, we listen to Mr. Hawk-nose," she sounded bored. "He talks about Latin and Erasmus (he's impressed with Mr. Erasmus). There's France, Italy (I never get it straight), the continent, the empire. Then I have time with Sarah or Mama, and go for a walk. Sometimes, I sneak out to play with the dogs."

Next, Paula touched on the role of religion in her life.

"We pray all around the clock. There's morning, midday, and evening prayers. You'd think God would get tired of it," she scoffed. "There are feasts and then fasts with no milk, eggs, meat, and nothing but fish. Lenten feast days are the longest. Day after day, we eat smoked eel, haddock, nothing but fish."

I asked her what religion she was.

"What kind of question is that?" she responded indignantly. "Mama says people try to make trouble with religion and God. We don't have any of that now."

"Who's the king?" I asked.

"We call him 'Majesty,'" she giggled. "He was at the party. Cat had to stay home. Wait 'til I tell her. He's got a voice like Papa's. He's handsome and far too grand for me to talk about. He jousts; he's athletic. They are proud of him. He's Henry VIII Tudor and we call him 'My gracious Lord.'" She smiled.

"His wife, Queen Catherine, is from Spain. She made Spanish [needle]work popular. Everyone loves them. How good and brave he is, and how kind she is. I'm not grand enough to be in that kind of company." Now she reminisced about the party. "My grandame was there at the party. Maybe they sent me to stay with her for Twelfth Night . . . ?"

Now I suggested that she recall another significant scene. "A page brought me a message. I don't want to talk about it," she was alarmed. "Someone's dead. It's John, my husband. There's parchment in my hands. I'm very unhappy and I'm pacing the room," she was noticeably distraught.

"I'm twenty-six. This is my home. I've been here for six years. I mustn't be upset in front of the servants. I'm very angry at him for dying." Now, she drummed her fingers anxiously. "The servant won't leave. Damn it. It's so hot in here. I want to go away from here, ride, do something.

"I'm walking through the front hall calling for James to get me a horse. My staff won't let me go. They're afraid I'll hurt myself if I'm left alone. I want to get out of here. I can't wail in front of the servants, like a peasant. James is polite, but he's getting in my way. I'll have to strike him in order to get him to move out of my way."

Now she began crying. "I don't understand. Nobody understands. He's the only one who understood me," she said sadly. "I crumpled up the note and threw it on the floor.

"I have children. Mary, Henry, and little Catherine.

What am I going to tell them?" she cried.

Leaving the tragic moment behind, we moved ahead six years.

"The curtains are drawn. I got to keep the house. The children are fine. Mary's fifteen and a fine young woman now. She's tall and going to be very pretty. Henry looks just like his father. Little Catherine is seven.

"I've been married again," she said. "He's good to me and the children. I suppose we're comfortable together." She rubbed her stomach. "It will pass. It feels different. I haven't hurt like this before," she grimaced. "Little Thomas is a fortnight [two weeks old]. If I can love the baby, I can learn to love Thomas. He's the duke's chamberlain. He's been in and out of my room, but they kept the children out.

"Everything hurts. I have pains in my stomach." Her face became contorted. "It's close, stuffy. I'm sitting up, tearing at the sheets and bed curtains." She's ringing her hands now. "They call for the doctor. Thomas is upset. I'm clawing at the sheets and curtains. There's so much blood everywhere . . . Do I have to stay here?"

"No," I told her. "Go to light." There she found pain-free peace.

Upon returning to full waking consciousness, Paula was of the opinion that this had been an ordinary middle-upper class English existence or comfortable gentry, although not nobility. But much had appeared strange to her—for example, she saw furnishings that were different from anything she had ever seen.

Most of all, she confided, she was puzzled by the girl's attitude, which was entirely different from her own. The young Elizabethan woman had been concerned with looks and parties, and hadn't cared about learning. She speculated that the sixteen year old had been sent to the London celebrations so that she could wheedle her way into court.

Remembering her reaction to her husband's death, Paula claimed that she had felt trapped, frustrated, and devastated, but couldn't let herself grieve in front of the servants. "They knew I would kill myself," she told me. She also remembered tortured thoughts of how she would tell the children about their father's demise.

After a loving marriage with John, she was startled that her next marriage had been one of convenience. She told me that she believed the duke, to whom her husband was chamberlain, may have been either Norfolk or Suffolk.

During the queenship of Catherine of Aragon (1509-1533), both Thomas Howard, Second Duke of Norfolk, and his son, Thomas Howard, Third Duke of Norfolk, held the title.[2] Charles Brandon was Duke of Suffolk during the entirety of Henry VIII's reign.[3]

My experts explained that men of status, such as landed gentry, or members of the professional class, such as lawyers or wealthy merchants, often held positions such as chamberlain to kings, dukes, and other nobility, handling their personal and financial affairs.

Paula's description of her surroundings were deemed accurate by the experts. Tudor wooden furniture tended to be stained almost black, and there were few carpets and chairs, except in wealthy homes. Most great houses did indeed have formal gardens. The armor experts commented, however, that armor wasn't normally displayed in the home, but kept and maintained in an armory.

In retrospect, Paula told me that she was unsure whether she had seen armor displayed or guards wearing armor in the hallway. She felt as if the young noblewoman in the regression didn't care either way, because guards, like servants, were "like wallpaper." This reminded me of her inability to know exactly how old she was at various times. This fact impressed several commentators as did the emphasis on prayers and fasting which would have been authentic and suggestive of a religious family.

A few distrusted the names "Hawkins" and "Cat," which parallel Sir John Hawkins, Elizabeth I's famous admiral, and Elizabeth I's well-known nickname for her governess, Catherine Ashley. Also, "Clara, Sarah, and Sally" appear to be unusual names for this time period.

Most of the experts, however, found many historical "hits." For example, Catherine of Aragon did indeed bring "blackwork" needlepoint to England from Spain and it became wildly popular among the well-to-do.

The French hood, an elegant headdress that curved around the forehead and down past the ears, was gaining popularity at that time. So were the gowns with hanging, fur-lined sleeves. The mention of books was also correct, as printed volumes increased in number as the sixteenth century progressed. Meanwhile, messages could have been written on parchment.

Paula also mentioned Erasmus, the Dutch humanist and writer, who was admired by both the king and queen as a proponent of new learning and female education.

As the century passed, it became more and more common for the daughters of the nobility and nouveau riche middle class to educate their daughters. Both Sir Thomas More and King Henry VIII were among those who did so, providing well-rounded educations for their own daughters. Both the princesses Mary and Elizabeth, as well as the king's niece, the Lady Jane Gray, were renowned scholars who read, spoke, and wrote in Latin and Greek, as well as French and English. It would certainly not have been unusual for Paula's previous personality to have been educated by a private tutor.

Although the family may have been of the middle class, having a chapel on the premises, a variety of servants, cleared land, and a music teacher were indicative of wealth and a conscious effort to move up the social ladder. This was entirely possible during the reign of Henry VIII. The Boleyns, for example, came from middle-class stock. Even members of the lower class might aspire to noble status. Cardinal Wolsey was the son of a pig slaughterer.

As the young girl said, the 1520s were indeed years when "people were trying to make trouble with religion and God." By 1530, the kingdom would be in the midst of the Great Schism—England's separation from the Catholic Church—fired by the king's desperation for a new wife who could bear him sons. When the pope continued to refuse Henry VIII a divorce from his Spanish wife, who was past menopause, the king broke his nation away from the papacy and founded his own Anglican church to sanction a divorce from Queen Catherine and a second marriage to Anne Boleyn.

The teens' parlor games in the great hall also met with approval by my experts. They identified one game as Blind Man's Bluff because the young woman was standing. However, if she had had to kiss the boy to get her hood back, it might have been a variant of the game called Forfeits.

In earlier times, the great hall was filled with musicians as the center of social activities that included Twelfth Night festivities. Social etiquette would have called for addressing King Henry VIII as "Your Majesty."

In the weeks following our meeting, Paula claimed that she had flashes of other lives. In one, she told me, she was trapped in a house fire. In another instance, she was washing her hands after working on red leather sleeves for one of her Landsknecht reenactors. When she watched the red dye go down the drain, she saw herself as a nurse trying to get a musket ball out of a Revolutionary War soldier's leg. "My hands were deep in blood and I could smell smoke, hear shouts, and see cannons," she said solemnly.

Paula said she also achieved a new sense of peace through the regression experience. She had been plagued with fears of being physically abused or even murdered prior to the regression. Afterward, she told me that the brief reliving of the two deaths at the beginning of the regression had caused her terrors to entirely disappear.

13

Tee

"A thing immortal as itself . . . "
—William Shakespeare, *1564-1616*

Always joking that he had been a court jester in a past life, Thomas Earl Morris, known to most as "Tee," was startled by an occurrence that took place several years ago in a museum in Washington, D.C. He can still recall the Mediterranean-style tapestries that lined the walls of the chamber, the massive banquet table, and the old chairs placed nearby. Being an actor by profession, Tee related its ambiance to the set of the film *A Lion in Winter*. This scene triggered a stirring feeling. "I swore

I'd been there before," he murmured in a hushed tone, adding that he'd felt he was in a dimly lit great hall with a fire roaring. "I felt like I was making people laugh. I even heard raucous laughter," he said. He described the incident as "creepy" and explained it away as "impossible."

Another of Tee's unexplained sensations occurred after his first visit to London. Although friends had warned him to "prepare for culture shock," he was amazed to find that he felt more at home in England than in his hometown. It was when Tee returned home from Britain, he said, that he got his dose of culture shock.

He also admitted to occasional "strange, déjà vu-like emotions," when he dresses in his Maryland Renaissance Festival costume. He claims to feel more comfortable in costume than in his current-day clothes. Describing his character as having the mind of MacGyver but blessed with the luck of Wile E. Coyote, Tee was unquestionably proud of his character creation, Quinton Edmund Devonshire. Quinton is a sixteenth-century inventor, toy maker, astronomer, and "academician of the paranormal" who investigates the "Q-Files," which is a medieval parody of the *X-Files*. Quinton can be counted on to do outlandish activities such as trying to fly or contemplating the ghosts in the Tower of London.

"The Renaissance Festival isn't an easy gig," Tee told me. The actors do improvisation on an outdoor stage with historical information using a British accent. He, like the other actors, use what they call "Elizabethan speak" for over eight hours a day, which includes three stage performances, intermingling with patrons in the village streets, and singing in the festival tavern. He has studied stage combat and explained to me that his role is part actor and part stuntman. "The Ren Faire schedule makes traditional acting look easy," he sighed. "Besides, I'm an actor who has done my historical research."

In spite of the long hours, Tee derives immense joy

from his participation. He does his job with dedication, flair, and humor, approaching it as "a great big Warner Brothers cartoon set in the Renaissance."

Tee has polished his performance technique to such a degree that he has now joined an improvisation troupe that performs in Alexandria, Virginia.

As an actor, Tee says he appreciates the structure of the Maryland Renaissance Festival. He explained to me during a preregression interview that actors and actresses audition for their parts. Once selected, the cast is coached and everyone has a role in a plot line. They rehearse all summer long.

Although Tee had never participated in SCA events, he had recently joined the Landsknechts (see chapter 1). His sixteenth-century character is Wolfgang Idlehartz, nicknamed "Dogfood." Wolfgang is a fresh-faced recruit who is anxious to make a name for himself. He confided that he feels more comfortable in his Renaissance festival authentic reproduction costume than in his Landsknecht uniform.

He recalled a dream in which he went to work at his regular job as a graphic artist wearing his festival garb. "The funny thing was that no one noticed," he smiled. Tee also told me he prefers the ambiance of the Renaissance Faire. Having a penchant for the romance of the Renaissance, it was the perfect setting for the blond twenty-six year old to meet his girlfriend, a vendor with blood-red hair.

In his mundane life, Tee lives in Laurel, Maryland, and holds a B.S. in mass communication and theater from James Madison University in Harrisonburg, Virginia. He has studied acting at the University of London and Shakespeare at the Globe Theater. Tee has also had formal instruction in fencing.

The performing artist told me that he was fascinated with pageantry, including that of medieval warfare. He said he admires the skill that war took in times past and that all participants had a fighting chance. "Today," he said, "with the push of a button, an entire city could be wiped out."

By the fifth grade, Tee says that he was infatuated with the King Arthur legend and the movie *Excalibur*—anything that has to do with the search for the Holy Grail. In high school, in Richmond, Virginia, he began playing Dungeons and Dragons. At that time, he wrote short stories based on his Dungeon and Dragon characters.

The movie *Dead Again*, which dealt with reincarnation, made Tee first consider the possibility that we live again. Tee also admitted that he was nervous about being hypnotized and what he might learn from the experience. I reassured him that it was harmless, then began the visualization exercises. He easily slipped into the hypnotic state and within moments was laughing at the shoes he saw himself wearing. They were black suede with small heels.

"It's nightime," he told me. "I'm angry about something. People are afraid of me and I don't care," he said. "I'm in an alley, slamming into a wooden door of a house trying to break it down.

"A fat guy behind me raises a knife and stabs me in the shoulder. I've fallen. I feel dizzy. I see a stained-glass window with circles, and white houses. I hear voices but can't see anybody, as if everybody's indoors."

Suddenly, Tee spontaneously awoke. After I relaxed him again into the hypnotic state, Tee saw himself in a pub, dressed in clothing and shoes similar to what he wears at the Renaissance festival, although he didn't have the same physical characteristics as he does now. The man had short hair, a beard, a moustache, and was tall and brawny. Tee is cleanshaven.

Next, he found himself to be a six-year-old boy, running through a flat field of high grass and dandelions.

"I'm barefoot and wearing trousers and a white shirt with puffy sleeves. My hair is kind of long and I'm laughing," he said gaily.

"My father is carrying a picnic. I'm happy to see him. He's wearing basic clothes like I am. He has a beard and his face has heavy round features, but he's not heavy-set."

Tee's joy quickly turned to sorrow as he jumped to the next scene. "He died of the plague. I'm too young to know what's going on," he related. "Now, I'm with an aunt. She has two little daughters. My aunt doesn't smile much; she's very conservative. My mother could have died in childbirth."

Shifting to the next significant event, he saw an ornate Catholic cross. "I'm inside a really big church, possibly a cathedral, and see other boys dressed in robes. I hear sounds echoing through the church. I'm trying not to fidget, but it's hard. I'm not happy to be here," the small boy said glumly. "My aunt put me here because she didn't want to bother with me. She didn't like me. I can't tell the time period."

When I moved him forward, the boy found himself at his own funeral. "I can look at the casket. I look pale. I'm no more than fourteen. There aren't many people here, no one close to me. Those who are here are annoyed that they have to be here. They just want to get it over with. My aunt paid for the funeral, but didn't come. My hair-cut seems twelfth or thirteenth century and I'm wearing a simple nightgown. Maybe I'm nobility since I'm being given a send-off with formal burial rites.

"I was sad and very private. I grieved myself to death. 'Not a happy lad,' they said. No one knew me. I felt pathetic and couldn't figure out why. I felt alone, but I don't understand why I died so young. It looks like I had a good life, but I died lonely. I regret that I didn't do something. I remember being happy when I was six, but I was scared of my aunt. I know I'm dead."

After a few moments of silence, he moved into another lifetime. Tee heard crickets and discovered himself to be alone in a village at night.

"I'm wearing a black wool cloak, high leather boots, and a wool doublet. I'm carrying a dagger and trying not to be seen. I can't see my face because I'm moving quickly, nearly running by some houses. I don't know where I'm going. I'm being chased. I'm at a dead-end," he whispered breathlessly. "I'm waiting. No one's coming. I'm listening, but don't hear anything. I think I'm all right. I pull the cloak around me, sit down, and fall asleep."

It wasn't clear whether the next event took place in this life or another one. Tee saw himself in the middle of a bazaar.

"People are milling about, calling out, and hawking their wares. I think I'm a trader in Morocco. I pay a merchant for something to eat. The meat is overcooked, but it will do. I'm anxious to get home.

"I look like Errol Flynn with a thin moustache, a goatee, long black hair, and chiseled features. I'm wearing colors and patterns, while others are wearing white robes. I stand out, but I don't care. I feel nothing can touch me as I walk toward the ship. I don't like the Moroccan smell. It's putrid."

He paused and I smiled. It seemed appropriate that an actor would describe others by comparison to other actors. He smiled, too, but for a different reason. "I'd better keep walking. I saw a belly dancer. It's too tempting. Kids are running around."

Without warning, Tee told me that someone jumped him from behind. He was wrestled to the ground. "This fat guy was going to hit me over the head with a club," he continued breathlessly. "He's angry at me. He's too white to look Moroccan. He's shouting. He thinks he got screwed in a trade deal.

" 'Look, what's done is done. You agreed to the deal,' someone told him." Apparently, business affairs were soon resolved with the angry merchant, and Tee made his way to the docked boat.

"I'm leaving today and I'm ready to go home. The ship is pretty. I'm proud because I own it. On the ship, the crew doesn't pay too much attention to me. The cargo is cinnamon. It smells neat wafting through the ship. We've got cramped quarters."

Arriving at his destination, Tee told me it looked similar to a painting of Boston harbor, although he thought the harbor he saw was in England.

"I'm coming off the ship. Everybody's going nuts. People are happy to see me. I'm meeting Queen Elizabeth. She's greeting me at the ship . . . Or is it at court? . . . She's proud and telling me what a good job I did. She looks like actress Miranda Richardson.

"I'm so casual about this. I don't get it. I'm so calm, happy, and mellow. She's raving about me. I'm down on one knee and it's getting sore. The Queen hasn't let go of my hand. Others are jealous. Her dress is gold with pearls and pretty big patterns. She's got brilliant red hair. I think she's flirting with me. No," he decided, "she's not, but she's excited that I'm there.

"I heard 'Sir Walter' and I turned around. I'm not positive that's I. It's a party and I'm talking with different people about the New World. I feel too flamboyant to be Sir Walter Raleigh. I thought that he was a stuffed shirt," he told me.

Tee sped ahead to a rendezvous with an exotic French woman. "I'm in private chambers with a woman. She's very pretty with dark, black hair and a French accent. She's happy I'm back. It's getting romantic; hot and heavy. Candles are lit, windows are open. I think we're lovers, not married."

The love scene faded and Tee told me he sensed the

wind blowing through his hair. Having sailed out again, he was in the ocean.

"I see water as far as the eye can see. I don't know where I'm headed, but I feel contented," he continued. Then the sea became turbulent.

"A storm comes up and tosses us around violently. I'm almost washed overboard, but I think I'm all right. The ship's in bad shape. I'd say we're drifting."

Speculating on the outcome, I directed him to the last day of his life. "I see my face and my decomposing body on the sea floor. I died at sea. It was a gruesome death. The ship is under water. Maybe the ship sank when we hit a coral reef. Half of the crew was wiped out by the savages on an island."

Now, I asked Tee to explore a different lifetime. "I just blew fire," he began. "I'm entertaining people inside the castle courtyard. It's like a carnival or festival. I hear music and hustle-bustle. I'm wearing what a court jester would wear—bright red and yellow with bells on my hat. I'm juggling now. The kids and adults love it.

"I see the nobleman. He's separated from the others. He's not paying attention to me. He's very serious. He looks like a Sean Connery with no hair, a bushier beard, and a more stern look on his face.

"I'm done with my act. A little servant girl is bringing me wine or water. She's very cute and about six. I'm visibly tired. I sit down under a tree near the stage. Someone walks up and says something about me sitting down and not working. 'Good Sir, with people such as you, my job would never get done.'

"Someone threw me a coin. I gave it to the little girl. An older, shapely girl approached me, smiled at me, and handed me a rose.

"People are dressed differently. Visiting nobles have bright colors of reds, blues, and golds. Women have exposed cleavage, puffy sleeves, and corsets. Families and servants are wearing simple work shirts and breeches in drab, earthy colors. There are so many styles that it's hard to describe."

Tee then told me that the period was a lot earlier than the last lifetime, identifying it before the 1100s. I urged that he go to the last day of that life.

"It's four years later. I see the girl who handed me the rose. She's crying. I got the plague. We had been married for a little over a year. We didn't have a family, but we were happy and I treated her nicely. I made my living as the court jester."

With that, I gradually began to bring him out of the hypnotic state. Tee had trouble opening his eyes and it took about ten minutes of strong, emphatic suggestions to bring him back to the twentieth century.

Since the first two lives were too sketchy to comment on, my historical commentaries began with the life of the teenager who felt unloved by his aunt.

It would have been common for an upper-class boy to have been a scholar at a cathedral's song school during the thirteenth and fourteenth centuries. He said that his father had died of the plague. The bubonic plague first came to Europe in 1347-1349, but there were periodic outbreaks of the plague until the mid-seventeenth century. The word plague can also be applied to any number of the era's infectious diseases.

There were problems with the clothing Tee remembered. My experts agreed that if the time period were the thirteenth century, the "trousers and puffy shirt" made no sense, nor did the nightgown. Costumer Susan Reed told me that when she read the transcript, she envisioned a seventeenth-century life because of the clothing and haircuts.

Although Tee had assumed that he was nobility because of the formal funeral, Catholicism had a formal set of burial rituals used for all levels of society. Tee also claimed to have seen a casket, presumably made of wood. However, the use of coffins for burial was not common—most people were buried inside simple shrouds.

There was a general agreement that the lifetime of the Elizabethan sailor seemed to be fanciful. Actress Miranda Richardson played Elizabeth in the popular British comedy, the *Black Adder,* and could have been called into Tee's mind to play the queen of his regression.

The idea that the sailor and trader might have been Elizabeth's great favorite is tantalizing. However, Tee's reference to Sir Walter Raleigh did not tally with the life of the real privateer, explorer, colonizer, scientist, and poet—but not merchant—who did not drown at sea, but was executed by James I on Tower Hill in 1618.

However, it should be noted that Sir Walter Raleigh's half-brother, Sir Humphrey Gilbert, did die at sea. He had been on an expedition to Newfoundland, where he claimed the land in the queen's name. On his return to England, he and his crew were lost at sea. It could have been reasonable for him to accompany his half-brother, Sir Walter Raleigh, to court. After all, Tee said he had heard the name "Sir Walter" but was uncertain whether that was directed at him.

It would also have been possible, although unlikely, for a merchant to have met the queen merely for opening a new trade route.

Some regression therapists postulate that when a person recalls having been famous, they may, instead, have lived at the same time or in proximity to the well-known individual. Because the notable person had a position of prominence in the affairs of the era, the other soul could potentially personalize its memories of them.

It is correct that there were various periods in the Middle Ages and Renaissance when Italian and French merchants traded with North Africa, especially post-thirteenth century, when the Moors were defeated and Gibraltar was open for shipping from the Mediterranean to the Atlantic.

However, several of my experts were dismayed at the mention of belly dancers at the bazaar, agreeing that such dancers would not have been seen on the streets of Morocco until the late nineteenth century. Also, cinnamon did not come from Morocco, but from Ceylon and eastward. One commentator wondered whether Tee had mistakenly referred to Morocco, instead of to Moluccas, the Spice Islands off Indonesia.

In Tee's defense, Paula Peterka acknowledged that as an actor, Tee might have been inclined to describe the people he saw during his regression in terms of other actors. She also thought it possible that a good income could have been derived from a cinnamon cargo. Additionally, she pointed out that England's harbor in the Elizabethan era did resemble the later Boston harbor. It was also unlikely, but possible, for a merchant to have met the queen if he had opened a new trade route. However, one inconsistency she found was a lack of guards on the merchant's ship to protect its precious cargo.

In Tee's last recalled life as a court jester, the majority of my experts identified it as fifteenth century or later, but not in the 1100s as Tee had thought. The puffy sleeves, corsets, and exposed cleavage all date the lifetime to a later period.

The description of the jester's clothes was similar to those worn by jesters of a later era—circa 1540. Again, placing the life much later than the twelfth century.

In spite of some anachronisms in Tee's descriptions, I recalled the other compelling evidence of his déjà vu experiences in medieval settings and costume and his familiarity with London. There was also Tee's compulsion to perform, getting his M. S., studying abroad, and working most of the summer's weekends at the Renaissance

Faire to support a strong inner impulse to immerse himself in the medieval past.

Whether Tee's recollections were a mix of fantasy or glimpses of genuine past lives, the trip was well worth the taking. When I followed up with Tee a few weeks later, he told me that his recurring nightmares about loneliness had ceased since our session together.

14

Craig

"Whose citizens do not age . . . "
—Vernon Watkins, *Welsh poet*

Wearing a coronet on his head, Corun McAnndra, Baron of Storvik, sat astride a throne in the great hall, bestowing awards and favors upon deserving subjects. As the local representative for the Crown or, as he described himself, "the front man for the king," he was jovially recognizing his subjects for their achievements and service. Amid the pomp and circumstance, he never failed to maintain a royal demeanor. But when not presiding at court, Baron Corun could be spotted holding a stein and singing mellifluously with some of his color-fully clad subjects.

The year, A.D. 1995. The event, the SCA Barony of Storvik's Post-Pennsic Revel in College Park, Maryland. I was in attendance that balmy September evening, along with his vassals from Washington, D.C., and neighboring Maryland counties.

The Baron's name, Corun McAnndra, is Irish-Welsh. Apparently, his historical persona has the ability to transcend a time period of between the mid-900s and the 1600s. He can apparently jump cultures, too. That night, he was dressed as a Mongol.

Corun later explained that after an incident at a Pennsic War where he had sought safety in a Mongolian household, he joined with those who had befriended him. After a six-month probationary period, he was officially accepted as a member of the "Dark Horde Moritu." "Moritu" is a Mongol word for "people who ride." The horde portrays a Mongol tribe of the thirteenth century, during the reign of Genghis Khan. Always loving horses, he devised a new story line for his character: he'd been a Celtic wanderer who hooked up with these nomadic horsemen.

Being a member of a Mongol horde resonated well with Corun—or Craig Greenbaum, as he is known in the mundane world. The computer systems engineer has expressed gratitude for his "andas," which means blood brothers and sisters. The close-knit group adheres to a strict code of conduct designed to respect, protect, and support each other.

As a youngster, Craig was fascinated with Chinese, Japanese, and eventually the Mongol cultures, and took up the study of three martial arts. He grew up on tales of King Arthur, Robin Hood, and Prince Valiant, which expanded into Norse and Greek mythology.

Craig was born half Jewish and half Gentile. Raised as

a Lutheran, he attended church-run schools in Toledo, Ohio. In high school, he became part of the Youth Christian movement, and later he turned to yoga, the Buddhist philosophy, and the search for self-realization. Since age twenty, he said, he had considered himself a Zen Buddhist.

This philosophy, coupled with his belief that life is a school and that there is always something wonderful around the corner, has sustained him through traumatic times. He has maintained a childlike wonder, which he believes has allowed him to look years younger than his age.

His lifelong interest in philosophy and religion, and his draw to the past, have not dampened Craig's enthusiasm for science fiction. Kiddingly, he described himself as "being born 500 years too late or too early."

At the time of our meeting, he had nearly completed a bachelor of fine arts degree in theater from Kent State University, Ohio. Additionally, he played the piano and guitar, sang Irish ballads, participated in English country dancing, and read Shakespeare. He has even sewn and embroidered his own garb, served as chronicler, or writer, of the barony's newsletter, and taught classes for fellow Scadians.

When I met Craig, the SCA had already held his interest for over twelve years, in part, because it allowed him to express his artistic and dramatic interests. Craig also liked the history, spirituality, and mythology interwoven throughout the various time periods.

The hobby's multiculturalism also appeals to Craig. He said he has observed, for example, that the SCA serves as a sociological outlet, for example, for blue-eyed blonds who enjoyed re-creating Arabic cultures, while an African-American Scadian might select a French persona.

To Craig, the SCA is "the grand escape" from the mundane, where, in one evening, one can intermingle with various other times and peoples. He feels more comfortable greeting people as "my lord" and "my lady" than with modern salutations. He has even caught himself bowing as his boss went by, arranging his "skirt" before sitting down, and bowing over a hand at a wedding reception.

When I asked Craig about the paranormal, he described his many déjà vu experiences. When he finds himself in such a state, he creates a "game" by deliberately trying to change some detail from what felt so familiar.

When I asked his views on reincarnation, he speculated that when we die, individual pieces of ourselves may reform and join others to create a new spirit. He also felt strongly about the validity of karma, the concept that we are responsible for our actions in these and other lifetimes. Craig believed that, for him, reincarnation was more of a possibility than the existence of heaven and hell.

After completing our interview, the Baron of Storvik stretched out and readied himself for hypnosis. After a period of relaxation, he began slowly and painstakingly.

"I'm outside, alone," he said quietly. "My boots are of soft leather. My loose-fitting, wool tunic is belted with a band. I have long dark hair and I'm not young, nor old."

His consciousness shifted to his surroundings. He continued, saying, "There are open mountains and no trees. I see a moor, heather, and goats. It's cold, but not yet winter. I'm standing and waiting."

This information took a great deal of time in coming. Hoping it would get easier, I directed him to the next scene.

"It's daytime, but it's dark," he told me. I'm in a forest with tall trees. There's a clearing. I see a campfire. Other men are sitting around. I know them; we're together.

Maybe it's a hunting party," he mused. "There are spears and bows, but no horses. The men are dressed in wool and fur cloaks. They are talking and eating meat."

His voice was nearly a whisper now, having changed from its rich, deep, animated resonance when awake. He appeared to be getting individual pictures with no movement or sound, although he could sense occurrences and imagine movement. Again, I moved him forward.

"It's daytime. I see someone with a helmet, shield, and spear. I think he's a Saxon, or maybe a Dane, with long blond hair. He's a middle-aged male with a cloak, leather, and mail. He's a stranger.

"The two from the campfire are just standing there. I think the blond man's a guide and that we're on a scouting party. We're meeting for protection. Maybe we're forming an alliance against a common enemy for mutual protection and mutual nonaggression. There are two different groups trying to live together and share the land. I am the spokesperson. We clasp hands." Craig sensed an undercurrent of tension, but not one of intense urgency.

There were still long pauses between the bits of emerging detail. Laboriously, he moved forward to another scene. "I'm alone on a rounded hilltop at a fort in the village. It's big enough. There are wood-thatched huts around in the fields of grains. I'm coming back from the alliance and I feel good. I'm at the gate. There's a long meeting hall, corrals for the animals, buildings, a smithy."

He proceeded softly. "I'm outside the long hall. There's light coming from there. It's supper time. Everybody from the village is there. There's a young woman wearing a blue dress with brooches, and long, blonde plaited hair. She's pretty. She's my daughter, my only child. My wife's dead. I'm the leader or 'thegn.'

"I have a hut in the fort. There's a wooden bed, a table,

and a bench there. The hut has a thatched roof with a center roof pole and a fireplace. My daughter sleeps somewhere else and her room is similar. It's near the great hall."

At this point, I felt it was time to move Craig to the last day of his life. He found himself in bed.

"I'm not sick, just old. We don't count [the years], but I'm old and gray. My daughter is married. There are others in the room, but they are indistinct."

With that, I directed Craig to progress to any other medieval lifetime he had lived. I was surprised when Craig announced he was now a young woman in her twenties.

"I'm wearing shoes with buckles, stockings, and a black floor-length dress with a white square collar. It has petticoats and buttons down the front. I'm wearing an apron and my hair is under a bonnet.

"I'm a serving girl in the scullery," he continued. "I'm making bread at the table. The kitchen is open. There are white walls with dark brown wood wainscotting. Blown glass windows with pressed yellowish glass panes look out onto the street. It looks like a town or small city, but I don't know where. This is a townhouse.

"In the dining hall, there are round plates on the fireplace and little sconces on the wall. There's a long, plain wooden table."

At this point, I suggested that the serving girl move into another room. When she wasn't able to comply, I wondered if she had been restricted to a certain area because of her station. She moved, instead, to the next scene.

"Now, it's evening and I'm in the dining room. I'm holding a platter, serving the mistress and her husband. She's plainly dressed, with a white-and-gray dress with lace and a bonnet. They're in their fifties or sixties. He's wearing an indistinct frock coat.

"I'm the only server. The meal is beef and bread. The plates, cups, and large serving plates are all pewter."

With that, Craig brought himself out of hypnosis with a jerk. Apparently, the life of the servant was dull and insignificant and he had felt no need to continue. Craig speculated that the life had taken place in Tudor England. Although Craig was knowledgeable in early Celtic history, he claimed to have very little knowledge of the culture of northern Europe of the sixteenth and seventeenth centuries.

He also told me that he had felt a greater sense of "real life" in his regression experiences than he did during re-enacting adventures, when he would only occasionally catch glimpses of authentic history.

As for the historical period of Craig's first recalled lifetime, my Dark Ages experts identified it as seventh-to-eleventh-century Scandinavian. Some of the experts, however, wished to place the life in Dark Ages Britain or Ireland where the Vikings settled extensively. They also found his descriptions of a "long hall," a meeting hall, and typical Saxon or Viking women's clothing to be accurate.

The term "thegn" or "thane" refers to a local chieftain, my experts explained. Also correct was Craig's mention of brooches worn by the blonde-haired woman. Scandinavian women wore large, convex brooches on each shoulder. Saxon women had discontinued this fashion; but still wore brooches—thousands of them have been found by archaeologists and metal detectorists in the United Kingdom, Europe, and Scandinavia.

Ann Longmore-Etheridge speculated that the hand-clasping Craig described could have sealed a mutual aid pact between a native Celt and a newcomer to the Scandinavian community. Vikings settled all over Scotland and particularly in the Danelaw area of England. They flourished on the Hebrides Islands, the Shetlands, and the Orkneys.

Bruce Blackistone agreed that the thegn would have slept within the compound, near or in the hall. However, he took exception to the hut Craig mentioned, preferring a more well-appointed bower or sleeping structure for the thegn.

As for the lifetime of the serving girl, the experts felt that the location was Flanders (Holland), the Netherlands, Belgium, or England, between 1570 and the 1680s, because of the woman's simple, plain "Protestant" clothing, the decor of the house, tableware, and the popularity of narrow townhouses in the Low Countries. White walls with dark brown wood wainscotting and sconces were very typical.

As for a time setting for this lifetime, most agreed it to be somewhere between about 1580 to 1700. However, the white square collar and buttons down front of the serving girl's dress made Paula Peterka suggest a later time period—the 1700s.

What appeared to be the drab life of a young scullery maid came as a surprise to Craig, the Baron of Storvik. Although his first recalled lifetime as the spokesperson for a group of Celts resembled his leadership role in the SCA and his Irish-Welsh persona, his lack of knowledge about this female life piqued his curiosity. I recalled Craig telling me about his enjoyment of cooking for a few people, but not for majestic feasts. Coincidental? Perhaps. Or perhaps a remnant from his life as a scullery maid.

15

Helen

"Fly falcons, tell tales, sing songs . . . "
—Robert de Blois, *13th Century*

Some of Helen Caldwell's earliest memories are of her fascination with Joan of Arc, the French Catholic saint. At the age of eight, she snipped off her doll's golden locks, dressed the doll in a white tunic, and renamed her after the saint.

As her friends watched the *Mickey Mouse Club, Romper Room*, and *Mister Rogers Neighborhood* on TV, Helen was devouring *Beowulf, The Canterbury Tales,* and the works of Shakespeare. While her friends wanted modern toys,

Helen wanted a Celtic harp. She remembered the other seventh graders thinking that she was "insane" for enjoying Shakespeare. Even her mother, who had majored in medieval history, contended that Helen was a "throwback to another age." As a youngster, Helen wrote romantic poetry and created Celtic knotwork. Long an admirer of King Arthur and Robin Hood, Helen had always yearned to be Maid Marian and envisioned herself with a bow slung over her shoulder. Later, she would dabble in archery.

While still a child, Helen designed fantasy drawings of whimsical ladies wearing exquisite, graceful gowns. Decades later, as a member of the SCA, she sews medieval garments for herself and others that bear a strong similarity to sketches she once conceived of during childhood play. Her skill as a seamstress has allowed her to support herself with work commissioned from other SCA members.

Helen was captivated with her first taste of SCA activities while working on her B.A. in theater at Florida State University and joined in 1990.

When I met the thirty-four year old in October 1995, Helen explained that the SCA provided her with a nurturing ground for writing poetry and songs, playing classical guitar, spinning and weaving, and continuing to design Celtic knotwork.

That fresh autumn afternoon, the beautiful, slender woman with long, dark flowing hair entered my office with her arm in a sling. Even in her twentieth-century clothing, I was struck by how much she looked as if she had stepped out of some medieval novel.

Matter of factly, Helen told me that she had injured her right arm during greatsword fighter practice. She was, as she described, "clubbed like a baby seal." Helen explained that she attended fighter practice to learn sword and shield techniques, normally donning armor several days a week.

With her next breath, the versatile woman told me that she had left her first batch of apple cider mead bubbling away in a carboy in her kitchen. For her sundry talents Helen had been presented the first kingdom-level Award of Arms for achievement in both the arts and fighting.

Helen, who belongs to the Shire of Highland Foorde in the Kingdom of Atlantia, is known to her fellow Scadians as Lady Mari ferch Rhodri, Welsh for "Mary, Roderick's daughter." Her persona is that of the daughter of a minor Welsh lord of the late twelfth to the early thirteenth centuries, whose family moved to France at the time of the Albigensian Crusades. With this persona, she was able to combine her interest in the Welsh culture with the romance of Queen Eleanor of Aquitaine's "courts of love." These sessions in court were forums for developing guidelines on such issues as how a knight should treat a lady and his fellow knight.

In fact, Helen said she loved the tremendously chivalrous and courteous way Scadians treat each other. She also appreciated the way they treasure life.

Although she described herself as an intense woman who enjoyed living life to the hilt, she said she had often contemplated the life hereafter. In fact, since she had been a teen, Helen had believed in reincarnation. She believed that God would not be wasteful of a soul who might not have perfected itself the first time around.

Helen was anxious to get on with the regression. She was already familiar with various forms of meditation and relaxation and went easily into a hypnotized state. I was flabbergasted when the first words out of her mouth sounded like French.

"*Le Jor!*" she said in response to my question of whether it was day or night. "What?" I asked dumbfounded. "The day," she said. I regretted drawing attention to her language as it apparently caused her to revert to English. She did, however, continue with a French accent. She was now a girl of fifteen.

"It's our home in Aquitaine," she went on excitedly. "Oh, I see Mama and Papa negotiating for my marriage. A lord has brought his son with him. They're from down near Montpellier, in a place that begins with 'Mont,' perhaps Montélimar. It's not too far from my home. It's in the Languedoc region in the southeast of France, and it's still part of Aquitaine. The son is three years older than I, and his name is Raymond. He's reserved but seems nice enough. He's a little shy and quiet, but not bashful. Mama says I should not worry because his father is just a lord and not a *vicomte* like Papa. 'They are a minor branch of a very powerful family, their fortunes could rise, and this is not a comedown for us,' she says.

"I will miss the Perigord, the country of my homeland, which is a small part of Aquitaine," the fifteen year old said wistfully. "There is still so much to negotiate, like my dowry. I have to have new clothes. I can't be the lady of the castle with the clothes I've been running wild in the past two years. I'm usually dressed in sturdy wool, have my blonde hair braided back, and wear gloves when I ride the gray mare through the forest. I'll have to settle down and concentrate on my weaving, Mama says—not ride breakneck through the forests of Perigord anymore.

"She says that I can wear silk for my wedding. This is the first silk dress to be made for me right from the start. Although I do wear fine linen and fine wool, I rarely wear silk, except when I've borrowed Mama's dresses for special company.

"It's funny listening to Mama talk," she continued gaily. "She's Norman English and had a well-arranged marriage. The Duchess, the Queen of England, arranged it. Mama was one of her ladies-in-waiting. She went to

Poitiers with the queen when she was having problems with her husband. My name is Aliaenor and I'm named for the Queen. It's hard to live up to the namesake of the Eagle [Queen Eleanor] because she always flew so high.

"I'm the youngest of seven. Two sisters died young. Mama says she's lucky to have had five to live and grow up. One brother is a monk. This is what he was meant for. He expected it. Maybe he'll be an abbot. My oldest brother will inherit. Two sisters are both well-married and raising families. They are blessed with sons. It's a good thing because their husbands will keep them. The way most men look at it, it's a great shame if a woman doesn't bear children."

Now, Aliaenor shifted to the scene of her wedding. Speaking as Aliaenor, Helen had me on the edge of my seat. Her articulate style, coupled with her animation and occasional emotional outbursts made her story even more riveting. I was astonished at the details that came alive as they flowed effortlessly from her mouth in a French accent. But my analytical side slipped into place. I had conducted other regression sessions in which the details came as naturally. However my subject was experienced in telling a story in poetry and song. She was also a seamstress of period costume, and so her delivery was indeed a treat.

I noted that Helen, who was comfortable with meditation techniques, had easily reached a deep level of hypnosis. When awake, Helen was also animated, artistic, articulate, and even "looked the part." Even though she had some historical background, I couldn't discount the emotional or soul connection she appeared to have made. My mind happily returned to Aliaenor's wedding day.

"It's a pretty day for a wedding. Perhaps it's May. There's the first hint of summer heat and a cloudless sky," she said excitedly. "My dress is pale yellow and blue silk.

What's underneath is pale yellow. The blue cyclas is the color of the sky.

"For once I don't have to wear a stupid wimple and veil. I'm a bride and a virgin, and I want to wear my hair loose and uncovered with just a circlet. That's my right," she insisted. "Mama calls me a spoiled brat." She laughed. "Mama says I have to get used to veils and wimples all the time after today. I won't be able to sneak them off in the woods. Fine. That's tomorrow. This is today!"

On her wedding day, the young woman experienced the gamut of feelings—from anxiety, fear, and resignation to pride and self-assuredness. Helen described Aliaenor as heartbreakingly young and deceptively fragile. She could feel Aliaenor's slight "bird-boned" build, coltish long arms and legs, narrow tapering fingers, and shoulders strong from riding.

Following the wedding, Aliaenor relocated. Marriage seemed to have been a sobering experience for the young woman.

"I like my new mother-in-law. I call her *ma mère*. She's very nice. It seems like I know her," she continued. "My new husband's now the lord. His father died shortly before we were married.

"He tries to be kind. I suppose I can tolerate him. He's nice enough, but he just doesn't say much. He lets me play my lute, in fact he encourages it, but I can't step out of the castle without an escort nor wander in the woods. Not that Mama ever liked that very much either.

"Married life's all right," she prattled on. "I don't see what all the fuss is about. Mama says in time I'll come to love him, but I don't. At least I have a child; a baby boy! He's not terribly strong or sickly, but he's small for his age.

"Mama was right that I work on my weaving. At least I can weave my woods and bring the forest into the fortress. Tapestry's my salvation, although I can't work on it a lot," Aliaenor said appreciatively. "So much needs to be done—be sure the flax is prepared and spun right for shifts, household linens, and wool cloaks. Those things we spin and weave. The nice fabrics we buy.

"One of the weavers is an old woman. She gives me a hard time. I have to find my mother-in-law. She won't listen to me. *Ma mère* says I'm too gentle for my own good.

"Besides weaving, I spend time in the garden and the kitchen, and time with my son. Sometimes my husband will let me go hunting with him. I'm an excellent equestrienne and hunt with falcons. He thinks I'm so fragile, but that's silly. I was in labor for twenty hours with our son. That's not so fragile!

"My husband works hard with his household knights, squires, and men-at-arms," she reported. "They drill hard in the bailey every day. Raymond says it's just a matter of time before there's trouble here.

"*Ma mère* is a Cathar, though she's not one of the perfects. The priests say Cathars are evil and do cruel things. It's not true, so we just ignore the priests, though I'm a good daughter of the Church. I go to mass. But I don't see what's so wrong about what *ma mère* does. She's good, kind, and doesn't spit on the cross, defile the host, or do any of the vile things that they say. But, I'll leave theology for the priests. That's their job."

Helen's, or rather Aliaenor's, story was spellbinding. It was as if she were starring in the movie that was unfolding before me. Anxiously, I suggested she go forward to a significant scene.

"My baby girl's dead. She was only a few weeks old. She fell asleep and didn't wake up," she said sadly. "I'm twenty and I should have another healthy baby by now.

"Michel, my son, is into everything. He's four now." The thought of her son lifted her spirits. "Raymond gave him his own wooden sword and shield. He terrorizes the barnyard and chases the dogs. He's really quite a sight," she said laughingly and progressed to another scene.

"My husband is taking me to Carcassone for the tournament. We're taking his mother with us," she continued. "The sky is overcast and the grass is green. I'm wearing a soft sage green wool gown and I feel the weight of my braids coiled up under my wimple. We've bought new silk, and spices, and kermes to dye wool. It's a beautiful deep rose. It was so expensive, but it was worth it. I'm tired of that madder red that makes me look sick. I prefer rich colors, fine fabrics, and a close cut in my clothes instead of lots of jewelry."

Next, she indicated that her husband was in the market for some military assistance and that, besides the shopping, perhaps the trip could prove to be a fruitful one.

"The captain of the men-at-arms is going blind, but Raymond will not pension him off because he is so proud. We should find someone to help him, but no one in the garrison has proved to be a good enough tactician. A good commander can picture the battle, seeing it in his mind's eye from above like a bird, and can anticipate from where the enemy will come. The captain can see things that way, but we have to find him help.

"The Grand Melee is this afternoon. Raymond hopes he will see someone promising here, although he's too busy talking politics with the other lords. The stands are crowded. *Ma mère* and I are watching.

"That Norman knight. What is he doing so far south? He's very good, very fast. *Ma mère* says he knows his tactics. He pulled one small group back, spread out, wheeled around, and sandwiched his opponents between him. His group won. It was much faster than normal.

"I just shocked everyone," she cried excitedly. "I pulled off my veil (but not my wimple and barbette) and waved it towards them. The Norman comes up and he takes it. I tell him that, if he wishes to stay in the south, my husband and I would be glad to retain his services. He called me 'Bella Donna.'

" 'You don't know my name,' he said. I replied, 'I don't need to know your name, my lord. All I need to see is how well you fight. But a name would be nice.' His name was Richard de Giscors, and he said he would be my liegeman through life and death. That's pretty. Someone taught him manners and courtesy. *Ma mère* asks how old he is. He's not even eighteen.

"Raymond is absolutely enraged with me about the veil and he hits me. 'You have no right to hit me for so petty a thing as that,' I yell. He says that he's of good mind not to honor the oath I made to de Giscors to retain him. I tell him that if he does, he will be dishonored. He says he won't pay his wage. 'Fine, I shall. We have need of him. You say that there is trouble coming. Your precious captain's going blind. How can he meet any danger if it should come? How would he be able to prepare for war, to lead in war if he cannot see?' "

Aliaenor sounded upset. "I really made Raymond angry. He's never beaten me before. I have bruises that will show on my face. But in the morning, Raymond will back me up. He doesn't like it, he's angry. He tells Richard that if he doesn't like his pay, he can argue it with me. They hate each other. Outraged, Raymond stalks off. He leaves the new liegeman to lead me off the dais.

"Richard says, 'He beat you. Why?' I tell him. He says, 'You are very loyal. Give me what you can afford to pay me. I'll take not a bit more.' I said, 'You could go elsewhere. Another lord could pay you more.' He replied, 'I gave you my oath yesterday. I will not take it back.' Fortunately for me, Richard collected some handsome winnings from the tournament circuit.

"He unbelts his sword, hands it to me, and kneels down. 'I repeat, I am your man through life or death. I won't leave unless you bid me go.' What else can I do but accept his oath. He's very proper. There's nothing in his behavior that Raymond could complain of. So, we go home."

Time passes. The incident has blown over. Aliaenor saw herself pregnant and then giving birth to a girl. The time, she believed, was around 1208. "She's healthy and very strong," Aliaenor said of her baby. "She never smiles, but is a very quiet baby. *Ma mère* calls her 'our little nun' because she is so grave. I name her Almucs.

"Raymond's often gone to Carcassone and Bèziers, the court of the Count of the Provence. Raymond may be the count's distant cousin," she continued. "At home, he's always grim. When he leaves, I'm always so glad. The air itself seems lighter when he's gone.

"There's a troupe of *jongleurs*," she said brightly. "They perform the songs of the troubadours. Sometimes they teach music as well. They are itinerant musicians, going from town to town.

"You want me to play for you?" Her laughter filled my office as she described picking up her lute. "All of a sudden, I feel Richard's watching me. Why? He does this often. I turn to look at him and he gets up and retreats into the shadows. It's very strange."

Now, she turned her focus back to her children. "Almucs is a strong little thing. She's growing fast. Michel is six now and big enough for his first pony. Michel, be careful," Aliaenor warns. "No," she screams. "His pony slipped in the mud and fell on him. He hit his head hard and he's not conscious."

Aliaenor kneels, holds her son in her arms, and weeps. Richard picks him up and carries him inside. "Michel is too heavy for me. He never wakes up but stops breathing after three days," she said, grieving, and described the feeling of exhaustion after not having slept since the accident.

"I suppose that means I have to sleep with Raymond again. I don't want to have another baby. The labor with Almucs was so hard. I suppose I have to try. He needs an heir."

On the heels of that tragedy, yet another befell the family. This led to further marital strife. "Almucs gets lung fever and is dead by Twelfth Night. I cannot conceive again. It's not like Raymond comes to my bed that often. He's dressed in crimson and black and is drinking heavily the dark red local wine. He's really becoming quite cruel. He accuses me of ugly things, like having an affair with Richard. It's absurd.

"No, I will not turn him out. The captain is blind as a bat. He can't see his own nose in front of his face. 'No, he's not my lover, courtly or otherwise! What is the matter with you? Do you think I'm a fool?' I scream. 'No, do not accuse me of being barren. You know perfectly good and well I am not barren. I have borne you three children. It's no fault of mine that they died. Well, you are the one who gave Michel that half-broken pony.'"

Raymond continued to beat Aliaenor to remind both Richard and her that she was his property. Aliaenor believed that he would have killed her except that he wanted to keep the good will of her family.

After the last heart-wrenching events, I encouraged Aliaenor to move ahead in time. Now, she centered her attention on politics.

"The pope has declared a crusade against the Cathars. This is foolish. Why are they doing this?" She was visibly distraught. "Richard is laughing. He says it's not about religion; it's about power, money, and land. The French king wants to annex Languedoc, Provence—all the south. He's a greedy man and always wants what isn't his."

Her hand moved to her mouth. She gulped and whispered. "A messenger has just come from our neighbors, our friends in Montpellier. Bèziers has been sacked. The entire town was utterly destroyed and every man, woman, and child is dead. All of them, Cathar and the faithful alike. They spared no one. What kind of animals are they?" she moaned. "They call themselves 'crusaders.' Christ Himself must hide His head in shame.

"The only good thing about all of this is that Raymond's almost never home. When he is home, he complains because I'm barren. I tell him that if he was home, perhaps I would conceive. Then he beats me some more," she continued. "He doesn't have time to worry about putting me aside. I suppose he's good enough to me. He doesn't begrudge me fine clothes and silks. He doesn't stop my music. He just beats me. *Ma mère* says I'm lucky. Other women get broken bones; I just get bruises.

"Richard doesn't think the crusaders will come. We're not that big of a castle. No one outside the family but Richard knows that *ma mère* is a Cathar. He talks to her often."

Then one summer afternoon, Aliaenor returned to her work. "The household is in the solar, a castle room that faces south. There are looms and ladies spinning. Apart from homespun linens for shifts, I have little new clothing. My clothing allowance goes to pay Richard's wages.

"I'm supervising the weaving. There are young girls here. Their fathers are in fealty to my husband. I'm teaching them things it's needful for a lady to know. *Ma mère* is with me. Guillaume, the captain, and Richard come in. They say the crusaders are inside the gates."

Suddenly, Helen's mouth opened and she screamed. "They think we are Cathars! They are outside, burning everywhere. They will destroy us if they can. I cannot let them. My husband is gone. It is just us. I have to command them. I don't know what I must do. I was not raised to this."

She wrung her hands anxiously. "We are not Cathars! Why are they here? What will they do? Burn us all? Richard says he will not let them burn any of us. I am glad for Raymond that he is in Provence, far away from here.

"We're setting up the table and drawing a map," she said breathlessly. "The captain of the men-at-arms is not strong enough to lead this anymore. The lieutenant stands beside me. *Ma mère*, Guillaume, Richard, and I draw a map of the castle, the land we sit on, and the way the land falls. We try to figure out which way they will come, which tactic they will take.

"I tell Guillaume to take *ma mère* and the ladies—they are all so young—high up within the keep. I must go to the walls. They are outside the walls. Richard says I should go to the keep. I say I will not. In my husband's absence, my place is on the walls where he would be. Its blazingly hot and a misery up on the walls this late June or early July day.

"We tell them we are not Cathars. We are not heretics. They do not care." She shrieked, " 'Do not let them take us!' I am afraid and the lieutenant holds me. He's telling me he will not let them burn me. But that's what the crusaders do to heretics. We have few archers, not enough.

"There's a hail of arrows arching down. I took a bolt—an arrow—in the lung. My blood is everywhere. They must have hit a vein. Richard holds me and calls me 'amica.' The blood's all over both of us. I feel his arms about my shoulders and hear his voice as blood fills my punctured lung, soaking the bodice of my gown." Her hand reached up. "I see him crying. I did not know that he loved me. The darkness swallows me up. I'm quite dead. They are carrying my body down into the keep and into the chapel."

She gasped. "They burn *ma mère* for being a Cathar. How little *ma mère* screamed in the flames. Perhaps she drugged herself when the castle fell. They take Richard as a traitor because he is a Norman. They leave everyone else alone. They behead him for treason because his father swears fealty to the king of France. They don't listen to what he has to say—that his father was in fealty to the king of England, so he had every right to be in fealty to a vassal of the late queen. Besides, he was in fealty to me and what does he do, abandon his lady? De Montfort doesn't care. At least it's over quickly, although his severed head is stuck on a pike."

Next, Helen recalled a lifetime in Gaul during which she, as a fourteen year old, gave birth to a boy who was the result of a sacred rite. While on a visit to her parents, Romans ambushed them, slaughtering both mother and child.

Now, Helen saw herself as a dancer at the Egyptian temple at Karnak. While dancing to celebrate the floods covering the fields, she stepped on a scorpion.

In her next lifetime, Helen was a bull dancer in Knossos. Blaming herself for the death of another dancer who had emulated her style, she carelessly slipped and was gored.

Finally, Helen came back into another medieval existence. "I'm barefoot and wearing a homespun, calf-length linen shift. I have longish, raggedy hair to my shoulders. I'm a little girl of four, nicknamed Alys," she said precociously.

"Teenage girls from the village are dancing around the fairy tree. We do it every spring. It's silly! The priests shake their heads. The girls want to get married and have babies. That's what my mama said. I'm too young. I have to be grown up first.

"All the girls from our village are here. They are wearing festival clothes. The gowns fit closely, lace up the front, and are pretty colors—reds, blues, and greens, and some yellows.

"Marie has flowers braided in her hair," she continues proudly. "She's my mother's sister, but is much younger. She's dancing in the circle. It's three steps to the left, then two to the right. Then they repeat. Sometimes they kick when they dance to the left. They're singing, but I can't hear the words.

"I'm supposed to be watching the geese, but it's too pretty a day to waste. I've got chores to do. I also spin every day, but that's okay because I can take it wherever I go. Mother taught me a couple of years ago, as soon as I could hold it and not drop it. When I turn five, she'll teach me how to comb the wool, so I'll know what it's supposed to look like. This is what mother does.

"They'll be done dancing soon. I have to get back to the farm or Mother will beat me. Whenever she thinks I'm being lazy, she beats me. Every few days, she smacks me on the back. The girl next door says her papa beats her black and blue if she doesn't do everything right the first time. We sneak off and play, but it doesn't happen very often.

"I watch the geese and make sure they don't run off. We spin wool for our own clothes," Alys said responsibly. Now, her thoughts turned to her family and home.

"It's just Mama, Jean, my eight-year-old brother, and I. Father is fighting with our French king. He's just a foot soldier. He's been gone a long time, since before the spring. Jean had to do all the plowing this spring. He got dreadful blisters on his hands. His hands were bleeding, but he got it all done. It's been a dry spring. We need rain. If there's no rain, at least we have lots of wool to trade, to get grain from Normandy, wherever that is.

"Every day, we're up as the sun's coming up," she continued. "I gather eggs while Jean starts the fire back up. Mama starts a breakfast of cooked grain and bread. We do all right for peasants, although others do better. They have more children and more help. I asked Mama why. She said that the other babies didn't live past the first few months. We were the only two who survived."

Presently, Alys's Aunt Marie, whose family was more

financially stable, visited them. She had news about a local girl. "Tante Marie says that her friend Jeanne has gone 'straight crazy.' She wants to cut off her hair to fight. She's a bit older than Marie. No one understands why she hasn't married yet. It's peculiar. I guess she doesn't want to. Mama told Marie to hush and not to give me any ideas. I'd like to go to war to protect father."

Suddenly, the conversation shifted. "They're talking about the abominable weather and how high the wheat should be now. Also, ways to hide the grain we hope to get, in case the army comes and tries to take it all. It's our country. We're the ones who have to wear ourselves to the bone growing food.

"Tante Marie says that the war takes husbands and sons away to die. I don't know what she means by dying. I've seen dead chickens. Besides the old and young, I haven't known anybody who has died.

"We talk about the usual," Alys went on. "How the orchards will do. Whether the flax is sprouting yet. What's to be done around the farm. How much taxes are due. Mama says she'll have to pay her taxes in chickens again. She said she'll give them the scrawniest ones. Her family deserves the fat ones.

"Marie said that the soldiers burned down the cities near Paris and killed everyone, even the children. They take everything, all the grain. I'm scared. I don't know who the other soldiers are, whether French, English, or Burgundian.

"Now, Marie's talking about the king. She's heard he's getting old and dying, and there're rumors that the dauphin is not the son. It's so silly. Who cares? I don't care who's king, just that we have food to eat and warm clothes, and that Papa comes home. Mama listens to Marie and shakes her head and says, 'That's in Paris. Let them worry about it. I've got crops to grow and children to raise.'"

The conversation ended and Helen, speaking as Alys, went to town.

"In the village, the homes look like everyone else's. Some have stone near the ground. The walls have big beams packed with clay and mud, and then white-washed. Some roofs are hay or straw; a few have slate roofs. Shutters cover the windows. We have an apothecary and a church. Every town has one.

"A few soldiers and knights are slowly coming forward on horseback. They're wearing armor and carrying their helmets. The sun glints off their bright armor. Pikemen on foot are carrying funny things like long-handled axes with points on them. They're wearing padded jackets. They don't look terribly tired.

"It's Papa. 'Mama, Papa's come home,' " Alys called out excitedly. "He says he can't stay. The place is pandemonium. Everybody has someone coming home." She laughed. "Mama says we'll kill the goose for supper tonight to celebrate.

"Papa doesn't want to talk about the fighting; he just wants to see the crops and livestock. He's not proud of some things that they've done in the war. I don't know the name of our town, but he said they've been lucky and only lost a couple of men in a few months. He has to go back in just a few days.

"He says that they're all mad. They care about things that don't matter. They don't care about whether the weather is good and the crops are all right, or if people live or die. All they care about is who's the bully on top of the hill."

After her father left, Alys's health became precarious. She coughed. "It's raining. I've got a nasty cough and I don't feel good. I've just turned five. Mama's trying to keep me in bed. She looks worried. She also said that we have to be careful with food this winter, but we should make it."

While she remained in bed, her thoughts turned to war. "War's the same thing over and over. Crazy Jeanne actually did go and join the army. She cut her hair and they gave her armor. She's lucky in a way," the child sighed. "Lots of people have lung fever and have died. Mama and I think I have it. She puts herbs on my chest and gives me broth. I'll either get well or I won't. But my fever keeps building and my lungs are filling with fluid. "They're wrapping me up. Mama's crying. Aunt Marie's crying, too. My brother's trying not to cry. They're carrying the body to the churchyard. Most of the village is there. Mama buys a few masses with a chicken or a goose. She can't buy a lot. A priest is here.

"I'm lucky to be out of that life," she philosophized. "So much is going so badly. France is nothing but a cesspool. With wars, it never stops. Better to die young and quickly, than grow up and fall into a foot soldier's path or die for brigands."

After awakening, Helen likened her hypnosis session to psychic drowning, feeling totally swept into the dramas of the lifetimes. In response to my questioning about her exposure to French in this life, she told me that she had been "lousy" at French, having had to repeat the class in college.

Helen also said that while on a prior visit to France, she had been captivated with the area where Aliaenor grew up, but loathed Carcassone. Several years before her regression, she also experienced a kind of déjà vu while standing over a table and drawing a map. During her regression, she felt that she "knew" the aging captain and mother-in-law in that life and saw their current faces superimposed on their ancient ones. She also believed she recognized her liege man Richard, who is now a formidable SCA swordsman. Additionally, although Helen had known that Simon de Montfort was in charge of the Crusades and that everyone was killed at Montségur, she hadn't known details about Bèziers and Carcassone.

After her regression, Helen did some research and discovered that the skyline of Carcassone was now modern and that walls were now of Victorian construction, a scene she would have viewed on her trip to Carcassone. But what she had "seen" in her regression was walls that looked older, a smaller citadel, and a skyline that had a variety of new and old buildings. Perhaps her visit to the medieval site had helped to trigger subconscious memories of the medieval city as it had been.

Her further research indicated that Perigord was in the southern end of the old duchy of Aquitaine, while Giscors was in a disputed section of Normandy called "the Vexin."[1] In the latter part of the twelfth century, she found that the lords of Giscors owed fealty to the dukes of Normandy and the English kings, until they renounced fealty to Henry Plantagenet, giving it, instead, to the French kings. Additionally, she said that the lords of Giscors were associated with the Knights Templar and inextricably linked with the Prière de Sion and the Cathars.

Helen thought that her citadel was in Montélimar, which she couldn't trace until one year after the regression, when she found it on the eastern banks of the Rhone. The closest names she found that matched the location she had in mind were Montréal and Minerve, with Montlieu nearby.

Helen deduced that Aliaenor's death would have been between A.D. 1210 and 1212, believing that she would not have been so terrified of being burned prior to hearing tales of the sack and massacre of Bèziers.

Helen believed that her mother had been Norman English and spoke both dialects of French. She speculated that Aliaenor's mother was probably from around Sussex near Kent, near the royal court where she was a lady-in-waiting to the queen.

She also theorized that her mother may have given birth to Aliaenor later in life or perhaps as a product of a second marriage, as she would most likely have been in attendance prior to Queen Eleanor's imprisonment by her husband, King Henry II. Helen surmised that there were gaps between the mother's pregnancies, with Aliaenor, being the youngest, having been born around 1185-'87. Queen Eleanor was still imprisoned by her husband until the late 1180s. So, Aliaenor's mother couldn't have been with the duchess past 1175.

Several of my experts frowned upon the idea that Aliaenor would have been exposed to the ambiance of courtly love. However, as others pointed out, Aliaenor was Queen Eleanor of Aquitaine's namesake and the daughter of a viscountess who had served the queen.

Helen agrees and believes that if Aliaenor's mother had been with the duchess at Poitiers, she would have been profoundly influenced by the "courts of love," which troubadours have said were instituted by Queen Eleanor and her daughter by King Louis of France, Marie, Countess of Champagne.[2]

While historians are skeptical about the actual existence of these "courts of love," they do acknowledge the troubadour poets who commonly sang of young men courting unobtainable women. Aliaenor, a married woman, fell into that category for Richard.

My experts located two places in the region with the prefix Mont, as Helen stated in her regression. Montauban, near the city of Toulouse, and Montségur castle, the famous last stand of the Cathars, built in 1206 for Raymond of Perella (his daughter Esclarmonde was among the 210 Cathars burnt alive when Montségur fell to the crusaders after a ten-month siege in March of 1244).[3]

Raymond was a common name in the area; indeed, Raymond of Toulouse was Count of Provence and another Raymond was Count of Bèziers (sacked in 1209 by the crusaders) and Carcassone (also sacked).[4]

Details in Aliaenor's life that came under suspicion included limiting the inheritance to the oldest brother. Apparently, this was not the standard southern French pattern. Instead, the land was divided among all the children and managed by one or two. Also, household knights and squires were less common in southern France than in other areas, and landholders there tended to rely on mercenary troops. A popular saying of the age was "the Franks to battle; the Provençal to the table." However, experts indicated it would not have been unusual to find a Norman knight in southern France.

The beheading of Richard for treason was questioned by some of my commentators. They felt that Richard's father's oath of fealty would not be binding on the son, and, therefore, he should not have been beheaded for treason. However, as Bruce Blackistone put it, "When a castle is taken by storm, legal niceties fall by the wayside." And as we have seen, "spare no one" was the crusaders' motto.

One of the military experts said he believed the style of tournament Helen described was advanced for the twelfth century, but correct for the preceding century.

Then there was the problem with the wimples. According to the fashion experts, Aliaenor's joy that she did not have to wear a veil and wimple on the day she married was correct—the error resting on the assumption that she already wore wimples and veils. Young, unmarried women were not expected to wear head coverings, which were the burden of married women.

Expressions of time were also an issue. People measured time in the Middle Ages by canonical "hours" of about three hours each. There were few clocks, none of them accurate, and most found in churches where it was important to know when to pray the correct set of prayers for a canonical hour. Aliaenor, for example, said that she had been in labor for twenty hours, when she should have said something like "from dusk until the following dusk." In her defense, I must once again state that the twelfth-century memory expressing itself through a twentieth-century mental filter may be the reason for these anachronisms. Neither case precludes the possibility that this is a past-life memory.

There was also some doubt about Aliaenor's comment that she went to mass and that this made her "a good daughter of the Church." This concept did not become defined until the Fourth Lateran Council in 1215, presumably after Aliaenor's death.

Details about which Helen was correct include the mention of kermes, a very expensive red dye. Aliaenor also talked about silk, which was then available from Spain—also extremely expensive. It would have been appropriate for a woman of Aliaenor's status to have married a man below her rank. This was often viewed almost as we view an investment that could pay off if the groom and his family were up-and-coming.

Helen self-dated this lifetime's end to between 1210 and 1212. This would make correct the presence of Simon de Montfort, the military leader of the crusade at the sack of the castle and Richard's beheading. Just six to eight years later, he would end up meeting death himself during the taking of Toulouse.

Helen herself was surprised when Aliaenor saw an upright loom—believing they would no longer have been in use in that era. This is not necessarily true, according to Susan Reed, who explained that while new-style looms began coming into use around the year A.D. 1000, it would not have been unusual to have retained a vertical loom.

What troubled some commentators were the references to famous persons in her regressions—Queen

Eleanor and the woman described as Joan of Arc. They thought it unlikely that she could have been exposed to two such notables.

Moving on to Helen's lifetime as the child Alys, if we are to accept that the woman "crazy Jeanne" was Joan of Arc (1412-1431), then the village the child lived in would have been Domrémy, in Lorraine. Alys's father was most likely fighting with the French King Charles VI, who died in 1421. Her mention of Charles VI places her in the fourth year before his death in 1421. The beginning of Joan's military career is believed to have been in 1427. Joan would have been too young to have fought with Charles VI.

Although unlikely, it should be taken into consideration that "crazy Jeanne" may have been an entirely different woman. My commentators told me that women have dressed as men and gone to war since the dawn of time. Legend says that Queen Eleanor of Aquitaine and her female entourage, for example, took part in a crusade to the Holy Land dressed as Amazons.

When husbands were away fighting other battles, it was traditionally the wife who became the official protector of the home in case of attack. For instance, Katherine of Aragon, the first wife of Henry VIII, ran a successful military campaign against the invading Scots while her husband was in France, fighting much less successfully for his ancient right to that throne.

The war the child recalled would have been the Hundred Years' War, a period of separate, almost contiguous campaigns to settle the quarrel between the English Plantagenets and the French, as to who should rule France.[5] (Henry VIII was the grandson of Edward IV, and his invasion of France can be seen as an unhappy postscript to this bellicose dispute.)

The spinning wheel was invented in the thirteenth century, but drop spindles were still used by the poor, and are to this day. Another problem area for my experts was whether a two-year-old child had the manual dexterity to drop spin and whether a four year old could drop spin proficiently enough to actually help her family. Ann Longmore-Etheridge rebutted the criticism by commenting that she had seen young children using drop spindles at living history events and that it did not matter whether Alys was proficient enough to be useful—what was important was that Alys practice to become useful one day. Susan Reed also added that Alys had said she would learn to comb wool at age five. Although this might seem an easier task, it does require more physical strength.

Another job that called for strength was plowing. Again, some commentators questioned whether Alys's eight-year-old brother had the strength to guide a heavy plow. Another countered by wondering if the boy actually goaded the ox while someone else plowed. It was customary for women to assist in the fields.

All agreed that for Alys to say she hadn't known anybody who'd died except for the young and old was unusual for a member of a society where healthy adults were cut down regularly by disease or accident. It was also rare, they said, for a small village to have its own church, but common for peasants to marry relatively late.

In addition, Lisa Steele, who specializes in medieval France, said that transcounty shipments of grain were fairly infrequent because of the sheer bulk of any reasonable supply, especially since almost everything was upriver from Normandy. Worse, if this really were fifteenth-century Lorraine, Normandy was in English hands and unlikely to trade grain to a French village. According to Lisa's research, there didn't appear to be a particularly poor harvest in Lorraine in the mid-fifteenth century.

Helen was correct in describing soldiers wearing padded jackets and carrying pikes and halberds ("axes with long handles"). It is also true that by the fifteenth century, many taxes and tithes were paid by coin, although most farmers still preferred to pay in grain or animals.

After her regression, Helen told me that the experience had been rather uncomfortably like an onion being peeled. She was glad to return to the more pleasant world of medieval reenacting. "Thank heavens there are antibiotics, laws for divorce and for the protection of battered women," she reflected gravely. "And no Inquisition." And with that, Helen grinned.

16

Weaving the Mystic Threads

"Thoughts that wander through eternity . . . "
—John Milton, *Paradise Lost*

In each and every case, the subjects who participated in my study acquired an obsession with the past that began when they were children.

At the age of five, Eric left the New York Metropolitan Museum in tears because he couldn't have a suit of armor. At seven, Ann became fixated with playing the six wives of Henry VIII. In seventh grade, Felicia taught herself the recorder with a strange sense of ease. After a consuming interest that spanned far back into childhood,

Karen was finally able to launch herself wholeheartedly into the study of French in eighth grade. As a youngster, Dori was fascinated by swords and faithfully transformed herself into Robin Hood each Halloween. Paula's interest in European castles steadily built throughout her childhood.

Rich played Dungeons and Dragons while in Boy Scouts, and Nick, Susan, and Tee were infatuated with the tales of King Arthur and the Knights of the Round Table. Craig's consuming interest became Norse mythology. Although she grew up reenacting the Revolutionary War era with her family, Katharine always preferred the time and work of Shakespeare and became involved in Renaissance festivals as a teenager. As a youngster, Helen found herself designing and sewing medieval fashion. In a burst of creativity, she chopped off some of her Barbie doll's hair, dressed her in a tunic, and changed her name to Joan of Arc.

All thirteen of my subjects were haunted by the Middle Ages or Renaissance as youngsters. During my earlier study on Civil War reenactors, I found that three-fourths of the participants were deeply attached to the era by elementary school age. Dr. Ian Stevenson, a respected reincarnation researcher, found that there is a profound connection with previous lifetimes in some young children until the age of seven, and this is consistent with both of my subject groups.[1] Stevenson's subjects, however, generally lessened their attachment to the people, places, and events of their past lives, while my subjects carried over their interest into adolescence and adulthood.

My subjects averaged seven years of participation in the SCA, Markland, Renaissance festivals, or other reenactment groups. Three-fourths of these seven women and five men were single. All but one had a minimum of two years of college; eight had bachelor's degrees, and three held master's degrees. Eight of their degree programs were related to the expression of their historic interests, including political science, textiles, French literature, and theater. Nearly one-third had careers related to history.

These statistics on career and educational interests are consistent with psychic diagnostician Edgar Cayce's theory of individuals bringing into their current lives the talents and interests from other lifetimes.[2]

During this assessment, I noticed that the medieval reenactors were younger and had completed more degrees than the twelve Civil War reenactors in my previous study. Only one-fourth of that group held history or related degrees, while one-third held jobs in the field. However, on average they had been involved in Civil War reenactment for fourteen years—twice as long as the medieval reenactors—and a much higher percentage were married.

Just as several of the Civil War reenactors in my study had looked more comfortable in their uniforms than in twentieth-century clothing, so, too, had medieval garb looked somehow more suitable than jeans or suits for Helen, Rich, and some of the others. Although I am told by other reenactors that this is a widespread phenomenon, it is not universal: some people wear the archaic clothes like naturals, while others don't. For those who do, it just seems right. Familiar. Like they've done it all before.

There were differences between the two groups reenacting such divergent periods of time. In general, I found the medievalists to be interested in the entire culture and lifestyle of the period, rather than focusing specifically on battles and troop movements, as was the case with some of the Civil War reenactors. Medieval groups also tend to be more of an outlet for socializing and dating, as many members marry within their ranks and have offspring for whom a weekend spent as a Viking or a Celt becomes a normal part of life from birth.

My subjects described medieval reenacting as a way to satisfy a wide range of needs. They cited gaining hands-on experience in archaic arts and skills, finding a supportive social circle, and earning recognition for their talents and dedication. Others discussed finding a "tribal" or community feeling, intellectual stimulation, and personal growth. It also serves, they revealed, as an escape from the real world, a forum for public education, and a vehicle for time travel.

Although one-third of the medieval group described themselves as "fun mavens," another third as "authenticity mavens," and the rest as a mixture of both, they collectively scored their degree of seriousness in reenacting at seven or above.

Many of these medievalists joined the hobby after attending an SCA or living history event, or Renaissance festival, or as the result of a friend who participated. Likewise, familiar clothing, situations, or people often become subconscious triggers for the spontaneous recall of past lives.

Three-fourths of my medieval subjects claimed to have experienced some sort of déjà vu or spiritual, paranormal, or unexplainable experience. Overall, they initially appeared more open to the possibility of reincarnation than the Civil War reenactors, who spoke with deeper philosophical caution. Prior to their regressions, the majority of the medievalists I regressed admitted open-mindedness about reincarnation. Four were already firm believers. Another was a vehement advocate of ancestral genetic memory.

After their regressions, during which all of the subjects reported past lives in the Middle Ages or Renaissance, over half of those who had not been totally convinced in reincarnation prior to their regressions told me their level of belief had increased by 20%. This was similar to the Civil War reenactors, three-fourths of whom were nearly 20% more willing to consider the possibility of reincarnation.

Like the Civil War reenactors, the medievalists also found their regressions much more "vivid" and "real" than their various reenactment experiences by an average of 40%. Unlike modern reenacting, where merriment abounds, under hypnosis, my subjects did not recall much feasting and frolicking. Instead, hardship, fear, frustration, and tragedy were the major themes expressed.

While in the hypnotic state, six of the medieval reenactors said they saw or experienced past-life memories as snapshots, with each setting distinct. Seven, or 54%, said they viewed their stories as a continuously running "movie."

This tallied well with my Civil War subjects who had a slightly higher number who described the memories as moving pictures, as opposed to photographs—a nearly 80/20 split.

During their regressions, four medieval and five Civil War reenactors noted that they were not able to make small changes in their "scripts," even at my direction. This, I hope, is an indication that I was not able to unduly influence them by the power of suggestion.

Of course, the most significant potential influence on these subjects was their own historical knowledge. On a scale of one to ten, with one being "no knowledge" and ten being "expert knowledge," the majority of subjects rated their level of knowledge on the era at above five. When assessing their knowledge of special interest areas such as embroidery or the making of chain mail, my subjects assessed these skills at an average of about seven.

Most also said they felt fairly comfortable acting and speaking as their "personas." This again begs the question of whether the past-life characters they recalled were merely additional theatrical extensions of themselves. Not surprisingly, the Civil War reenactors had also rated themselves above average in their ability to do first-person dialogue in character.

After the regressions, I asked my subjects to estimate the percentage amount of their past-life recollections that they felt could have been created from their current historical knowledge. The average estimate was 55%.

Not surprisingly, the Civil War reenactors had also rated themselves high in their knowledge of the Civil War and extremely high in their knowledge of reenacting. Their knowledge gave them the ability to observe great depth of detail during their regressions.

In comparing the level of detail in their past-life accounts given by the eight people who had been in medieval groups the longest (anywhere from five to sixteen years, the average being 10.5 years), the average level of detail was double that of the five newer people who had been involved an average of 1.9 years.

There was also a vast difference, nearly 30%, between the two groups in their rating of prior historical knowledge of the information that came through during their regressions. This does appear to indicate that the level of detail in a regression may be directly tied to the amount of "living" a reenactor has done in the setting of reenactment camps and other events. However, this could also indicate an enhanced ability to recognize details unique to the time period that a less-experienced participant might observe during regression, but fail to describe due to unfamiliarity.

It should also be noted that my medieval experts found nothing out of place with the past-life memories of three subjects, as well as one recalled life of a fourth subject. Of these, two were relatively new members who rated themselves extremely low in historical knowledge, while the older members had also rated their historical knowledge moderately low.

In comparing the medievalists' regression scenarios with their invented reenacting personas, I noted that in eleven cases, in at least one of each of their recalled lives (some remembered more than one), there was a broad cultural similarity—for example, both the persona and the previous incarnation lived somewhere in the British Isles. In seven cases, there was some connection with the persona's social role, function, skill, or belief system. For instance, Tee recalled having been a court jester in his fifth recalled lifetime. He is now a Maryland Renaissance Festival comic.

Additionally, six subjects recalled lifetimes in the countries of their own ancestry. This could mean that the subjects were drawn to reenact subconscious ancestral memory. Or that they once again returned in a similar culture.

This is in keeping with Eastern and Western reincarnation theories—for example, the Edgar Cayce psychic readings—that our actions, biases, and prejudices continue from lifetime to lifetime.[3] It is also consistent with past-life therapy literature which underscores our observance of recurring thought and behavior patterns.[4]

This leads us to consider the possibility that healing can result from re-creating former, often painful, patterns in the hope of identifying and breaking them, and then creating new life-enhancing patterns in their place. Evidence shows that historical reenacting, even without past-life regressions or a belief in reincarnation, is an excellent technique for inner healing.

Ten of the medieval regression subjects (one recalled a lifetime outside the Middle Ages) traced present-day fears, phobias, and health concerns back to lives recalled. Of these, four reported positive changes in these areas following their regression experience.

Nick, who learned through regression that he had been beheaded, was released from one type of debilitating migraine. Paula, who may have died at the hands of a vicious man, no longer had a fear of being victimized. Tee, who said he died of loneliness as a medieval teen, noticed that his recurrent nightmares about loneliness ended. Dori, who remembered losing an infant in childbirth during a past life, was no longer fearful of giving birth. Two others claimed to have found a new sense of confidence and support while several described the regression as spiritual or enlightening. All but one could identify how the regression experience positively affected their personal lives.

Over half of the Civil War reenactors noticed that their regressions changed their perspective on reenacting. Also, three of their recalled war deaths or woundings possibly relate to health problems today.

Among my Civil War subjects, I found only one (a woman) who recalled changing sex. Among medieval reenactors, over half—five females and two males—kept the same gender in medieval lives. The other six recalled lives as both sexes. Of the six, three had more lives in their current sex, two women had more male lives, and one man had both a male and female lifetime. Counting the lifetimes that fell outside the medieval time frame as well, five subjects still only recalled lives as the same sex they are today.

In compiling the social classes represented in my subjects' past lives, I discovered that all but two fit into either religious (one), gentry or nobility (eight), middle class (four), or lower class (twenty-eight). I also found that social class during the Middle Ages was not always dependent on financial status. There was also some fluidity and upward mobility—especially during the sixteenth and seventeenth centuries—a time of great religious and social upheaval.

To determine the social levels of my subjects' past incarnations, I selected certain characteristics for each type. "Gentry/nobility" possessed tracts of land, were knights, fought on horseback, held a title, or spoke of other circumstances suggestive of the upper class. For example, this included both the bastard son of the duke and the lonely boy who had been sent to a monastery school. The middle-class criteria included any lives in which the individual was well-learned, a professional, or an international trader. Included in this category were the wife of the university professor, the wife of a chamberlain, the daughter of a well-to-do merchant, and the wife of a merchant.

The lower class was made up of yeomen—those who held land with tenants under them, artisans, sailors, soldiers, and peasants—who held a strip of land for themselves. Also included were the entertainer, the tavern owner, several servants, and the nomad.

Of those who recalled a life as nobility, all—save one—also recalled being lower class in other lifetimes. The percentage breakdown of past lives, according to medieval societal standards, was 2% religious, 19% gentry, 9% middle class, 65% lower class, and 5% undetermined.

These percentages are similar to those of the massive past-life study reported in the late 1970s by psychologist and researcher Dr. Helen Wambach. Wambach's study included 1,100 subjects with 1,088 reported past lives, approximately 44% of which were in the Dark Ages, Middle Ages, and Renaissance. Wambach found that nearly 67% of the remembered lives were lower class and 28% were middle class.[5] While my upper-class percentage was higher and my middle class was considerably lower, I suspect that these differences reflect our own criteria for categorizing our subjects' recalled social class as well as our individual decision-making on some of the more vague descriptions.

Interestingly, in this life, five medievalists have earned titles, roles of nobility, or won outstanding awards. Three of these recalled having had lives of nobility. A baroness today was a servant then, while four subjects who remembered positions in the gentry class in the past have no titles or positions in today's medieval reenacting. Noble classes accounted for one-fifth of my subjects' recalled medieval lives. This is the same percentage I found among Civil War reenactors—only two of ten soldiers were officers. But those of noble birth were not left unscathed. Two were killed in the crusades, several endured loveless marriages, and another may have been slightly retarded. One died of melancholia as a youth, while another recalled a gruesome death at sea. In Wambach's regression study, she also discovered that those who reported upper-class lives did not recall them as having been particularly pleasant.[6]

Many of the lower-class lives were also painful and deplete of glamour. There were remembrances of eating bugs as a delicacy, smelling putrid odors, and lifetimes of drudgery, poverty, and struggle.

All of my subjects experienced emotions and physical sensations, often vividly describing what they saw, felt, or heard under hypnosis. They expressed fear, anxiety, anger, and grief, as well as physical pain. This is comparable to the memories of my Civil War reenactors. Nine of ten Civil War soldiers recalled not knowing where they were going, being hungry, thirsty, and tired, suffering cold and the exhaustion of forced marches. Many graphically described their fear during battle and the agony of wounds that led to their death—or which a lucky few survived.

Over half of the recalled medieval lives did not contain a mention of religion. This could be seen as startling, considering how much of a role the church played in everyday medieval life. In some cases, the individual could have been so consumed with personal issues or had such brief lifetimes that day-to-day religion seemed unimportant. Of the nineteen lives that did contain references to religion, one was a monk or religious assistant; one worked for an archbishop; one was a crusader, another a member of the order of the Knights Templar. There were twelve Catholic lives. Mentions of other religions included Catharism, Muslimism, Calvinism, and Protestantism. There were two references to pagan rituals and another (possibly a Mongol life) touched on folk and herbal healing.

As for literacy, personalities in 14%, or six lives, were able to read—although four of those (all females in those lives) described themselves as only reading a little. Of those, two said that their husbands were much better at reading. Two said they learned what little they knew from a family member. One woman remembered being able to read practical things, but was unable to write. Only one woman recalled having a tutor and could read some Latin. Of the five who said they could not read, one man, the mercenary, claimed that his wife could read some, although he could not. In thirty-two lives, there was no mention of reading whatsoever.

Lives in medieval times did not, on average, last long. The average age of the population was between seventeen and twenty-one (thirty years in the 900s, according to one source), and the average age of death around thirty-four. However, death statistics are misleading. It must be remembered that more than 50% of all children died before age five. Young women frequently died in childbirth and young men by violence. And then there were the plagues. The Black Death alone killed one-fourth to one-half of the Occident's population between 1347 and 1352. All of these factors tend to obscure the fact that many people lived well into their sixties and beyond.

The age-of-death statistics of my subjects were in agreement. Of the forty-three recalled medieval lives, sixteen remembered personalities who were either murdered or judicially killed, while five died in accidents such as fire, being hit by a cart, and bitten by an asp. Six died of illness, four of old age, and one as the result of childbirth. In twelve cases, there was no mention of the type of death. In Wambach's past-life study, she determined that about 21% of the medieval deaths were violent, 15%t were accidental, and 60% died of natural causes.[7] In my study, 37% died violently, 12% by accident, and 26% died of natural causes (including childbirth). Although the levels of violent death reported by my subjects is slightly higher, it is possible that, in the regression process, subjects gravitate to traumatic deaths to resolve the issues behind them. Wambach agreed, finding that the subjects that reported regressions to violent deaths resolved many of their fears and phobias.[8]

In eleven lives, or 26% of the cases, people died between the ages of five and twenty. Of those, seven died before reaching fifteen. Of those who died by age twenty, six were killed, two had fatal illnesses, two had accidents, and one died of "loneliness" which we must tag as a natural cause. Apparently, violent deaths among youth are still prevalent today. Wambach uncovered a statistic from the New York City Health Department that in 1976 murder was the cause of 53% of the deaths of nonwhite youths from fifteen to twenty-four, while another 33% died from accidents.

While alive, the medieval personalities found themselves in a variety of settings—from forests to farms, from poor huts to grand households. Only six past-life characters appeared to have lived in an urban setting. A medieval urban area could be characterized as having its own charter, being independent, and customarily having trade, merchants, and markets. Two clear examples are Robert Murray (Ann Longmore-Etheridge), who dwelt off the Edinburgh "High Street," and the female servant (Craig Greenbaum) who lived in a city townhouse. Rural locations consisted of villages clustered around the seats of nobility. Thus, a life in a castle or monastery would be classed as rural.

Assessing the geography of my subjects' past lives, eight lives of forty-three were too nonspecific to determine a geographic area. Of the other thirty-five, the British Isles carried the preponderance of lives, with seventeen, or nearly 50%. The next most popular locale was France with four lives, the Netherlands with two, Poland with two, and two "Saxon" lives of uncertain geographical setting. Italy, Denmark, Germany, Palestine (visited by the French crusader), the Middle East, Mongolia, China, and Japan had one past life each.

The breakdown of the seventeen lifetimes in the British Isles includes four of nonspecific locale, seven in England, five in Scotland, and one in Ireland. Today, personas from the British Isles are popular among medieval reenactors and living historians. Although there was a profusion of recalled lifetimes in the British Isles, most subjects recalled lives in other locations as well. Of those whose lives weren't too vague to identify, only Helen returned in both of her medieval lifetimes to France. Her other lives, which fell outside the medieval time frame, were from completely different localities and cultures.

But whatever the locations of their past lives, these experiences were far more real than their current medieval activities. As Helen Caldwell put it, "Reenacting is a *game* in which we try to exemplify and re-create only the finest points of the medieval era. My French lifetimes were too gritty for that." Or Nick Neville, who said "that reenacting is joy and feasting. The regression experience was vivid memories of strong emotions and pain." Or Tee Morris's comment, "The Ren Faire is a 'safe' environment compared to the 'reality' of my regression." Ann Longmore-Etheridge found "absolutely everything" different about the regression in relationship to her participation in Renaissance festivals and living history events. According to Rich Weissler, "Reenacting is fun and still mostly me. Neither regressions were fun! The 'person' in my second regression was 'mentally dull.' "

Craig Greenbaum found a greater sense of real life in his regressions that he finds only fleetingly at some reenacting events and never at Renaissance festivals. Susan Reed, who focuses on authenticity, savored the period details and lack of modern distractions in her past lives. Katharine Bradley's observation was, "In doing festival activities you can only speculate what life was like. In the regression, I got a feeling for what it was really like!" For Felicia Eberling, the regression was "reality" as differentiated from modern history reenactment activities which she described as "dress-up parties." Felicia says that her reality base doesn't shift by means of the hobby. At the Renaissance festival, which she describes as "an entertainment gig," she finds the magic in making music, not in time/space shifts.

In their hobby, these medievalists try to somehow recreate the past, focusing on the joy. But are they really trying to heal ancient experiences etched on their souls and the soul of the collective unconscious? Is it somehow a catharsis? Were they reliving their own past lives or dipping into ancestral memories? Were their memories just pieced together from their imaginations and/or knowledge? What did they plunge into when they submerged themselves in their subconscious under hypnosis?

The purpose of this study was not just to seek answers. It was as much about exploring the questions themselves. Why are we motivated to do what we do? Why do these reenactors choose to pour their time, money, and emotional resources into musty antiquity?

While these regressions do not prove that reincarnation exists, the beliefs of those who participated in the study changed dramatically after their regressions, because what was unearthed for them during the regressions was far more graphic and lifelike than what they had previously known. Could their emotional past-life experiences have been an indication of the eternal nature of the soul?

I cannot help but wonder if identifying subconscious motivations, possible past lives, and "soul lessons" are just the primary step that allows us to move through and beyond the emotions that these memories stir. Perhaps we need to step out of the old armor that has protected us on our weary journey through time. Perhaps it is time to dissolve our swords of hatred, violence, and separationism—emotions that have led to warfare. Instead of conflict, we have the opportunity to choose the new tools of forgiveness, truth, love, and compassion with which we can transcend our experiences and transmute our pain. This is indeed the fertile soil for growth and expansion of the soul in its journey through time. As we do this, we can create a reality based on harmony rather than conflict. In so doing, we will not only heal ourselves, but uplift humanity.

Perhaps the medievalists who chose to voyage with me, as well as other reenactors, as they continue their medieval hobbies, will now occasionally stop and listen for the echoes, however faint. Whether they whisper to them through the trees or dance with the sparks of a campfire, or reverberate with the clanging of armor or the laughter and merriment of a great and glorious feast, perhaps they will hear something ancient that stirs them. And perhaps the next time guests visit a Renaissance festival, they can allow for a few quiet moments to look within and feel or hear their own echoes from medieval halls.

17

A New Home

"Times' glass breaks . . . "
—Vernon Watkins, *Welsh poet*

As dawn broke, we silently pitched a cluster of Viking A-frame canvas tents among the towering trees. A chill hugged the air. Some of the participants armed themselves by digging a firepit, while others unloaded the last of the provisions.

Round, colorful shields with iron bosses rested against stumps and rocks. Off to the side of the camp, a wooden ferrying boat, named the *Gyrfalcon*, had been pulled ashore, its yellow sail bellying in the breeze. The small vessel's oars were being lashed together to form one of the tents.

As we transformed the clearing into a Viking encampment, there was talk of the strict criteria for authenticity expected of all competitors. Several years earlier, I was told, the Viking camp had lost points because a female reenactor was observed with shaved legs.

The Military Through the Ages (MTA) competition is held each March at Virginia's Jamestown Settlement, a reconstruction of the 1607 stockade that grew into the first successful English settlement in the New World. Competing groups span history from the Dark Ages to the Vietnam War.

Before the first patrons arrived, at nine a.m., that mid-March Saturday morning, all the colorful encampments were in place, participants were dressed in authentic garb, and each unit had become its own bubble of time, frozen on a single day of a great military campaign. These included the campaigns of Caesar, Napoleon, Boudicca, Kaiser Wilhelm, and U.S. Grant.

With my medieval past-life study months behind me, the magic and mystery of medieval reenacting continued to enchant me. I had "played" with the Scadians and wandered among Renaissance festival entertainers. Now, I was invited to participate with living historians in a competition. Finding this a fitting conclusion to my project, I happily donned the garb of a Viking.

For us, it was the early spring of A.D. 860 in the Viking Camp. Nicholas, the son of my hostess Ann, was romping in the field behind camp with other Norse youngsters. Nicholas, age four, who had attended his first MTA in a basket at the age of one month, was carrying a wooden sword. His Viking name was "Snorri," an authentic appellation, and also apropos, as he had snored through all his early events.

Meanwhile, the Viking adults conversed with newly

arrived visitors, explaining that our camp was situated on Jeufosse Island, Francia (France). During the preceding decade, this Viking encampment on the River Seine had been a base for the Danes and Norwegians who laid waste to the Frankish countryside. The Norse women and children had now come south to join their men at the island stronghold. The Vikings' plan was to attack Paris to the southwest, then to permanently settle the land they had stolen from the Franks.

Guards, dressed in chain mail and nasal helms, armed with axes and short swords, alternately stood watch near the booty taken from the raids on sacked towns. Silver ingots, arm rings, coins, Byzantine glassware, gold bullion, and glass beads spilled from a wooden sea chest. A jeweled reliquary had been stolen from a monastery. The old bones inside—what the Franks called "relics"—had been thrown out because they weren't even good enough to feed to the dogs. Fittings from ornate book covers were being made into jewelry, while other stolen books were to be ransomed. I detected disdain in the voice of a Viking woman as she commented that the god of the Franks was a weak, silly god. After all, was he not a god of peace while the Viking god, Thor, was a strong god of war?

Turning my attention to the fire pit, I watched as a woman bent over a heavy iron cauldron hanging from a tripod. The pot looked ancient, but had been newly commissioned from a blacksmith for the fee of $250. The cook stirred the stew inside, which consisted of desiccated—and now rehydrating—onions, parsnips, mushrooms, carrots, lentils, turnips, cabbage, and oat groats. Suspended from a second tripod, a smaller riveted caldron held chunks of rabbit and shallots in a vegetable broth. A huge leg of goat roasted on a spit. Trout, heads and all, were spread out on top of the oak wood embers. At the other end of the pit, a second rabbit was roasting, while wine, stolen from a monastery, was mixed with fruits and spices and mulled in a ceramic pot.

Joining the others, I helped form dough into little balls and then flatten them out with my hands. The resulting flatbread, which consisted of flour and a little liquid for binding, looked like a small pancake. Sylvanna (Ann) fried it on a griddle. Making leavened breads in a travelling camp was almost impossible, hence this Viking equivalent of modern hardtack.

I helped myself to some of the cooked, warm flatbread. It was delicious when spread with honey or goat cheese. Throughout the day, I would return to the collective board to snack on dried cherries, apples, plums, and pears. Like the others, I ate from a wooden trencher and drank from a handblown "beaker" glass, which had no stand, demanding that the user hold it until the beverage inside was consumed. Others in the camp drank from waxed cattle horns and wooden bowls.

While enjoying my repast, I sat on a sea chest covered with a sheep skin and stared down at my feet. I wore pig suede turn shoes—slippers sewn inside-out to hide and protect the seams. Because they were several sizes too large, I had stuffed them with uncombed wool. Others stuffed theirs with grass and straw, although some were lucky enough to have nålebound socks (nålebinding is an archaic single-needle knitting technique).

My clothes were simple: I wore a light brown linen tunic that came to my ankles, and a shorter camel-colored wool tube apron with a band of card-woven decorative trim at the neck. To create this trim, a deck of wooden cards pierced with holes had been carefully threaded. As the weaver shuffles the cards in a repeating pattern, the design emerges.

The other Viking women and I also wore two large bronze tortoise shell brooches on the front straps of our aprons. Usually, the brooches were connected with a string of glass, ceramic, and carved bone beads. Dangling from chains held by the brooches, women wore toiletry items such as an ear spoon (for removing wax) and tweezers, as well as other utilitarian items, including a needle case or shears. Primary wives wore the keys to the family's supply chests dangling from their brooches as well. Viking men could have several wives as well as concubine slaves. Although I wore the brooches, a necklace, and a dangling cowry shell—a souvenir from a male relation's travels—I wore no keys. For the weekend I was Birgita, Sylvanna's unmarried cousin.

Over my clothing, I wore a light blue, wool Anglo-Saxon yoke cloak to keep me warm during the early morning hours. It was fastened at the shoulder by an iron penannular brooch, the Dark Age equivalent of a big safety pin. My hair was covered with a linen cap that tied under the chin. It had been copied from examples found in York, England, and Dublin, Ireland—both Viking cities.

Several times during the day, I wandered outside the Viking time bubble to visit other encampments. The well-researched and documented culture, dress, and atmosphere of each period was visually stunning. The energy, talent, commitment, and spirit of each living historian was equally captivating.

After passing through the reconstruction of the James Fort, I entered the more modern encampments, all set on a gently sloping hill that led down to the river. Suddenly confronting the Civil War encampments, I now felt like a primitive being, and the soldiers and their hoop-skirted wives seemed very strange indeed. But when I approached them, we again became old friends.

I chatted with them about the Battle of Antietam and other war-related events I'd become familiar with during my previous study, in which I worked with re-enactors' memories of past lives during the Civil War. I had developed a deep affection for the 1860s while conducting the study and evidence research. Now, as before, when I mentioned the study and resulting book, *Echoes from the Battlefield*, some of the soldiers related strange déjà vu experiences they'd had on the battlefield, experiences that made them wonder.

Now, however, I had just finished a new study on Dark Ages, medieval, and Renaissance reenactors. As dusk approached, I knew I had to get back to the Viking Camp. I smiled wistfully at the Civil War gents and ladies in their finery and said my good-byes.

As I trudged up the path back to the opposite end of the camp—and the time spectrum—I felt a little like Dorothy with her red slippers. Looking down at my oversized, pig suede turn shoes, I reminded myself that my new home was far away in the past. As I tripped over my rawhide shoelaces for the thirtieth time, I chuckled to myself. Up ahead, I saw our Viking Camp. I heard Snorri laugh and I waved at Sylvanna and the other Viking women who were sitting around the fire.

Glossary

Consider these your medieval regression crib notes. Thanks to Kathy Norvell and Susan Reed for supplying the definitions.

Clothing

BARBETTE: A linen chin-band passed from one temple, down, under the chin and up to the other temple. Worn with a fillet—a crownlike linen band—and wimple—a fine white linen or silk scarf that covers the neck. Wimples are still worn by some Catholic nuns.

CHEMISE: A shift or underdress. Usually white, it was worn under the outer garment.

COTEHARDIE: A garment that fits the torso, shoulders, and arms, replacing the tunic by the fourteenth century. Men's cotehardies often came to mid-thigh, while women's were floor-length with full sweeping skirts. By the end of the fourteenth century, it was the preferred undergarment for the "houppelande."

CYCLAS: A fashionable overgarment for men and women, similar to a tabard. Initially worn as a simple length of material with a neck hole and side seams sewn only from the waist down.

DAMASK: A reversible fabric in figured weave.

DOUBLET: A man's close-fitting jacket with sleeves, worn over the shirt in the fourteenth to sixteenth centuries. Hose were held up by ties that were attached to the doublet.

FRENCH HOOD: A unique, half-circle headdress supposedly introduced into English court fashion by Anne Boleyn upon her return from the French court in the 1520s.

HENNIN: Worn in many European countries during the late 1400s, the cone-shaped headdress rose to four feet in height and was draped with a veil.

HOUPPELANDE: A garment with large, hanging sleeves, massive folds, and broad sweeps of material. Women wore floor-length houppelandes, while men's houppelandes could be found in lengths varying from floor-length to thigh-length.

JERKIN: A short, close-fitting coat or jacket for men, often sleeveless and worn over the doublet, from the sixteenth and seventeenth centuries.

KERMES: A red dye made from the dried bodies of certain Mediterranean insects.

KILT: Scandinavian in origin, it means a garment like a long tunic, hiked up above the knees for ease of movement.

LAMELLA: A metal plate as used in armor.

LORICA: A large, square shield carried by Roman soldiers.

MAHEUTRES SLEEVES: Sleeves padded into shoulders, ca. fifteenth century.

MAIL: A flexible body armor made of small metal rings, scales, or loops of chain.

PATTENS: Wooden clogs or sandals that add height and keep the wearer's feet out of the mud.

PLATE ARMOR: By the 1400s, suits of plate armor were designed to cover the entire body. Steel helmets, gauntlets (gloves), and shoes completed the outfit. A suit of armor could cost as much as a small farm.

POULAINES: Pointy medieval shoes, frequently very long, ca. fifteenth century.

SURCOAT: An overgarment, often sleeveless.

TABARD: A short-sleeved, blazoned cloak worn by knights over their armor to protect it from the sun and dust.

Jobs, Roles, and Functions

CHAMBERLAIN: Bedchamber attendant for royalty or nobility; a chief officer in the household of a nobleman; a high official in certain royal courts. Also, a treasurer.

FARRIER: A blacksmith who shoes horses.

JONGLEUR: A wandering minstrel of the Middle Ages in France and England.

LIEGE MAN: In feudal law, a vassal or subject, bound to give service and allegiance to the liege lord, who is entitled to the loyalty.

MARSHALL: A household official in charge of ceremonial aspects of any gathering or one in charge of the staff who cared for the horses.

MONIER: An official appointed to strike and produce coins. He was required to put his name on the coins that he struck.

PERFECT: A spiritual leader of the Cathar faith. Initiated by a baptism of laying on of hands and having an understanding of the full teachings. Considered an adept and part of the Cathar hierarchy.

STEWARD: A household official charged with the general administration of household affairs. The royal Stuarts of Scotland were descended from a king's steward.

Other Terms

BAILEY: The outer wall of a medieval castle or any of the walls surrounding the keep or space immediately within the walls of the castle.

CATHARS: Members of a religious sect who were persecuted for heresy.

CLOSE: An enclosed area, like a quadrangle, close to a cathedral bordered by the archdeanery, deanery, and residences. Also, an open space partially or wholly enclosed by a group of dwellings.

DREKKAR: A Viking longship.

ERASMUS OF ROTTERDAM: A mid-sixteenth-century philosopher.

FRUMENTY: A dish of wheat boiled in milk and usually flavored with sugar, spice, and raisins.

GREAT HALL: Main living space of a Dark Age nobleman's dwelling, in which eating, sleeping, and entertainment occurred. Later, the term for the banquet hall or gathering area in a castle or house.

HIGH STREET: The main street of a town.

HIGH TABLE: The head table at a feast where the nobility and presiding guests were seated.

MAIN CHAUD and BLIND MAN'S BLUFF: "Parlor games," the former played while seated, the latter played while standing up.

MATINS: The service of public morning prayer. The first of the seven canonical hours.

MOOT: An early English assembly of freemen for discussion, deliberation, or to administer justice.

MUNDANE: What Scadians call everything and everyone still part of the twentieth-century world.

PICTS: A northern Scottish tribe who painted their bodies blue for battle in which they fought naked.

POPERY: A hostile term for the doctrines or rituals of the Roman Catholic Church.

PUND: A pound, before A.D. 900.

QUINTAIN: A post with "arms" sticking out—one with a board or "shield" and another with a sandbag to knock the rider off the horse. Used in jousting practice.

REVEL: A gathering devoted to dance, drama, conversation, and refreshments.

RUSHES: In the absence of rugs or carpets, rushes (reedlike plants) were strewn on floor and allowed to pile up. Periodically, they were swept out and changed. Usually they were full of rotting food, bones, and bread crumbs.

SYLKIE: A seal that can take human form.

TA: A possible expression of self-mockery.

THEGN: A Saxon or early Scottish title meaning "leader." Also spelled "thane."

TIERCE: The third of the seven canonical hours.

WATTLE-AND-DAUB: A common house construction method in the Middle Ages. Rods or poles were interwoven with branches or reeds (wattle) then covered with mud or clay (daub).

The Historical Commentators

Bruce Blackistone: Bruce describes himself as a full-time civil servant, a part-time blacksmith, and a seasonal Viking ship captain. In 1970, Blackistone founded the Markland Medieval Militia and became its first "Warlord." He is the author of *Beowabbit,* a parody of *Beowulf,* and a contributor to Dick Brown's *Hagar the Horrible's Very Nearly Complete Viking Handbook.* He produced and acted in Markland's educational film *The Battle of Maldon,* based on an Anglo-Saxon poem. His historical areas of expertise are the early Middle Ages with an emphasis on the Vikings, Anglo-Saxons, and the history of technology. Bruce holds a B.A. in history from the University of Maryland, College Park.

Craig Greenbaum: Craig's expertise is in Asian cultures and philosophies. He has studied three martial arts and considers himself a Zen Buddhist. The computer systems engineer has a nearly completed B.F.A. in theater from Kent State University, Ohio. In his reenacting hobby, he is able to use his many talents—singing, dancing, playing musical instruments, and acting.

Stephen Hick, M.S.: Stephen's medieval research has focused on fourteenth- and fifteenth-century European swordsmanship, especially that of Germany and Italy, including combat, comportment, codes of chivalry, oaths of fealty, training for squires, and table service. His monographs have been included in the *Encyclopedia of World Sports.* Hick is also a student of Japanese martial arts, with particular emphasis on the sword and other weapons. Hick holds an M.S. in computer science from the City University of New York.

Ann Longmore-Etheridge: A journalist and magazine editor, Ann holds a B.A. in history from George Mason University, Fairfax, Virginia. Her areas of intense historical study include the Viking age (ca. A.D. 800-1100); the reigns of Henry VIII, Edward VI, Mary I, and Elizabeth I (ca. A.D. 1500-1600); the expansion of English settlement in the New World; and the lives and times of the Brontë sisters.

Joann Moran, Ph.D.: Professor of medieval and Renaissance history at Georgetown University, Washington, D.C., Dr. Moran specializes in the social and intellectual aspects of medieval history. She has authored several books and has lectured on topics ranging from the Arthurian legends to the lives of medieval women, as well as mysticism in the Middle Ages.

Susan Reed, M.A.: Susan is a historical costuming consultant with an M.S. in textiles from the University of Maryland, College Park. She has been a member of the Society for Creative Anachronism, Inc. (SCA), for over sixteen years. In addition, she has researched the domestic culture of the Middle Ages and has an interest in medieval religion.

Kathy Norvell: Kathy is an expert on medieval costume, dance, and cooking. She also specializes in fifteenth- and sixteenth-century British Isles history. She holds a B.A. from Towson State University, Maryland.

Paula Peterka: A computer systems analyst for the Internal Revenue Service in northern Virginia, Paula holds a B.S. in political science from the University of California, Los Angeles. She has done extensive research in European history during the Middle Ages and the Renaissance, specializing in England under the Plantagenets and the Tudors, and the Holy Roman Empire under Maximilian I and Charles V.

Larry Peterka: Also a computer systems analyst for the Internal Revenue Service, Larry attended Fresno College and Fresno State University where he received degrees in photography and the administration of justice. He joined the Hanford Renaissance of Kings Cultural Arts Committee in 1980 and helped found the Tudor Rose Society, a nonprofit corporation for the promotion of medieval and Renaissance education and arts. He is an expert in European medieval and Renaissance history.

Lisa Steele, J.D.: A Massachusetts attorney since 1991, Lisa specializes in appeals and tax litigation. She holds a B.A. in international relations from Mount Holyoke College and a J.D. from the Western New England College School of Law. Her articles have appeared in *Medieval France, Fief,* as well as various law reviews. Lisa has lectured on manorial economics, landholding, and French history.

Jeff Tyeryar: Jeff defines himself as an amateur historian with a special interest in pre-conquest, Anglo-Saxon England. He studied medieval history, the Anglo-Saxon language, and theology at George Washington University, Washington, D.C., where he received a B.A. in history in 1982. He is also a 1994 graduate of Catholic University Law School.

Reenactment Events and Involvement

Further information on medieval reenacting and participating in Middle Ages living history events can be obtained by contacting the following organizations:

The Society for Creative Anachronism, Inc.
P.O. Box 360789
Milpitas, CA 95036-0789
SCA members can be contacted on the World Wide Web at http://www.sca.org/

Renaissance Festivals: Call your closest faire for auditions. Theatrical auditions are listed in some local papers. To find a faire near you, contact:

Renaissance Herald
Renaissance Publications
P.O. Box 95
Riverside, CA 92502
(909) 943-7333
E-mail: http://www.rennfest.com

Markland Medieval Mercenary Militia, Ltd.
P.O. Box 715
Greenbelt, MD 20768-0715
Markland Hotline (301) WAR-O-WAR [301-927-0927]
The Markland home page is: http://www.markland.org/

The Markland Viking Camp
c/o Ann Longmore-Etheridge
P.O. Box 164
Myersville, MD 21773

La Belle Compagnie
c/o Robert Charrette
1402 Summerset Place
Herndon, VA 22070

The following group has sister organizations in California and Pennsylvania:
Das TeufelsAlpdrücken Fähnlein
Landsknecht Mercenary Reenacting
P.O. Box 503
Annapolis Junction, MD 20701-0503

Note: For medieval historians and history buffs, more academic information can be found in the newsgroup: soc.history.medieval

For information about past-life regressions, contact:
Association for Past-Life Research and Therapies, Inc. (APRT)
P.O. Box 20151
Riverside, CA 92516
(909) 784-1570

Reincarnation International, Ltd.
P.O. Box 10819
London. SW13 OZG
Tel/Fax: 0181-241-2184
e-mail: reincarn@dircon.co.uk
web site: http://www.dircon.co.uk/reincarn/

For information on speaking engagements or private sessions, contact Barbara Lane at:
P.O. Box 25502
Alexandria, VA 22313
e-mai: Echoes11@aol.com
web site: http://members.aol.com/echoes11/barbara.htm

Endnotes

Preface
Mystical Medieval Threads

1. The Pre-Raphaelite movement was formed in 1848 by a group of talented artists who felt that English art was at a low ebb. The Pre-Raphaelites thought to infuse the stale aesthetics of the era with art inspired by nature which would instill character and veracity to their work. By the 1850s, Pre-Raphaelite artists were heavily inspired by the Middle Ages, which appeared to embody both the purity of simpler times, as well as moral concepts such as chivalry, brotherhood, and honor.

Chapter 1
Dreamers and Dream Sellers

1. See *The Renaissance Herald* by Tom Wilson.

2. See *The Renaissance Catalog Magazine* by Gael Stirler.

3. See *Smoke and Fire News* and *Smoke and Fire Co.,* by Donalyn Meyers and David Weir.

4. Alvin Klein, "It's Theater All Day Long," *New York Times*, Sept. 4, 1994, p. 11.

5. See *Italian Comedy: The Improvisation, Scenarios, Lives, Attributes, Portraits, and Masks of the Illustrious Characters of the Commedie Dell'arte* by Pierre Ducharte.

6. James Redfield, *The Celestine Prophecy: An Adventure*, p. 22.

7. See *The 1994-1995 Ohio Edition of the Uproots Directory* by Jonathan Crocker.

Chapter 2
Past-Life Therapy—Historical Perspectives on Healing

1. See *Beyond the Ashes: Cases of Reincarnation from the Holocaust* by Rabbi Yonassan Gershom.

2. See *A Tribe Returned* by Janet Cunningham.

3 See *Mission to Millboro* by Marge Rieder, Ph.D.

4. See *Echoes from the Battlefield: First-Person Accounts of Civil War Past Lives* by Barbara Lane.

5. See *Lessons in Living Throughout the Ages* by Richard Levy, Ph.D.

6. See *Past Lives—Future Lives* by Bruce Goldberg.

7. See *Life Patterns: Soul Lessons and Forgiveness* by Henry Bolduc.

8. Roger Woolger, Ph.D., "The Signs of the Times and the Time of the Heart," *Journal of Family Life*, Fall, 1995, pp. 26-35.

9. Roger Woolger, Ph.D., *Other Lives, Other Selves: A Jungian Psychotherapist Discovers Past Lives*, pp. 9-12.

10. See *Journey of Souls: Case Studies of Life Between Lives* by Michael Newton, Ph.D.

Chapter 3
Susan

1. See *The Intelligent Travelers Guide to Britain.*

2. See *The English Heritage: Guide to English Heritage Properties.*

3. Charles W. Ferguson, *Naked to Mine Enemies: The Life of Cardinal Wolsey*, p. 27.

4. Ibid., p. 190.

5. Ibid., p. 27.

6. Ibid., p. 20.

Chapter 4
Nick

1. See *Bartholomew's Motor Map of Britain.*

2. See *The Wars of the Roses* by Elizabeth Hallam.

Chapter 6
Ann

1. See *The Concise Oxford Dictionary of English Name Places*, 4th ed., by Eilert Ekwall.

2. See *Mary, Queen of Scots* by Antonia Fraser.

3. See *The Concise Scots Dictionary* compiled by Alexander Warrack, p. 1911.

Chapter 12
Paula

1. See *Anne of Cleves* by Mary Saadler.

2. Leslie Stephen and Sydney Lee, eds., *The Dictionary of*

National Biography, vol. 2, p. 1,126.
3. Ibid., vol. 10, pp. 62-64.

Chapter 15
Helen
1. Elizabeth Hallam, ed., *Plantagenet Chronicles*, p. 45; map of the Duchy of Aquitaine, p. 44.
2. Marion Meade, *Eleanor of Aquitaine: A Biography*, pp. 246-254.
3. See *Albigeois et Cathares* by Ferdinand Niel; and *The Albigensian Crusade* by Jonathan Sumption.
4. *The Albigensian Crusades*, Joseph Strayer; *Map of Occitania in the 13th Century.*
5. See *The Hundred Years' War: The English in France, 1337-1453* by Desmond Seward.

Chapter 16
"Weaving the Mystic Threads"
1. See *Twenty Cases Suggestive of Reincarnation* by Ian Stevenson, M.D.; and "Reincarnation: Field Studies and Theoretical Issues" by Ian Stevenson, M.D., in the *Handbook of Parapsychology* by Benjamin Wolman, ed.
2. See *Many Mansions* by Gina Cerminara.
3. Noel Langley, *Edgar Cayce on Reincarnation*, p. 84.
4. See *Regression Therapy: A Handbook for Professionals, Vols. I and II,* by Winafred Blake Lucas; *Past-Lives Therapy* by Morris Netherton; *You Have Been Here Before* by Edith Fiore; and *Past Lives—Future Lives: Accounts of Regressions and Progressions Through Hypnosis* by Bruce Goldberg.
5. Helen Wambach, *Reliving Past Lives: The Evidence under Hypnosis*, p. 115.
6. Ibid., p. 118.
7. Ibid., p. 141.
8. Ibid., p. 144.

Bibliography

Ansari, Masud, Ph.D. *Modern Hypnosis: Theory and Practice.* Washington, D.C.: Mas-Press, 1991.

Ashelflord, Valerie. *Visual History of Costume: The Sixteenth Century.* London: B. T. Batsford, Ltd., 1983.

Baigent, Michael, et al. *Holy Blood, Holy Grail.* New York: Delacorte Press, 1982.

Beattie, Nancee, ed. *Tournaments Illuminated,* 113: Winter, 1995. Milpitas, California: Society for Creative Anachronism, Inc.

Bogin, Meg. *The Women Troubadours.* London: Paddington Press, 1976.

Bolduc, Henry. *Life Patterns: Soul Lessons and Forgiveness.* Independence, Virginia: Journeys into Time, Inc., 1994.

Boucher, Francois. *20,000 Years of Fashion.* New York: Harry N. Abrams, Inc., 1966.

Burckhardt, Titus. *Moorish Culture in Spain.* New York: McGraw-Hill, 1972.

Capellanus, Andreas (Parry, John Jay, trans.). *The Art of Courtly Love.* New York: Columbia University Press, Parry Pub., 1960.

Cerminara, Gina. *Many Mansions.* New York: Sloane, 1970.

Crocker, Jonathan, ed., et al. *The 1994-1995 Ohio Edition of the Uproots Directory.* S. Hero, Vermont.

Crowl, Philip A. *The Intelligent Traveler's Guide to Historic Britain.* New York: Congdon & Weed, Inc., 1983.

Cunningham, Janet. *A Tribe Returned*. Crest Park, California: Deep Forest Press, 1994.

Ducharte, Pierre. *Italian Comedy: The Improvisation, Scenarios, Lives, Attributes, Portraits, and Masks of the Illustrious Characters of the Commedie Dell'arte*. Mineola, New York: Dover Publishers, 1965.

Ekwall, Eilert. *The Concise Oxford Dictionary of English Name Places*, 4th ed. Oxford: Oxford University Press, 1960.

——————. *Guide to English Heritage Properties*. London: English Heritage, 1993.

Ferguson, Charles W. *Naked to Mine Enemies: The Life of Cardinal Wolsey*. New York: Little Pub., 1958.

Fiore, Edith, Ph.D. *You Have Been Here Before*. New York: Ballantine Books, 1978.

Fraser, Antonia. *Mary, Queen of Scots*. New York: Delacorte Press, 1978.

Gershom, Rabbi Yonassan. *Beyond the Ashes: Cases of Reincarnation from the Holocaust*. Virginia Beach, Virginia: A.R.E. Press, 1992.

——————. *From Ashes to Healing: Mystical Encounters with the Holocaust*. Virginia Beach, Virginia: A.R.E. Press, 1996.

Goldberg, Bruce. *Past Lives—Future Lives: Accounts of Regressions and Progressions Through Hypnosis*. New York: Ballantine Books, 1982.

Hallam, Elizabeth, ed. *Plantagenet Chronicles*. New York: Weidenfeld & Nicholson, 1986, pp. 44-45.

——————. *The Wars of the Roses*. New York: Weidenfeld & Nicholson, 1988.

Klein, Alvin. "It's Theatre All Day Long." *New York Times*, Sept. 4, 1994, 11.

Lane, Barbara. *Echoes from the Battlefield: First-Person Accounts of Civil War Past Lives*. Virginia Beach, Virginia: A.R.E. Press, 1996.

Langley, Noel. *Edgar Cayce on Reincarnation*. London: Howard Baker, 1969.

Levy, Richard, Ph.D. *Lessons in Living Throughout the Ages*. (Unpublished manuscript.)

Lucas, Winafred Blake, Ph.D. *Regression Therapy: A Handbook for Professionals, Vols. I and II*. Crest Park, California: Deep Forest Press, 1993.

Meade, Marion. *Eleanor of Aquitaine: A Biography*. New York: Penguin, 1991.

Meyers, Donalyn, and Weir, David. *Smoke and Fire News*, and *Smoke and Fire Co*. Grand Rapids, Ohio: Smoke and Fire News, 1996.

Netherton, Morris, and Shiffrin, Nancy. *Past Lives Therapy*. New York: William Morrow, Inc., 1978.

Newton, Michael, Ph.D. *Journey of Souls: Case Studies of Life Between Lives*. St. Paul, Minnesota: Llewellyn Publications, 1996.

Niel, Fernand. *Albigeois et Cathares*. Paris: P.U.F., 1976.

Payne, Blanche, et al. *The History of Costume: From Ancient Mesopotamia Through the Twentieth Century*, 2nd ed. New York: Harper Collins Pub., Inc, 1992.

Redfield, James. *The Celestine Prophecy: An Adventure.* New York: Warner Books, Inc., 1993.

Rieder, Marge, Ph.D. *Mission to Millboro.* Nevada City, California: Blue Dolphin Publishing, Inc., 1993.

Saaler, Mary. *Anne of Cleves: Fourth Wife of Henry VIII.* London: Rubicon Press, 1995.

Seward, Desmond. *The Hundred Years' War: The English in France, 1337-1453.* New York: Atheneum, 1984.

Stephen, Leslie, and Lee, Sydney, ed. *The Dictionary of National Biography, Vols. 2 & 10.* Oxford: Oxford University Press, 1959.

Stevenson, Ian, M.D. *Twenty Cases Suggestive of Reincarnation.* Charlottesville, Virginia: University Press of Virginia, 1974.

_____ . "Reincarnation: Field Studies and Theoretical Issues," in Benjamin Wolman, ed., *Handbook of Parapsychology.* New York: Van Nostrand Reinhold Co., 1977.

Stirler, Gael. *The Chivalry Sports: Renaissance Catalog Magazine.* Nantucket, Mass.: Phantom Press.

Strayer, Joseph. *The Albigensian Crusades.* Ann Arbor, Michigan: University of Michigan Press, 1992.

Sumption, Jonathan. *The Albigensian Crusade.* London: Saber & Saber, 1978.

Wambach, Helen, Ph.D. *Reliving Past Lives: The Evidence under Hypnosis.* New York: Harper & Row, 1978.

Warrack, Alexander, ed. *The Concise Scots Dictionary* compiled by Alexander. Dorset, England: New Orchard Editions, I.td., 1911, 1988.

Wilson, Tom. *Renaissance Herald.* Riverside, California: Renaissance Publications (Aug., 1995).

Woolger, Roger, Ph.D. *Other Lives, Other Selves: A Jungian Psychotherapist Discovers Past Lives.* New York: Bantam, 1987.

_____ . "The Sign of the Times and the Time of the Heart": Keynote lecture given to the Dutch Foundation for Reincarnation. Amsterdam, April 1994, in *The Journal of Family Life* (Fall, 1995).

_____ . "The Troubadour Cult of the Feminine," in *Caduceus* (28), 34-35.

For Further Reading

Barker, Elsa. *Letters from the Light: An Afterlife Journal.* Hillsboro, Oregon: Beyond Worlds Pub., Inc., 1995.

Blackistone, Bruce. *Beowabbit.* Takoma Park, Maryland: Canta Pub, 504 Ethan Allen Ave., 1977, 1983.

Bowman, Carol. *Children's Past Lives: How Past Memories Affect Your Child.* New York: Bantam, Doubleday & Dell, 1997.

Bradley, Marion Zimmer. *The Mists of Avalon.* New York: Ballantine Books, 1982.

Browne, Christopher. *Hagar the Horrible's Very Nearly Complete Viking Handbook.* New York: King Features Syndicate, Inc., Workman Pub., 1985.

Cannon, John, and Griffiths, Ralph. *The Oxford Illustrated History of the British Monarchy.* Oxford: Oxford University Press, 1988.

Chartier, Roger, ed. *A History of Private Life III: Passions of the Renaissance.* Cambridge: Belknap Press of Harvard University Press, 1989.

Duby, Georges, ed. *A History of Private Life II: Revelations of the Medieval World.* Cambridge: Belknap Press of Harvard University Press, 1988.

Holmes George, ed. *The Oxford Illustrated History of Medieval Europe.* Oxford: Oxford University Press, 1988.

Ives, Eric W. *Anne Boleyn.* Oxford: Basil Blackwell, Ltd., 1986.

Kruta, V., et al., ed. *The Celts.* New York: Rizzoli Press, 1991.

Leon, Vicki. *Uppity Women of Medieval Times.* Berkeley, California: Conari Press, 1997.

Margeson, Sue. *Norwich Households: Medieval and Post Medieval Finds from Norwich Survey Excavations, 1971-1978.* Norwich, England: East Anglian Archaeology, 1993.

Roesdahl, Else, and Wilson, David M., eds. *From Viking to Crusader: Scandinavia and Europe 800-1200.* New York: Rizzoli Press, 1992.

Ryan, Michael, ed. *The Illustrated Archaeology of Ireland.* Dublin: Country House, 1991.

Somerset, Anne. *Elizabeth I.* New York: St. Martin's Press, 1993.

Steele, Lisa. *Medieval France.* Amherst, Massachusetts: White Rose Publishing, 1994.

Steele, Lisa. *Fief.* Amherst, Massachusetts: White Rose Publishing, 1997.

Webster, Leslie, and Backhouse, Janet, eds. *The Making of England: Anglo-Saxon Art and Culture AD 600-900.* Toronto: University of Toronto Press, 1991.

Weir, Alison. *Six Wives of Henry VIII.* New York: Grove Weidenfeld, 1991.

White, Stewart E. *The Unobstructed Universe.* New York: E. P. Dutton & Co. Inc., 1941.

A.R.E. PRESS

The A.R.E. Press publishes quality books, videos, and audiotapes meant to improve the quality of our readers' lives—personally, professionally, and spiritually. We hope our products support your endeavors to realize your career potential, to enhance your relationships, to improve your health, and to encourage you to make the changes necessary to live a loving, joyful, and fulfilling life.

For more information or to receive a free catalog, call

1-800-723-1112

Or write

A.R.E. Press
P.O. Box 656
Virginia Beach, VA 23451-0656